Praise for *The Chemistry of Connection*

'I love this book. *The Chemistry of Connection* literally "connects" history, science and philosophy, and really everything in a beautiful tapestry that goes right to the heart of human existence: the power of connection that makes life worth living. It is the love that binds us all not only to our most intimate ones, but to all of humanity and, truly, to all of life and beyond. He brilliantly and articulately reveals the science of how we are made for love and connection, as we hinted at years ago in our book *Natural Highs*. He then inspires and instruct us on how to apply that knowledge to create and enhance our experience, so that we are fully alive. Happiness is not what we have, it's how deeply and well we connect – or, in Patrick's words, to go "from lonely to alone to all-one". Highly scholarly but an easy read and very funny.'

Dr Hyla Cass, former Assistant Clinical Professor of Psychiatry at UCLA School of Medicine and author of *The Addicted Brain*

'*The Chemistry of Connection* affirms that exploring our consciousness can lead us to happier, fuller and more integrated lives, realizing "our highest potential as human beings". Drawing on ideas from Sufi philosophy and the ancient tantric traditions of India, together with the chemical enhancement of psychedelics, Patrick illuminates myriad pathways to happiness, all united in fostering greater connectivity.'

Amanda Feilding, Director of the Beckley Foundation

'Patrick Holford is a national treasure. *The Chemistry of Connection* illustrates once again his genius at taking complex subjects and cutting-edge approaches to every aspect of health, and making them not only accessible but compelling. He ignites in his readers the spark to find out for ourselves what it means to be fully human in the most celebratory and divine sense.'

Leela Miller, yoga teacher and spiritual activist

'In this book I found a lot of surprising new, useful information, updating me professionally and personally – even for a basically healthy, meditating senior like me with a lifetime of expertise in mind–body and spiritual and psychological work.'

Beverly Feinberg-Moss PhD, Clinical and Health Psychologist near Boston, Massachusetts

'Patrick Holford brings together the clarity of his scientific intellect with his spiritual awareness to offer us a powerful, clear and deeply insightful manual for living a truly balanced and awake life. Whether you're just beginning your journey or are well along your path, you'll find wisdom and inspiration in these pages. The guidance in this book v... will stay with you for a long time to come.'

Sally Kempton, author of *Meditation for the Love of It*

'Patrick Holford's *The Chemistry of Connection* should be required reading for all students of medicine, nutrition and nursing, and for all professionals in the National Health Service. His work should cause a paradigm shift. It is vital we recognize that consciousness is the universe awake to itself. Reality is purposeful. Unfortunately big pharma and its agents (usually "doctor-journalists") will probably either ignore or try to demonize Holford's work. Ho-Hum!'

MALCOLM STEWART, FORMER PRIEST, UN PROJECT DIRECTOR, HEAD OF RELIGIOUS PROGRAMMES FOR LONDON WEEKEND TELEVISION AND AUTHOR OF *PATTERNS OF ETERNITY* AND *SYMBOLS OF ETERNITY*

'After teaching thousands how to eat themselves healthy, Patrick Holford has turned his attention to the place where religious beliefs meet the atheistic materialists' position that we carbon-based systems are fated to come to an irrevocable stop. He brings back reports of chemically induced visions and mystical ego death experiences, juxtaposed with the wilder shores of physics and quantum theory where the scientific and the mystical share territory. Exploring important questions about the nature of reality, this shaman proves a warm and open-hearted guide offering wonder, hope and certainly more healing.'

JEROME BURNE, AWARD-WINNING MEDICAL JOURNALIST, CO-AUTHOR OF *TEN SECRETS OF HEALTHY AGEING* AND *FOOD IS BETTER MEDICINE THAN DRUGS* AND EDITOR OF HEALTHINSIGHTUK.ORG

'I fully endorse the *mens sana in corpore sano* philosophy that Patrick so persuasively elucidates in this inspiring book. What I found really compelling was the degree to which he illustrates that these are not just issues about human health and wellbeing, but that there are political and social issues that need to be addressed if humankind is to benefit from this historically unique opportunity to create a more just, peaceful and healthy global society. Patrick's book gives us the ammunition to fight and win this battle... peacefully.'

CRAIG SAMS, CO-FOUNDER OF WHOLEEARTH FOODS, GREEN & BLACKS AND CARBON GOLD BIOCHAR, AND FORMER CHAIRMAN OF THE SOIL ASSOCIATION

'Patrick is a prolific and respected writer for a reason – he is passionate and knowledgeable and wants to share this to transform the world. This book is a clear and grounded guide on how we can reconnect – which is what we all want. An inspired balance of knowledge and practice, based on his own experience and learning, to empower us so we can each do this for ourselves, and he doesn't hold back on what we need to do.'

JONATHAN SATTIN, FOUNDER AND MANAGING DIRECTOR OF TRIYOGA, LONDON

'This is an impressive book – well researched and incredibly comprehensive. The author is expert with a vast range of knowledge, and he draws meaningful parallels to modern-day challenges of both individuals and society as a whole. It is unique in that it brings spiritual wisdom traditions together with recent scientific discoveries. At the same time, it reads like a personal journey and is brought to life with anecdotes, stories and the experiences of the author.'

LAINIE HENEGHAN, MANAGEMENT CONSULTANT

The
CHEMISTRY
of
CONNECTION

Other books by Patrick Holford:

6 Weeks to Superhealth
Balance Your Hormones
Beat Stress and Fatigue
Boost Your Immune System (with Jennifer Meek)
Burn Fat Fast (with Kate Staples)
Food Glorious Food (with Fiona McDonald Joyce)
Food is Better Medicine than Drugs (with Jerome Burne)
Good Medicine
Hidden Food Allergies (with Dr James Braly)
How to Quit without Feeling S**t (with David Miller and Dr James Braly)
Improve Your Digestion
Natural Highs (with Dr Hyla Cass)
Optimum Nutrition Before, During and After Pregnancy (with Susannah Lawson)
Optimum Nutrition for the Mind
Optimum Nutrition for Your Child (with Deborah Colson)
Optimum Nutrition Made Easy (with Susannah Lawson)
Say No to Arthritis
Say No to Cancer
Say No to Diabetes
Say No to Heart Disease
Smart Food for Smart Kids (with Fiona McDonald Joyce)
Solve Your Skin Problems (with Natalie Savona)
The 9-day Liver Detox (with Fiona McDonald Joyce)
The 10 Secrets of 100% Health Cookbook (with Fiona McDonald Joyce)
The 10 Secrets of 100% Healthy People
The 10 Secrets of Healthy Ageing (with Jerome Burne)
The Alzheimer's Prevention Plan (with Shane Heaton and Deborah Colson)
The Feel Good Factor
The Homocysteine Solution (with Dr James Braly)
The H Factor (with Dr James Braly)
The Low-GL Diet Cookbook (with Fiona McDonald Joyce)
The Low-GL Diet Counter
The Little Book of Optimum Nutrition
The Low-GL Diet Bible
The Optimum Nutrition Bible
The Optimum Nutrition Cookbook (with Judy Ridgway)
The Stress Cure (with Susannah Lawson)

The

CHEMISTRY

of

CONNECTION

Five Keys to a Richer Happier, Fulfilling and Meaningful Life

PATRICK HOLFORD

HAY HOUSE

Carlsbad, California • New York City • London
Sydney •Johannesburg • Vancouver • New Delhi

SUSTAINABLE FORESTRY INITIATIVE
Certified Sourcing
www.sfiprogram.org
SFI-01268
SFI label applies to text stock only

*If perception were cleansed every Thing
would appear to man as it is, Infinite. For
man has closed himself up, till he sees all
Things thro' narrow chinks of his cavern.*

WILLIAM BLAKE

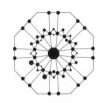

Contents

Preface   xi

Acknowledgements   xvii

Introduction: From Disconnection to Connection   xix

PART I: CONSCIOUS CONNECTION

  1. Elements of Life and Death   3

  2. Love Is the Proof That Consciousness Is Shared   9

  3. The Chemistry of Culture and Consciousness   29

  4. Say No to Drugs   51

  5. Doors to Enlightenment   65

PART II: THE FORM OF CONNECTION

  6. The Mind–Body Connection   81

  7. Methyl Magic and the Brain-Makers   97

  8. Generating Vital Energy   105

  9. The Earth Connection   117

 10. The Shape and Sound of Connection   133

PART III: HEART CONNECTION

 11. Opening the Heart   157

 12. Community Spirit   177

 13. Men and Women – *Vive la Différence*   191

PART IV: THE ULTIMATE CONNECTION

    14. The Alchemy of Sex and Spirit   207

    15. Five Keys to Connection   223

Exercise Appendix

    Clearing Emotional Charge   227

    Negative Transference Exercise   230

    Healing the Body Visualization   234

    Diakath Breathing™   236

    Lalita Meditation   238

    Erotic Orange Exercise   241

References   243

Recommended Reading   251

Resources   255

Index   263

About the Author   275

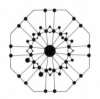

Preface

Have you ever noticed how the course of your life turns in unexpected directions due to strange coincidences or connections? I had one of these back in the 1970s when I was taking a year off before heading to university to study economics. I had decided to visit India, romantically in search of the meaning of life. After receiving the required hepatitis B injection (gamma globulin), I returned home and was sitting in my bedroom when suddenly 'I' was experiencing everything as a mass of energy, a vibrant, alive waveform, seemingly infinite and eternal. There was no body, no room. Then I was back in my bedroom, as if nothing had happened. I cancelled my trip to India. There was no need to go.

Consequently I switched to studying psychology, thinking I would perhaps become a psychotherapist. I had first been turned on to bigger questions in life through reading the legendary books of the great writer Hermann Hesse, author of *Siddhartha* and *The Glass Bead Game*, who brought ideas of Eastern mysticism into the Western mind, then the works of psychiatrist and psychotherapist Carl Jung. I spent the summer before university travelling and studying Psychosynthesis, a therapeutic approach based on the teachings of Roberto Assagioli which gave birth to the transpersonal psychology movement. However, as I soon discovered, the academic field of psychology was desperate to establish itself as a 'science' and shunned any metaphysical questions, preferring a materialist and behaviourist approach to life. I remember asking if we were ever going to do anything on love being a key driver or connector in human life. No chance! Even Freud and Jung were covered in a mere lecture. It was all about rats in mazes and behavioural theory.

However, having been forced to study brain chemistry and its impact on behaviour in quite some detail, I bumped into some research on high-dose B vitamins having a remarkable impact on schizophrenia, which got me into nutrition. More unexpected turns...

Now, 37 years later, having established the Institute for Optimum Nutrition, which catalysed the new profession of nutritional therapy in the UK and abroad, written the same number of books on nutrition and established a charity, the Food for the Brain Foundation, dedicated to exploring the link between nutrition and mental health, I have realized it is time to get back to the meaning of life.

In my twenties I was very much involved in studying and practising various mystical philosophies, primarily as a student of Oscar Ichazo of the Arica School®, which exposed me to the Neoplatonic philosophy of the Greeks and the Sufism of Islam, much of which was influenced by Neoplatonic philosophy. Then in my thirties I immersed myself in Siddha Yoga, exploring the philosophy of Vedanta and Kashmir Shaivism with various trips to India and also one to Tibet. Since then I have continued to explore, albeit part time, our true nature and highest potential as human beings.

The Dalai Lama once said that all people have two fundamental desires: to be happy and to be free of pain. I propose that happiness is what happens when we connect with something, someone or ourselves. It could come in the form of a sip of wine, a piece of chocolate, a coffee, a hug, a lover, a cat, an idea or a piece of music or art. It could be looking good in new clothes, having great sex, closing a deal, getting paid, buying something, winning something, receiving recognition, resolving an issue and/or experiencing an inner feeling of completeness or even a peak experience, a profound expansion of consciousness, an experience of ultimate unity, a connection with a higher intelligence or God.

In most cases, happiness comes with the fulfilment of a desire – gaining something we want or feel we are lacking. This kind of happiness is rather short-lived. It can be explained as fulfilling a 'reward' circuitry with the release of the brain's feel-good chemicals, notably dopamine and endorphins. As a consequence, we seek more – more money, more chocolate, more sex, more love, more clothes, more achievement, more praise. In short – *more*. We live in a culture of more. It is the basis of the materialism that runs through the veins of the 21st century. But is there ever enough? And are the people who 'have everything' really happy?

> *Is there a mountain of delight*
> *that would fulfil my insatiable appetite?*

Some people *are* happy, truly happy, with much less. Their happiness isn't seemingly dependent on stuff. It is an inner happiness. They glow and are not easily perturbed by the changing fortunes of life. That is what I am interested in, not only as a subject of enquiry, but for myself and for everyone.

When we surveyed the habits and beliefs of the superhealthy in my 100% Health Survey online at www.patrickholford.com, which has involved over 100,000 people to date, I further researched the top 100 to find out their health secrets. Of these highest-ranking health scorers, 96 per cent said they had a clear sense of purpose or direction in life, 75 per cent described themselves as happy and 61 per cent felt fulfilled. I wrote about this in my book *The 10 Secrets of 100% Healthy People*. Most had good relationships, kept fit, did vital energy-generating exercise, meditated or had some kind of spiritual practice, considered their relationship to nature important, had a good diet and took supplements. The key seemed to be *connection*, be it to others, the Earth or a higher purpose.

Psychologist and former nurse Elizabeth Register, who is associate professor at the College of Nursing at the University of South Carolina, is somewhat of an expert in connection. Her conclusion is that quality of life is largely about connectedness[1] and she has compiled a scale of connectedness that is now being used to measure how people feel.

In her view, there are six aspects to being connected.[2] These are:

1. *Being metaphysically connected:* Having an awareness of yourself within a larger Universe.

2. *Feeling spiritually connected:* Being aware of a higher power and/or searching for meaning and a purpose in life.

3. *Being biologically connected:* Optimizing your functional capacity and participating in activities that relate to promoting and maintaining your health.

4. *Feeling connected to others:* Enjoying human interpersonal relationships that are free of spatial or temporal constraints.

5. *Being environmentally connected:* Working to connect yourself with your personal living and natural environment.

6. *Feeling connected to society:* Having a relationship with a personal social system, your extended family and community and the global community of society.

You can find out how connected you are with my online Connection Quiz at www.patrickholford.com/connectionquiz, which shows you in which aspects you are strongest and weakest. It gives you a score for the five zones of connection, the five keys we will be exploring here, the total score being the sum of them all. The five keys are:

1. *Sexual, sensual and erotic connection* – expressing yourself as a sexual and sensual being, in touch with your own enthusiasm for life, true to your longings and desires, enjoying the pleasures of the senses.

2. *Body and Earth connection* – being in touch with, respecting and nurturing your body with good nutrition and energy-generating exercise, and respecting and protecting the Earth through conscious living.

3. *Social and self connection* – being in touch with your heart, your love and deepest feelings and reaching out in your social group, society, humanity and animals as sentient beings to make this world a better place.

4. *Intellectual connection* – having clear thoughts, beyond fears, limiting beliefs and limitations, openly enquiring and questioning and learning and tapping into the wisdom of the intellect, the source of insights and the illumination beyond the thinking mind.

5. *Spiritual connection* – being in touch with the field of being, the consciousness in which everything is happening, your pure awareness, the all-pervasive benevolent intelligence that is your essential nature.

All of these, working together, make a sixth, the ultimate experience of living in a state of connection.

This book explores elemental, chemical, psychological, social, philosophical, ecological, sexual and spiritual avenues in the search for a deeper understanding and experience of connection. It also uncovers connections between cultural, scientific and spiritual traditions in the search for higher understanding. It is written very much in the spirit of enquiry and I would ask you to read it in that spirit. Because I have delved into many domains on which I am no expert, I have interviewed those who are. I therefore apologize in advance for any omissions or errors of understanding – these are all mine. If I am wrong, please let me know. Similarly, if I have inadvertently offended anyone's beliefs, please accept my apology.

Ultimately, this book has one purpose, which is to lead you to an experience of greater connection in your life, be it personal, transpersonal, social or global. In many chapters I give you avenues to explore. There are also practical exercises, meditations and contemplations that you can do to enhance connection. Take what works for you. Your feedback on what works and what doesn't is always appreciated through my Facebook page.

It is through connection that we have the greatest opportunity to resolve personal conflicts, enjoy a fulfilling life and create a global society that works. More than anything, we are going to need a united humanity to resolve the global conflicts and catastrophes that may be heading our way, whether due to war, economic collapse, overpopulation, disease, food or water shortage or climate change. It is to this united and connected humanity that I dedicate this book.

Wishing you the best of health and happiness,

Acknowledgements

My sincere gratitude goes to my teachers: Oscar Ichazo of the Arica School®, the late Muktananda, Gurumayi and the Siddha Yoga swamis, meditation master Sally Kempton, the late Dr Abram Hoffer for his remarkable contribution to psychiatry and unravelling the chemistry of psychedelics, the visionary psychiatrist Stanislav Grof, Professors David Smith and Helga Refsum for their wisdom on methylation and Alzheimer's prevention, Tim Laurence of the Hoffman Institute, Malcolm Stewart for his wisdom and generosity in sharing his work on cosmic geometry, his extraordinary experiences and so much more, Nora for her assistance, Rosie Stewart for her guidance on social connection, Sophie Sabbage for her wisdom and bravery, Gavin and Gaby at the HeartMath Institute, Danny, Duncan and Luciana for sharing their stories, Rupert Sheldrake for his pioneering ideas on morphic resonance and challenging the scientific status quo, Marc Gafni for his radical take on Eros and wisdom on Judaism and the Kabbalah, Alla Zaki for his guidance on Islam and Sufism, Damcho Dyson for her insights into Tibetan Buddhism, Ashnandoah for her generosity in sharing her remarkable art, Brian Russell for his illustrations and help with the artwork, Mike Heneghan, Mukti Mitchell and Pennell Rock for their suggestions and support, Nancy Treharne for her editorial guidance, my wonderful wife, Gaby, for her honest feedback and support in giving me the space to immerse myself in this subject, my super-efficient manager and editorial assistant, Jo, Steph for getting it out there, and the team at Hay House including Michelle, Julie, Lizzie, Jo, Ruth and Tom – thank you for your film editing – for making it happen, also Leanne for her wonderful designs including the cover, and Barney Wan for his guiding eye.

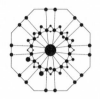

Introduction

From Disconnection to Connection

There is a dis-ease in the Western world that is so all-pervasive that it is not really perceived as such. It is like water to a fish. It is a malaise that comes from the core of the modern world despite all its scientific progress, affluence and technology. I call it *disconnexia* – a state of disconnection.

It is reflected in the ever-increasing rates of mental illness – depression, stress, anxiety, insomnia and failing memory. These problems are, according to the World Health Organization, the most prevalent health issues globally in the 21st century. Followed by obesity and cancer. We have not scored well, despite all the apparent progress of modern medicine. Nor do we appear to be happier. Globally, there are now more suicides each year than violent deaths.

As a consequence, though we are the most advanced and 'successful' species on the planet, we have a very real chance of self-destruction. We have eliminated 99 per cent of the animal species previously on this planet and 90 per cent of its oxygen-producing rainforests. The oxygen in every other breath we take is generated from algae, largely in the sea, yet we are in danger of not only destroying the conditions necessary for algae to generate oxygen but also of depleting the already small reserves of fish stock and coral habitats.

We are even destroying each other at a rate of half a million murders a year, with seemingly futile wars about religion, land, ideology, oil and money. It isn't love but money, we are told, that makes the world go round. Yet global money markets teeter on the edge of collapse, with almost every country owing billions or even trillions of dollars to who knows whom.

We are also destroying ourselves. So many mental and physical diseases have, at their root, disconnection. Cancer, for example, involves a breakdown of a cell's behaviour in respecting its boundaries with other cells. Diabetes and fatigue are breakdowns, disconnections, in how the energy in food becomes energy in the body. Alzheimer's may well result from a breakdown in methylation, the connecting principle of the body and brain that helps our system micro-adjust (*see Chapter 7*). Depression – which is often anger without enthusiasm, or feeling cut off, often the consequence of not speaking our truth or living a life true to who we are – is a disconnection from our own nature or a biochemical disconnection brought on by a lack of omega-3, vitamin D or B vitamins and too much sugar or caffeine.

Few of us are actually content. Most are brainwashed into a kind of mindless existence. Many are living a horrible life on the edge of survival. The gap between the rich and poor is growing wider. Our culture, indeed our species, our ecology and our biosphere are getting ever closer to the tipping point of no return.

We were warned of this outcome by great visionaries such as George Orwell in *1984* and Aldous Huxley in *Brave New World*, yet here we are living, or starting to live, the nightmare.

Why should this be? Apparently we are more connected than ever, via TV and world news, mobile phones, the internet and social media. So much so that the average person checks their phone at least every 10 minutes and answers work-related e-mails on holiday. But what kind of connection is this? In a survey, one in 10 young adults in the USA admitted to having checked their smartphone during sex![1]

Twenty-first-century living literally puts us on high alert, so that we expect constant stimulation. Few of us can sit still. In a recent study at Harvard,[2] volunteers were exposed to an unpleasant electric shock, which they said they would pay to avoid. Then they were left alone for 15 minutes. No company, no smartphone. Just their thoughts. Twelve out of 18 men and six out of 24 women gave themselves up to four electric shocks. Two thirds of men pressed the button. One man gave himself 190 shocks to relieve the boredom!

That is how desperate we are for contact and stimulation. Yet on the other hand there is a move to encourage 'mindfulness': to let go of thoughts, sensations and perceptions and focus on the space behind and between them, like the space between breaths – to 'mind the gap', so to speak.

It's ironic that this is exactly what most people are afraid of. Of having nothing to do, nothing to think, no button to press. They suffer from what I call 'out-of-contact-itis'. Even falling asleep can be difficult. They need continual engagement, constant stimulus.

Almost two-thirds of travellers on urban trains and buses have their head buried in their phones, texting, playing games – anything to keep their mind occupied. In cities, the pace of the modern world sells us permanent stimulation, plus the drugs to keep us there. Caffeine sales just keep rising. Two billion cups of coffee are drunk every day worldwide, 70 million in the UK. The number of cola drinks is even higher. At least 1.7 billion Coca-Colas are drunk every day, and that's just one brand of caffeinated drink. With the demise of the other major stimulant drug, nicotine, sales will no doubt keep on rising. Caffeine keeps you wired, which is, I guess, the next best thing to the true state of connection.

All this adrenalin, non-stop, every day, wears us out. We are meant to produce adrenalin, and the longer-acting adrenal hormone cortisol, infrequently, in response to a real stress – hunting dangerous animals for dinner or avoiding being eaten for dinner. It triggers the 'fight, flight' syndrome – actually it's the 'fight, flight, freeze, f**k, food' syndrome.

Both compulsive food and sex can be part of this stress addiction, hence the growth in obesity and pornography. As a result, we are wired and tired, channelling any energy into nervous energy and away from digestion and repair. Even though we live longer, we age faster and suffer decades of decrepitude. The average woman in the EU is destined to spend 10 years disabled, meaning unable to climb 10 steps.

Being constantly on the go is draining. One in five of us now needs to take time off work due to the ill-effects of stress. We try to fix the problem with caffeine, alcohol, drugs, sex, more things, more money, more power. We try to escape with endless TV, dramas, alcohol and other numbing drugs. But the problem is getting worse, not better and that is, I believe, because of something so insidious that it has a real danger of killing us. It is the loss of understanding of who we truly are.

As an Englishman, born, bred and educated with a degree in psychology, I have some ideas that my culture has embedded so deeply within me that I simply assume them to be true. One is that 'I', that is, my thinking mind, am separate from the material world that surrounds me. Another is that my mind is in my head, that my very consciousness is some kind of trick of the neural circuits of my brain, and that it will therefore be extinguished at the point of death. Given these assumptions, what purpose is there to life other than to have fun and accumulate wealth to provide security and pass on to one's children?

Yet all these assumptions are wrong.

First, there is no material world as we see it. No one, despite hundreds of years of looking, even with such extraordinary instruments as the US$13 billion Hadron Collider, which is capable of crashing particles more than a trillion times smaller than the eye can see, has succeeded in finding actual matter.

Also, for the mind to exist in the brain, the brain must store memory, yet no one has found that either. The hunt is on, though. There are theories that memories are stored in the space in between brain cells and a £1 million award has recently been given to British neuroscientists in recognition of their work in understanding memory.[3] But no 'hard disc drive' has been discovered, no pattern of activity across the neural network established that we could say is an actual memory. There's no explanation for why we remember that girl or guy who turned our eye.

We assume that we 'see' the world in our brain, but no one has shown this to be true either. No one has shown an inverted image projected on the inner screen of the mind.

Furthermore, many people have 'seen' when they have been completely unconscious, or even braindead. Many have left their body and seen it lying there.

Following on from this, there is no actual evidence that consciousness is extinguished at death. We are born with it, but we don't know where it comes from, nor how it expands and unfolds.

So-called science, philosophy and medicine just avoid these questions because their models are completely inadequate to answer them. However, many people, religious and otherwise, have had a direct experience of a force, a power, an intelligence far greater than, and including, their own consciousness. Some call this God.

For those who have experienced this, 'it' is undeniable. For those who haven't, well, some hope for it, others don't. Yet there is an emerging science of consciousness and of how to access the transcendent, the 'spiritual' realm of existence that connects everything and makes sense of the mystery of life. Many are unaware of this new research, because it has become almost taboo to talk about these things, not 'PC'. I call it LGBTM – 'lesbian, gay, bisexual, transgender and mystical'. Yet we have an innate yearning for learning about our true nature.

In the meantime, some find solace in so-called science, believing that intellectual pursuits and technological developments, founded on the myth of objectivity, can solve all society's ills given enough time and money. Of course, we are rapidly running out of both. And few of us realize just how broken and subverted most science is, distorted by ulterior motives of profit. Key psychological and medical studies, which

The Chemistry of Connection

drive clinical practice, have proven unreproducible.[4] The 'gold standard' of randomized controlled studies is little more than the Emperor's new clothes, yet governments, pressured by commercial interests, base policies on this elaborate storytelling. Science as we know it is all too often an extension of marketing – funded by those who can see a way of making money out of a new discovery or technology.

Modern medicine is a prime example. It has generated a trillion-dollar drug industry, yet it cannot stem the tide of cancer, diabetes, obesity or Alzheimer's, to name a few of the modern man-made diseases. Those blinded by the illusion of medical science believe we will find the cure for these diseases with new drugs. Meanwhile, our societies are crippled by the cost of medicine, which consumes a quarter of our taxes, yet few ask why we are so unhealthy despite an overabundance of food. Perhaps something as simple as food may be the answer, a question I explored in my book *Food is Better Medicine than Drugs*, co-authored with award-winning medical journalist Jerome Burne.

Some find solace in religion. Yet this too is in decline. Islam has been hijacked. Christianity is crumbling. Their philosophies are weak in the face of atheistic scientism (AS), the new religion in the West, a product of materialistic rationalism. Yet modern philosophers also fail to truly connect with who we are and why we are here. Instead they weave illusory webs that ricochet with implausible and complex theories that no one understands or even less experiences.

Some look to the East, to India and Tibet, yet both are rapidly being taken over by industrialization, their ancient cultures homogenized in homage to the West. China, the home of communism, is now a hotbed of materialism. Modern drugs and hospitals are fast replacing traditional medicine. Taoism is on the wane. Japan, the home of Zen, now has deeply embedded social issues, not least of which is the rapid decline in sexual desire, couples and children.

Few know that our Western culture, which originated in the Greek cultural revolution, is the source of much of the deepest wisdom of the East. The philosophies, psychologies and theologies of the Neoplatonic schools, once they had been kicked out by the dominant Roman Christian power base, put down roots in the Sufism of Islam and crossed into Kashmir, re-emerging in India as Shaivism and in Tibet as the highest Dzogchen teachings. The Greeks themselves were influenced by the Egyptians, Zoroastrians and, before them, Sumerians. However, the wisdom of the Greek philosophers was perverted in the so-called Age of Reason and the good bits buried.

Fortunately, the higher wisdom of these ancient 'gnostic' schools has not been lost, just forgotten. And it includes how to access a vast and connected inner world that shatters the illusion of our separateness.

We are, as a fact, much more connected than our culture leads us to believe, *and* more powerful and capable of making this world a better place – but not without a serious 'system upgrade', a radical reframing based on true science and experience, not belief. Only this, I propose, can create ethical, political and social systems that can work.

So, what is connection all about? I propose that connection is what happens when 'I' and an 'other' become one. It is an arc of consciousness. We, as a separate entity, get lost in a moment of connection. We get lost in art, music, sport, nature, the taste of chocolate or the act of sex. When that connection concerns an object, or even an idea, we recognize it as 'beauty'. When it involves a sentient being, we call it 'love'.

I once heard love defined as 'the greatest level of connectedness'. It can extend out from an individual, or a family, to humanity, animals, the world, *everything*. This 'big' love is what spirituality and religion are meant to be about.

Whatever the level of connection, we all seek it. We all love. We are all positively moved by some things and disturbed by others. And we have all lost something that connects us to each other, to the Earth, to our body and to our true self.

How can we reconnect? How can we be happy, healthy, brimming with joy and loving life? How can we learn to work together, play together, make this world a better paradise?

In my opinion, first we have to 'unthink' a few things to make space for something better to unfold. As Einstein said, 'The problems we have created cannot be solved at the same level of thinking we were at when we created them.' It is not new facts, new discoveries, new technologies that we need, it is new vision. As Marcel Proust said, 'The real act of discovery is not to find new lands, but to see with new eyes.'

PART I

CONSCIOUS CONNECTION

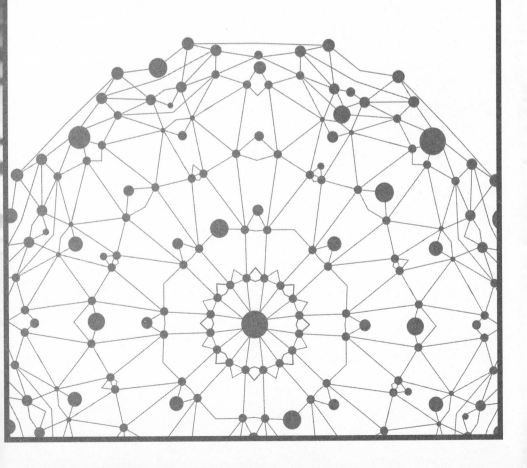

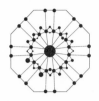

Chapter 1

Elements of Life and Death

We are sandwiched between two great fires – the fire of the Sun and the fire at the centre of the Earth. All the elements that make up our world, including the air we breathe and the water that flows through us from the sky to the Earth, come from space – they originate from exploding or dying stars. Life, health and death are a flow, a transmutation of these elements from pure formless energy into the classical 118 elements of the periodic table *(see Figure 1)*.

The visionary Russian chemist Dmitri Mendeleev saw how all the elements were related in a pattern according to their atomic weight. In 1869, when he had this realization, most of the elements had not been discovered, but now Mendeleev's periodic table of the elements has been completed.

These elements combine in many ways to form our world. Air is mainly nitrogen and oxygen and converts to carbon dioxide. Water is made up of hydrogen and oxygen. Sugars and fats – our fuel – are carbon, hydrogen and oxygen. Protein, which gives us structure, includes nitrogen and sulphur. Methylation, the process that keeps our body's chemistry in balance, depends on methyl molecules made up of carbon and hydrogen. These five elements – carbon (C), hydrogen (H), oxygen (O), sulphur (S) and nitrogen (N) – make up 96.5 per cent of our body. We are CHOSN.

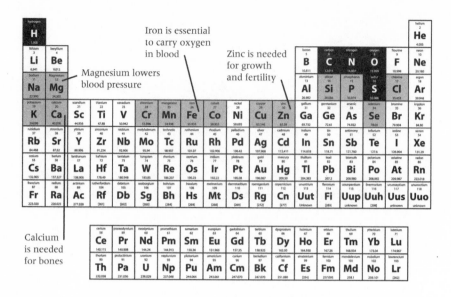

Figure 1: The periodic table. Highlighted black are the five elements that make up 96.5 per cent of our body.

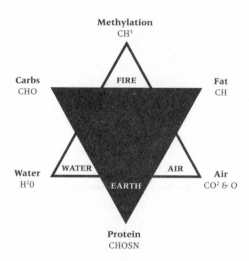

Figure 2: How the macronutrients we depend on are made from the major elements

Cycles of Life

Life sacrifices itself to life in a continuous cycle. Carbon, for example, is captured from the air (as carbon dioxide), stored in the soil and the sea, taken into plants and algae, consumed by people, animals and fish, then exhaled back into the air. Eventually our bodies decompose, or are burned, and nourish the soil. Dust to dust, ashes to ashes, as the saying goes. Effectively, we are stardust made out of billions-of-year-old carbon.

As mentioned earlier, the oxygen in every other breath we take comes from algae. Vast colonies of *Emiliania huxleyi* algae (*see Figure 3*) occupy the oceans, appearing from space like clouds in the sea, capturing carbon and calcium to make wheels within wheels and releasing oxygen. That is why the oceans are even more important than the Amazon jungle for life on Earth.

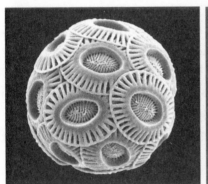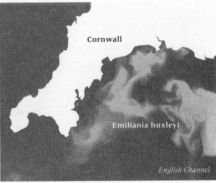

Figure 3: Electron microscope image of Emiliania huxleyi (left)
(© Natural History Museum London, Science Photo Library) and
colonies of it off the southwest coast of England (right)

The world also has a cycle of fire, or light, ultimately from the Sun, which is trapped in plants in carbohydrate and fat. It binds together the elements of carbon, hydrogen and oxygen like chords made of individual notes containing the vibrations that drive our biological processes.

Oxygen lights the fire in our cells' power plants, the mitochondria, releasing the Sun's energy in food to energize and support life.

These mitochondria are the great-grandchildren of bacteria. They have joined the fold, the unity we call our body. But that body also contains 10 times more bacteria than living cells. Where it starts and ends is a matter of debate. Are the bacteria in our gut and on our skin part of us?

There's a nitrogen cycle too. Air is 78 per cent nitrogen and 21 per cent oxygen, yet oxygen gets all the credit. However, it turns out that we can't use oxygen without nitrogen. Nitric oxide (one nitrogen and one oxygen atom) has to be attached to the haemoglobin in red blood cells before oxygen can be delivered to the cells of our body. It also relaxes our arteries. (This is not the same as nitrous oxide – two nitrogens and one oxygen. That is laughing gas, which makes us laugh then pass out. It's an anaesthetic, and bad news, because it stops us absorbing vitamin B12.) Lightning makes plants grow by sending nitrogen into the Earth.

We have a reserve of nitric oxide under the skin which is released when exposed to the Sun. That's why sunbathing actually lowers blood pressure. Then, of course, there are the multitude of benefits from the Sun's synthesis of vitamin D in the skin.

Wherever we look, there is a fundamental balance and connectedness between us and the world around us.

Energy in Space

The atoms making up that world are full of energy, each one a potential atomic bomb. The energy, ultimately, comes from the Sun. Each second the Sun, made of hydrogen and helium, produces as much energy as 100 trillion atomic bombs the size of the one used on Hiroshima, Japan, or the equivalent of 1,000,000,000,000,000,000 sticks of dynamite. One second of the Sun's energy is enough to meet all the UK's power needs for 10 million years!

Looking at atoms in more detail, each one has a centre, a nucleus of protons and neutrons, and a differing number of electrons orbiting in rings around the nucleus.

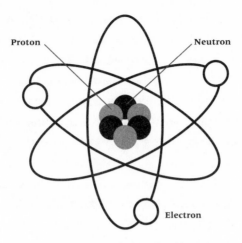

Figure 4: Subatomic particles

But all these atoms are largely empty space. Their subatomic particles are themselves largely empty space. They are apparently made of quarks, and quarks are vortices of energy. No one has found actual matter. It is all energy in space. We are all energy in space. Our world is energy in space.

Energy and Space

These two fundamentals – energy and space – are reflected in all the philosophies that have explored the nature of existence. They are represented by the male and female principles. God and Goddess. Shiva and Shakti. God the Father and the Holy Spirit. Jehovah and Shekinah. The absolute and the relative. Nothing and everything. Subject and object. The knower and the known.

In the Indian tradition, the god Shiva represents consciousness – the field of awareness in which everything happens. Every thought, feeling, sensation, perception – smell, sight, sound – happens in awareness. It is the screen on which the movie of life is played from birth to death. The screen itself is empty, void. It is the shadow of the creator, onto which is projected the creation.

The goddess Shakti is power, energy, atoms, elements, the dance of life, the material world. The Greeks called her Moneta; the Romans, Mater. Money and the material world come from this root. In Sanskrit, Maya is the creative force. In the Inca tradition, this female power is called Pachamama. Light, like a rainbow, manifests colours and forms. Like a movie. The Indian sage Swami Muktananda, when asked about the meaning of life, said, 'It is a play of consciousness.' Shakti dances for Shiva's delight.

Maya is also defined as the power that makes the real seem unreal and the unreal seem real. The world of manifestation is illusory in the sense that everything is energy.

It is ironic that atheistic scientism says that everything came out of nothing with the Big Bang, while the established religions say that God created everything out of nothing. At least they agree on something.

While not believing in miracles, the AS view is that everything can be explained by one great big miracle: the Big Bang. One wonders what was going on before the Big Bang. The physicists are onto this.

The AS position is that all of creation is just a product of chance, the unfolding of the rules of the Universe. But that just passes the buck, doesn't it? Who created the rules?

The Sufis, the mystical arm of Islam, agree. 'Hu created the rules,' they say. Hu is the name of the ultimate state of union between the Creator and Creation.

Hu?

We'll come back to this later, but now let's return to the field of awareness, of consciousness. All our experience happens there.

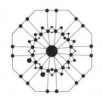

Chapter 2

Love Is the Proof That Consciousness Is Shared

Have you ever experienced not being conscious? In deep sleep, you might say, but think about it. Have you ever actually experienced deep sleep? Or unconsciousness? You are conscious when awake and conscious when dreaming. Are you conscious in between? Can you say, truly, *experientially*, that there is an in-between?

We create our world, our time and space, by streaming together moments of *now*. These are snapshots, memories, like frames in a film. This is how we mark and make time. If we were experiencing nothing – no thought, no feeling, no sensation, no perception – would we 'remember' anything? Perhaps that *is* what happens in deep sleep: nothing. So there is nothing to remember.

Where is Memory?

For our external and internal world to be 'real' – the sacred ground for the belief in materialism – two things must be found: matter and memory. No one has found matter, as we have seen, despite hundreds of years of searching. And no one has found memory either.

The standard assumption is that memory is a kind of trace that is stored in the brain. But there is no part of the brain that acts like a hard drive. To make matters worse, the memory of caterpillars remains intact when they have metamorphosed into moths, despite a complete degradation of the nervous system leaving nothing left to store memory in – if it is in the brain, that is. Similarly, people can suffer from or be born with extensive brain damage yet still remember. As can flatworms. In an extreme example of this, Dr Michael Levin at Tufts University in Boston, Massachusetts, trained flatworms to avoid a light stimulus, then chopped off their heads, thus removing their brains. Now, flatworms can fortunately regenerate their heads, and when these did so, they could still remember their training.[1]

Sure, you can mess up the brain and no longer function properly or seemingly remember some things. In the same way, you can mess up a TV and get interference or no signal at all. But that doesn't mean memory is held in the brain any more than *Coronation Street* exists in the TV.

Time is Relative

Memory requires the concept of time. Which is of course relative. As Einstein said, 'A man spends an hour with a pretty girl. It seems like minutes. He has to do the washing-up. It seems like hours. That's relativity.'

Time is also influenced by culture. The Amondawa tribe in the Amazon, for example, don't have the concept of time and space that you or I have. When they were discovered by researchers from Portsmouth in 1989, Chris Sinha, a professor of the psychology of language at the University of Portsmouth, commented,

> *We're really not saying these are a 'people without time' or 'outside time'. Amondawa people, like any other people, can talk about events and sequences of events. What we don't find is a notion of time as being independent of the events that are occurring; they don't have a notion of time which is something the events occur in. The Amondawa language has no word for 'time', or indeed of time periods such as 'month' or*

'year'. The people do not refer to their ages, but rather assume different names in different stages of their lives or as they achieve different status within the community. There is no 'mapping' between concepts of time passage and movement through space. Ideas such as an event having 'passed' or being 'well ahead' of another are familiar from many languages, forming the basis of what is known as the 'mapping hypothesis'. But in Amondawa, no such constructs exist.[2]

The only 'time' that exists is the present – that's why it's called 'the present'. I remember reading Baba Ram Dass's book *Be Here Now* back in the 1970s. Since his near-death experiences (more on these later), my friend Malcolm Stewart prefers to 'be everywhere always' in reference to his sense that everything is connected.

This is also what new ideas in physics are proposing with the apparent discovery of the zero-point field, an ocean of microscopic vibrations that appear to connect everything in the Universe like an invisible web. Even the 'empty space' I talk of isn't really empty.

Researcher Lynne McTaggart explores this in her books *The Field* and *The Bond*. The idea of connecting fields, whatever they may or may not be made of, is also consistent with biologist Rupert Sheldrake's proposal of the existence of 'morphic fields', which link related things together in space, and 'morphic resonance' as a means of connecting across time, with intentions in the future acting as 'attractors', much like magnets pulling us towards a certain future, and learnings from the present becoming part of the morphic resonance, affecting us all in much the same way as what Carl Jung referred to as the collective unconscious.

If we are all connected in this way, where does our individuality come into the equation? According to the Advaita philosophy, a school of Hindu philosophy, we create the idea of 'my mind' from thoughts; the idea of 'my body' from sensations and feelings; the idea of 'my bodymind' from thoughts, feelings and sensations; and 'the world out there' from perceptions: sights, sounds, smells and sensations. Our total experience is made up of thoughts, feelings, sensations and perceptions, and all this is happening in the infinite field of awareness or consciousness. In fact it is inseparable from consciousness, which is all-pervasive. There is no distance between a thought and the field of direct awareness that we call 'I' that it is happening in. For example, what is the distance between you and a thought, or a sound, or a sight? Advaita says that all that we experience happens within our awareness, or consciousness, and, ultimately, that everything is consciousness.

Rupert Spira writes eloquently about this philosophy in his book *The Transparency of Things* and also offers experiential trainings. In a sense, this philosophy anchors us in pure being and the awareness that is always present.

A New View on Vision

As well as reconsidering memory, and therefore time, we also need to review our view of vision. We are told that it is purely a function of the eye and the brain: that light enters the eyes and is translated into a 3D colour image in the brain. It's a nice theory, but there's no evidence for it. No one has found an image in the brain.

An alternative (and much more intuitively sensible) notion is that rather than seeing things in the brain, we see them where they actually are. Our attention reaches out to the object of our focus. The field of our mind, or in this case vision, includes our brain but also includes what we are looking at. This idea also explains irrefutable phenomena such as how we know when someone is staring at us. Rupert Sheldrake has done extensive research on this, which is explained in his book *The Sense of Being Stared At.*

Another big problem for the conventional view about vision is 'out-of-body' experiences. Too many people have seen what was going on around them when their eyes were closed and they were technically unconscious and in some cases more or less braindead. I was sharing this idea with an anaesthetist when he told me this story:

The anaesthetist was going to anaesthetize a 60-year-old faith healer for repair of an inguinal hernia. He reassured the gentleman that he would take good care of him and that everything would be fine.

The patient replied, 'Don't worry, I shall be keeping an eye on you!'

Needless to say, the anaesthetist was sceptical and enquired, 'How will you do that?'

The patient's answer was that he would 'travel outside' his body and observe the operation from up in a corner of the operating theatre!

This was too strange to believe, but the faith healer said that he would arrange a 'sign': 'At 6 p.m. precisely I will drop my blood pressure and slow my pulse rate, but only for 30 seconds so as not to cause further alarm.'

The operation proceeded smoothly, but at 6 p.m. precisely the patient's blood pressure dropped and his pulse slowed.

Just as the anaesthetist was reaching for the atropine to raise the pulse rate, it rose again and, together with the blood pressure, returned to normal levels.

In the recovery room after the operation, when quizzed about this 'sign', the patient replied, 'Well, doctor, I told you that I would do this and indeed I saw you reaching for a drug after 30 seconds ... and then I saw you relax again as I corrected the condition. I was watching you from up in the corner of the operating theatre.'

So, how is vision happening in someone who not only has his eyes closed but is also unconscious enough to be operated on? And what about a person in a coma?

My friend Malcolm Stewart is a man whose knowledge of mysticism, philosophy and theology is extraordinary. He is, among other things, an expert in cosmic geometry, the author of two books, *Patterns of Eternity* and *Symbols of Eternity*, and has done fascinating research into the patterns that connect life across all the realms of existence. He also once spent a very interesting six weeks in and out of a coma following a rather severe sub-arachnoid aneurism, a kind of stroke, which he was not expected to survive. Six times he was recorded as being at the severest coma-scale level (level 3 on the Glasgow Coma Scale), where a person can't hear or feel anything and their pupils don't dilate or react to light.

According to his wife, Nora, 'Malcolm kept going into the highest coma scale, meaning he was not present. This would last for anything up to three days. The doctors were perplexed. They were expecting him to die, but he didn't.'

Malcolm recalls, 'The doctors wanted me to stop going out of the body, so they asked Martha, my daughter, to tell me to stop. I had found a way to go in and out of the body. You just have to go up!'

I asked him what he recalled.

My experience was being without a body for a time – at various times actually. I was floating around, looking down, not from very high, about 15 metres [50 feet]. I could see the countryside and it was green. I think it was around Woking.

I could see the faces of many people. I had the feeling that they wished me well, had prayed for me or had sent me love. I had the feeling that I was being buoyed up on all these prayers and love.

Malcolm had been a supporter of the Ahmadiyya Muslim community, based in Tilford, southern England, whose motto is 'Love all, hate none.' When they heard that he was in a coma, the Caliph sent a message to his millions of followers asking them to offer their prayers for him. Prayers were also sent from the Aricans, a mystical school based on the teachings of Oscar Ichazo, of which Malcolm is a member. A mass was conducted at Lourdes, too, as Malcolm was ordained as a Catholic priest.

'I do have the feeling that I am a sample of what can be done for a person,' he said.

One thing I realized was that there was no sound. I was seeing things but there was no sound. I'm interested in that because 'in the beginning was the Word'. When we come into the body, there is sound. But when we're not in the body, there is no sound.

He also recalls a river of golden light:

This golden flow form was going from left to right, and I was above it, although I don't know what the 'I' was that was seeing it. It had flows and vortices with golden, reddish, yellow and orange hues. It was a living form. It is the dynamic principle of everything. That's how I see it.

Coincidentally, in my out-of-body experience when I was 18 I also witnessed a scintillating, living, pulsating flow of golden energy. I too had the feeling it contained – it *was* – all of life, and that everything was energy and was conscious. It was an eternal and infinite experience.

Eternal and Infinite Consciousness?

Malcolm, like many others, experienced and witnessed proceedings despite having a seemingly close to dead brain. Is there any evidence that death of consciousness exists?

As I was editing this chapter, a friend of mine told me of her brother, Duncan, who was bringing his wife, who was dying of cancer, home from surgery when he had a massive heart attack that nearly killed him. Duncan himself explained:

I was rushed into surgery for a quadruple bypass. They rip open the sternum and take the heart out and put you on total life support. You're not really biologically living. It's like suspended animation.

I was in another dimension completely. It was like being on a huge LP which was this life and other lives, and I was sliding across the lives like different tracks with reminiscences of past experiences. I knew I was going to the edge but was really fine with this. Then the movement slowed and the groove I was in became much more enveloping and visual. I went into a dimension of Jerusalem, which I knew because I'd been there many times, but it was like a mystical Jerusalem and I was being summoned for an interview, so to speak. I met a very impressive young male from the ancient world and a young child whom I knew immediately as Max, my two-year-old nephew whom I had never met but had seen in a photograph.

As we gathered in this space it concentrated and became like a living DNA spiral. It was divine coherence, and we – that is, Max, the ancient one and I – all got spliced into it. The clear message to me was that this was God's love for creation. It was awesome.

There was a sound like an immense deep wave, like a sub-tone, a power, a kind of 'Om'-like hum, a pre-music of a voice speaking only of beauty. It had a wave form totally in synch with a very active spiral with lots of spirals within it, and the three of us were connecting at slightly different points. Gold, silver, sometimes slightly pink, lilac – the colours were living energies that appeared golden or silvery. The whole atmosphere was pulsing with colours, like the river of life. It was a communication of absolutely everything. It was scientific down to the last detail with an immense heart vibration of love. I was seeing the meaning of what I was hearing – that this was God's love for creation. It was completely thrilling.

Then it asked me whether I wanted to return to the body or excarnate. I was shown the benefits of being in the body. It is the optimal density to really move into being, rather than merely being aware of existence. I said, 'Yes.' Then I was back on the LP and instead of sliding to the edge, I zipped right back to the hole in the middle and dropped back into my body. It was a dead body, like cold clay, and I tasted chalk. And I couldn't move and yet I had complete recollection of the experience.

I asked Duncan how his near-death experience had changed him.

I've been in an altered state ever since. The crown of my head feels 'filamental' – gentle, flickering, almost playful. It is a very visceral experience. I'm going through a very slow 'resurrection', unravelling some of my earlier life experiences, and I'm rather enjoying it. It has deepened my knowing to a natural state. I know we have a destiny but it is absolutely crucial how you are with it. When you know there is destiny and you accept it, and meet it, rather than resisting it, it is grace. Grace is fate.

A year later his wife died. I asked how his experience had altered that transition.

I wanted to get strong so I could help my wife, who was dying. There was an incident when she fell down the stairs and I crawled across to her and said, 'We are completely fucked.' We cracked up laughing. I called it a death tango flooded with love.

I have been totally helped to know that the core of existence is being, and being is love. You are aware of the 'self' being gone … and this life is gone, but there is a lot of you that does not die. Death is not 'it'.

Recently I met Max for the first time. He was just as he was in the experience. Complete déjà vu. It was amazing. I almost felt my heart breaking. It was something very pure.

Another insight into the nature of life comes from the near-death experience of Eben Alexander, a neurosurgeon who was declared as close to braindead as you can be following a rare meningitis infection. In his book *Proof of Heaven* he described his very lucid experiences. At one point he felt he was:

…something akin to a fetus in a womb. In this case the 'mother' was God, the Creator, the Source who is responsible for making the Universe and all in it. This Being was so close that there seemed to be no distance

between God and myself. Yet, at the same time, I could sense the vastness of the Creator, could see how completely miniscule I was in comparison. 'Om' was the sound I remembered hearing associated with that omniscient, omniprescient, omnipotent, and unconditionally loving God, but any descriptive words fall far short.

He, too, was accompanied by someone – 'a beautiful girl with high cheekbones and deep blue eyes'. She was no one he knew. Or so he thought. But he had been adopted, and four months after his recovery, having reconnected with his birth sister Kathy, he received a picture of his other sister, Betsy, as a young girl. Betsy had died and Eben had never met her or even known she'd existed.

There was no mistaking her, no mistaking the loving smile, the confident and infinitely comforting look, the sparkling blue eyes. It was she.

Atheistic scientists (ASs) propose that consciousness is a trick of the brain, extinguished at death. But there is really no evidence for this – quite the contrary, as the experiences of Malcolm, Duncan and Eben suggest.

Dealing with Your Own Death

I don't want to achieve immortality through my work; I want to achieve immortality through not dying.
Woody Allen

At the height of the 100% Health Club, a forum I have been running for people pursuing optimal health and longevity (*see Resources*), I was feeling a bit uncomfortable about this desire to postpone or at least resist the inevitable. We are, after all, all going to die. Would a healthier, more honest approach simply be to accept that fact?

In many traditions it is believed that your time of death is predetermined. And an Indian swami once told me, 'You health-food freak, you are going to look so silly when you die because you'll have nothing to die from.'

So I invited the brilliant psychotherapist Nan Beecher-Moore to present a workshop called 'Dealing with Your Own Death'. She had been running this for psychotherapists who, she said, arrived all gloomy but left all lit up. In the workshop you would complete the unfinished business in your life, consider what you would do if you only had a year to go and write your own obituary, among other things.

We had very few sign-ups. Then a week before the workshop, Nan went and died – presumably well prepared. Bless you, Nan.

My favourite death is that of the local holy man Zipruanna, who died in Nasirabad in India in the 1930s. One day he knocked on the door of a family in the village and asked if he could have a bath and a meal. He washed his body, then fed his body, and on completing his meal, he said, 'Zipru is leaving. You can cry now, but it won't make any difference,' and closed his eyes. He was gone.

What I love about this story is that he washed his body, fed his body, then left his body. His was a conscious death, without fear.

Play It Right

Oh Lord, I am lost for words to say
the meaning of death I wish to convey.
It is not that she leaves the world for us to grieve
But that the world in her leaves for her soul to be freed.

It is not that the she, the body, departs
But that the elements of Earth, water, air and fire
Merge into the ether of God's heart.

We come from God, so shall we return.
There is no dying to be done.
Just Mother and Child becoming one.

Against life's lessons we struggle and fight
And, in the end, return to light.
It is not that life is day and death is night,
It is all a play, so play it right.

I do believe that all fears ultimately stem from the fear of death or the fear of losing the sense of self, as in going crazy, and that fear is a driving force in dis-ease of both mind and body. 'Love is letting go of fear,' writes Jerry Jampolsky in his excellent book of the same title.

The medieval poet Rumi said, 'I died a mineral and became a plant. I died a plant and rose an animal. I died an animal and I was man. Why should I fear? When was I less by dying?'

Ho Hum

As a Christian, it is interesting that Eben heard the sound vibration 'Om', as did Duncan. 'Om' is known as the primordial mantra and may be what is referred to in 'in the beginning was the Word'. The Aborigines also say the world is sung into existence.

'Om' is actually 'AUM'. 'AU' in Sanskrit is written as 'O'. 'A' corresponds to the waking state, 'U' the dream state and 'M' the state of deep sleep. At the end of 'AUM' is a pause, a silence. This represents the state known as Turiya, or Infinite Consciousness. 'Om/AUM' is said to be the sound of the Universe.

If you were Greek, you might say 'I am Alpha and Omega.' The long 'aaaah' and the 'ooomega' are the origin of vibration and the beginning and end of the Greek alphabet, from which we create words, and in turn the conceptual world. 'All-ah' is a launch point to the absolute. Tibetan Buddhists in the Dzogchen tradition focus on the Tibetan symbol for 'A' (*see below*), although I like to use the @ symbol to develop one-pointed concentration, free of thought. Isn't it strange how this symbol has become the pivot between the individual and the 'global' in our digital world – patrick@googlemail.com?

Figure 5: Tibetan (left) and modern (right) symbols used in the 'A' meditation

Of course, the ASs get very uncomfortable with all this 'Om'ing, let alone the 'G' word and the idea that consciousness is not a product of the material brain and does not stop at death. 'Ho hum,' they might say. But that's not far from the mark either. 'Om' is the hum of the Universe and in Sufism Hu is the name of God. It is also the first breath, the first word or sound, in Egyptian mythology: the 'Hu-M'. From the absolute nothing comes everything.

Energy in Vibration

'In the beginning was the Word, and the Word was with God and the Word was God,' says the Bible (John 1:1). 'All material existence is just energy in vibration,' say the physicists. This is not a religious belief. It is what they have discovered.

Einstein was fascinated by the nature of light. In his famous equation, energy equals mass (matter) multiplied by the speed of light squared ($E=mc^2$), he predicted that if you sent one piece of matter, an atom, at the speed of light into another piece of matter at the speed of light, at the point of collision they would become energy. When a 'particle collider' was finally built, that's what happened. Einstein was right. It was amazing! So how did we use his insight? We built nuclear bombs.

One of my teachers, Dr Linus Pauling, was a student of Einstein's. The only person ever to have won two unshared Nobel Prizes, as well as acquiring 48 PhDs, he brought Einstein's level of thinking into the field of chemistry. He won his second Nobel Prize for campaigning for, and achieving, a ban on nuclear bomb testing.

But to return to the nature of light, where does light actually come from? We say the Sun. The dying words of Turner, the painter of light, were: 'The Sun is God.' All life ultimately comes from the Sun. It is far from an 'inanimate power station', as we are taught in 21st-century scientism. It is vast, mysterious and majestic, holding our whole planetary system together in its 3 million kilometre (1.9 million mile) wide field.

Somehow, the Sun generates more heat at the outer layers than in the centre. It is said such is the complexity of the interactions that occur there that each photon, each unit of light, generated in the Sun takes seven years to leave and head for us. The Sun that we see is 1.4 million kilometres (900,000 miles) wide and exactly 400 times the diameter of the moon and 400 times further from the Earth than the moon. This remarkable coincidence is why, in a solar eclipse, the moon exactly obscures the Sun.

The Romans worshipped the Sun as God, IGNA-tus, which is the origin of words like 'ignite'. The Vedic Indians worshipped it as Surya (Sun) and AGNI, representing fire. The Zoroastrians and before them the Egyptians worshipped it as God: Ra.

The Masai god is NGAI. With every rising and setting Sun they say, 'ASANGAI' – 'Thank you, Sun, thank you, God.' In Tibetan Buddhism NGA means 'powerful'.

Whether or not it is God, there are many very good reasons to consider the Sun intelligent, a conscious force in the Universe, as Greg Sams' book *The Sun of gOd* proposes with great substance and conviction. Even top NASA rocket scientists, with their complex calculations and precision engineering, would be happy to launch a satellite into space and keep it in a stable orbit for 100 years. The Sun has been doing this for the Earth and the other planets of the solar system for 4 billion years. It is certainly a lot more intelligent in this respect than we are.

We have so much to be thankful for. As Galileo once said, 'The Sun, with all those planets revolving around it and dependent on it, can still ripen a bunch of grapes as if it had nothing else in the Universe to do.' Those seeking 'enlightenment' might start, like the Masai, with a 'Thank you, Sun' at dawn and dusk.

Quite apart from the light of the Sun during the day, though, where does the light come from when we dream in the pitch-black night with our eyes closed? That is a question worth exploring.

In his book *The New Science of Spirit*, David Ash says that energy travels in a wave or a vortex. This mirrors the golden wave or flow form of both Malcolm and Duncan's out-of-body experiences, as well as my own. Think of a beam of light that spirals into itself in a vortex, like a ball of wool. That's what the physicists are finding in subatomic particles. Atoms, the 'stuff' of matter, are vortices of energy. As are we, the world and all the planets. We perceive our body and our world to be 'solid', but really everything is waves and vortices of energy. The vortex movement is often seen in the natural world. Even the planets, which are often thought to be orbiting the Sun, are actually spiralling in a vortex around it, while it moves along at 70,000 kilometres (43,500 miles) an hour![3]

It's worth bearing in mind that everything we are speaking of here is conceptual. These are constructs: concepts of time and space, atoms and elements, memories and matter. Our conceptual world is made out of words. Buddhists call it 'the relative truth'. Indian philosophers call it the Matrika Shakti. It is energy moving into vibration, into sounds and syllables, words and concepts – the matrix of existence. In the classic *Matrix* film the 'real' world turns out to be a projection fed into the neural circuitry of the brain. The 'real' world is virtual.

It is mind-boggling, but sometimes, to enter into the mysteries of connection, it is better to have a boggled mind.

Fundamental Beliefs

A true scientist, regardless of belief, would want to explore these fundamental questions and phenomena. Some are, and it is interesting that advances at the edge of astrophysics and microphysics are remarkably consistent with the teachings of the deepest mystical traditions.

The two fundamentals – pure being, the ground of everything, and consciousness, or, making it personal, our consciousness – can be arrived at experientially and logically through reason. The Greek philosophers did this and all the major spiritual traditions have done so too in their own ways.

Yet there is a wave of young AS proselytizers who haven't thought this through at all. Instead they seem to believe in the pre-existence of a set of laws floating around in the quantum Universe that can, or will, explain everything and do away with any need for a father figure God with a long, white beard. On the father figure God bit, I agree, but if there is a natural order that explains everything, what is that resting on? What is the origin of these natural laws, what is our fundamental nature, what gives meaning to life? These are the questions real philosophers seek to answer but today's ASs avoid.

A classic example of this is the lamentably bad book *The God Delusion* by Richard Dawkins, which starts by trying to show that Einstein was an atheist and goes on to say that if he was, we should be too. Really? Here are a couple of Einstein's quotes:

> *I maintain that the cosmic religious feeling is the strongest and noblest motive for scientific research.*

> *That which is impenetrable to us really exists. Behind the secrets of Nature remains something subtle, intangible and inexplicable. Veneration for this force beyond anything that we can comprehend is my religion.*

Now that doesn't sound like an atheist to me.

Dawkins then denies that any transcendental experience or higher intelligence exists, without offering any evidential support other than his own lack of experience. This is a bit like saying sex doesn't exist just because you've never had it. His philosophical arguments are equally dodgy. David Bentley Hart exposes the basic inadequacies in his logical argument in his books *Atheist Delusions* and *The Experience of God: Being, Consciousness, Bliss*. These are 'must reads' for any aspiring atheist, as are the Greek philosopher Proclus's book *Elements of Theology*, based on Plato's metaphysics, which provides the reasoned basis for the unity of everything, and Plotinus' *Enneads*.[4]

However, the fact that Dawkins' book has sold so well really shows how the fundamentalist AS point of view has become a substantial sub-culture in the 21st century. We have been sold the idea of the thinking 'I' and the material world: 'I think therefore I am.' It's a quite alienating approach with little sense of connection, and paves the way for greed and isolation and a lack of respect for the Earth.

With the loss of any transcendental meaning, material accumulation has become the meaning of existence: 'I buy therefore I am.' And why not, if who I am is just a carbon unit with a finite existence and a consciousness extinguished at death?

I find this concept not only absurd, but also deeply depressing. How much of the world's anger and depression comes from this belief? How much is generated by the rub between religious and atheist fundamentalists forcing their dogmas onto others – the battle of AS versus IS?

The fundamentalist atheist view incorporates notions of the selfish gene – survival of the fittest – which feed into rampant hubristic materialism and capitalistic exploitation, endorsing greed and eroding social ethics. With no regard for our true human spirit and nature, this worldview fuels a Cromwellian crusade to crush not only organized and often corrupted religion, but also any concept of God or a higher intelligence, or even the study of essential theological questions. It's a kind of 'thought police' as described by Orwell in *1984*. However, it is unscientific to ignore phenomena that cannot be explained by materialistic models. Thus, while rightly challenging fixed religious dogma, the less well-educated fundamentalists hypocritically fail to challenge the dogmas of materialistic science.

This atheistic culture also demotes the imaginal world of dreams, myths, deities, archetypes, angels and demons that is embedded in the philosophies of more 'connected' cultures, for instance Tibetan or Aboriginal, and inherent in the psyche of children and in what we might naively call 'medieval' religious philosophies such as the Sufism of Avicenna or Surhawardi, which has greatly influenced Iranian Islamic culture. This internal world has been replaced by an endless need for external images – TV, computer games, movies with more than their fair share of superheroes, X-Men, villains and mythic and sci-fi worlds – and the bridge between the 'real' world and our inner world, accessed in dreams and more easily by children before their brainwashing is complete, is increasingly blocked off. We feel this loss of inner space and project outwards with dreams of a sci-fi future, or immersion in mythical fantasies, or accumulation of stuff. We project the contents of our 'mind' into the World Wide Web then spend hours peering into it, looking for answers.

An Alternative Proposition?

There has to be a different way. And there is. The essential principles of the main religions are: love thy neighbour, treat others with respect and turn the other cheek. Whether or not you are religiously inclined, these connecting principles seem like a useful set of guiding ethics.

They are also in harmony with what the Greek Platonists reasoned was our true nature. Their view was that all desires ultimately led to, and were fuelled by, the transcendental desires for truth, beauty or goodness.

Why do we have these desires? Could it be because they lead to the ultimate ground of connection?

Wake Up

Wake up,
Put on your bodymind,
The world, it needs you now.
Someone must fetch the water, light the fire
And milk the cow.
Illusory as it all may be,
The game must be played and plays in me.
So get up, put on your bodymind
And make a cup of tea.

Love is the Proof...

The essence of consciousness, says Oscar Ichazo, is 'that which recognises itself'.[5] When one consciousness recognizes another consciousness, we experience love, be it a moment of connection with another sentient being or an immersion in the beauty of nature or an internal experience of consciousness recognizing itself. This is also called *samadhi*, that is, consciousness of consciousness. That's what Zen is all about.

According to Advaita philosopher Rupert Spira, 'Love is the proof that consciousness is shared.' It is an arc of shared consciousness, a shared field of awareness. I aspire to being in this expanded state on a more permanent basis. It is my fundamental desire. Does this make me a fundamentalist or, even worse, a fanatic?

The word 'fanaticism' comes from *fana*, a Sufi term for what happens when the individual ego, or sense of self, merges with the absolute. Rumi did this in a moving meditation than involved whirling faster and faster. The dance of the whirling dervishes, practised to this day, is a very specific internal meditation that, if done right, creates an experience of profound unity, a still awareness in the centre while the world spins, like planets orbiting the Sun or electrons circling the nucleus of the atom. That awareness, separate from the perceptions of the senses, is always still. As a consequence, when you stop whirling, there is no dizziness – *nada*.

Rumi said, 'When a man's "I" is negated (and eliminated) from existence, then what remains? Consider, O denier.'

Is this the ultimate connection?

The Beach

I'm a million miles from base,
Lying on a vast deserted beach,
In endless time and endless space,
Listening to the beat
Of his majesty, the roaring sea,

Washing his beloved's feet.

Bowing to the gentle sea,
Dressed in pure white sand,
Mother Earth asks, 'Will you be with me?'
And takes him by the hand.
He says, 'From now until eternity.'

God blesses them with the Sun's light,
So the sea can make the clouds,
And spins them fast to seal their fate,
So every day turns into night,
Protecting them from the Sun's fiery kiss,
Reminding them each night what they miss.

Wherever these two meet is a sacred place,
Whether gentle rain or
a complete downpour,
A riverbank or an ocean shore,
A waterfall or a babbling stream.
These are the places I like to be.

These places remind me that
My body is from the Earth,
My thoughts are from the sky,
My feelings are from the deep blue sea,
My spirit from the light.

I'm walking on the beach,
Knowing I have everything I need –
Food to eat, water to drink,
Air to breathe and time to think,
And the sacred Earth beneath my feet –
Knowing every moment is complete.

Chapter 3

The Chemistry of Culture and Consciousness

A s water is to fish, human relations are our 'second nature'. How we relate, including our ethics, morals and values, forms the basis of our culture. Some cultures have rules about relationships and behaviour that make them seem odd from a different cultural perspective. But what gives birth to a new culture?

Cultural Revolutions

The most significant cultural revolutions include the Sumerian, Zoroastrian, Egyptian, Vedic, Greek and Roman, and, in South America, the Mayan and rather short-lived Inca culture, part of the Quechuan culture, which continues to some extent today. As we have seen, our Western culture, including concepts such as democracy, stems from the Greeks, while our imperialism could be said to be a product of the Roman culture.

Each of these cultures had a shared vision and a unifying experience which culminated in a new set of concepts and rules for life. Most, interestingly, each also involved the use of a mind-altering substance. This was an area I explored when I was researching my book *Natural Highs* with psychiatrist Dr Hyla Cass, then Assistant Clinical Professor of Psychiatry at UCLA School of Medicine in Los Angeles, California.

In India almost 4,000 years ago, the Vedas – Hindu philosophical texts – extolled a plant potion called *soma*, considered to be God in plant form. It was their sacrament. Central to Zoroastrianism in Persia, at around the same time, was a potion called *haoma*. Thanks to Alexander the not so Great, who slaughtered the peaceful Zoroastrians, including all the priests who passed down their wisdom and plant potions verbally, we don't know what *haoma* was. Similarly, the magic formula of *soma* is lost, although theories abound, from mushrooms to a mixture of plants, including Syrian rue, which inhibits the breakdown of DMT (more on this in a minute).

The ancient Greeks, from Aristotle to Plato, took part in an initiation called the Eleusian mysteries, which involved consuming a rye-based drink. What exactly happened is also a mystery, thanks to the rather over-zealous Christians who destroyed the great Library of Alexandria along with several hundred thousand scrolls, but historians believe the drink contained the ergot-rye fungus, a natural source of LSD.

Egyptian cultures used the blue lily, henbane and mandrake, which were also favourites of European so-called witches, half a million of whom were wiped out in the witch-hunt that started in the 13th century.[1] The witches made an ointment, placed it on a stick, absorbed it through the mucus membrane of the vagina and 'flew' in visionary hallucinations, sometimes meeting spirit guides in the form of a black cat. When they were tortured during the witch-hunts, this became popularized as witches flying on broomsticks with a black cat. Interestingly, the puma or jaguar, which is often witnessed in *ayahuasca* and *achuma* experiences (*see page 36*), is the sacred animal of the Incas, and their headquarters, the city of Cusco, was originally built in the shape of a jaguar.

In the Americas, the Mayans discovered that certain mushrooms and the 'sweat' from the skin of certain toads contained powerful hallucinogens. The mind boggles as to how this was actually discovered.

Probably the earliest use of 'magic' mushrooms predates even this, going back to the Siberian peoples of northeast Asia, who later crossed the Bering Strait to colonize the Americas. They revered the highly toxic *Amanita muscaria*, or fly agaric, the red and white spotted mushroom that Alice took to enter Wonderland in Lewis Carroll's classic story. To this day a herbal brew known as *yage* or *ayahuasca* is still used widely by South American shamans, while the shrub *ibogaine* is used in West Africa.

Some Native American tribes from the Quechuan tradition, of which the Incas were the high priests, use the *achuma* (San Pedro) and *peyote* cactus, both natural sources of mescaline.

In the West, the mostly widely used drug is alcohol, the favourite of the Romans. The most widely used entheogens (mind-expanding substances) are 'designer drugs' – manufactured compounds such as MDMA/Ecstasy and LSD, which have been tried by an estimated quarter of all 16- to 24-year-olds.

Recent studies of volunteers on LSD or psylocybin show the whole brain lit up, with areas that don't normally talk to other areas, cross-connected.[2] If the brain is vastly more connected what is going on at a chemical level? How do these drugs work and what can they tell us about the chemistry of connection?

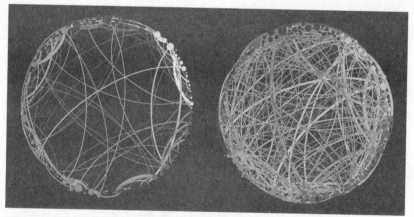

Figure 6: A simplified visualization of connectivity between functional areas and networks in the brain during the resting state under placebo (left) and psilocybin (right). Petri et al. (2014) (Used with permission of the Beckley/Imperial Research Programme, directed by Professor David Nutt and Lady Amanda Feilding) See colour section.

How Entheogens Expand the Mind

The brain naturally produces a mind-expanding substance called DMT (di-methyl-tryptamine), which acts much like one of the brain's neurotransmitters. This is clearly part of our design. There are DMT receptors in the brain by the seventh month of foetal development. It is thought to be primarily produced or stored in the pineal gland, along with serotonin and melatonin. It may be central to dreaming.

The pineal, which is at centre-stage in the brain, is light-sensitive in many animals and is necessary for them to be connected to the environment and the ebb and flow of day and night, as well as seasonal changes. Indian mystics consider the pineal to be our 'third eye' or *ajna* chakra (*see page 172*), an antenna, if you like, for 'inner' light. It may be the light source when we dream. René Descartes considered it to be the seat of the soul.

We know far too little about the role of the pineal gland, let alone about what DMT does, mainly because funding for research was shut down in the backlash against LSD, another fascinating chemical, back in the 1970s.

For this reason, we are indebted to Dr Rick Strassman, clinical associate professor of psychiatry at the University of New Mexico, who jumped through all the legal, political, financial and scientific hoops to research the effects of DMT by injecting volunteers with it and recording their psychological experiences and subsequent development and the effects it had on their brain chemistry. The whole story of this research was published in his extraordinary book *DMT: The Spirit Molecule*.

To cut a long story short, Strassman's decade of meticulously recording the experiences of volunteers taking DMT under rigorously controlled conditions has led him to hypothesize that there are other realms of existence or experience (as physicists are now proposing) and that DMT is possibly somehow involved in helping us access them. He believes that DMT release from the pineal gland may facilitate critical 'transitions' such as birth, death and near-death experiences, as well as dream states and peak experiences, and possibly be stimulated by the surge in adrenalin that occurs at birth and often in the approach to death.[3] In almost all the volunteers in Strassman's studies, DMT facilitated an expanded awareness leading to a greater sense of connection.

As freaky as this sounds, it is based on objective scientific exploration. However, to truly explore something, especially in the realm of our experience, it's best to do it. So I got hold of some DMT and vaporized it.

After one long inhale, much like the countdown after an anaesthetic – 10-9-8-7-6-5-4 ... wham! I was propelled into another world, equally real as this except with more striking kaleidoscopic colours and shapes. Then, roughly seven minutes later, although time was not perceived in the same way, I was back. It was quite a trip!

What had happened to me chemically?

Our brain filters out the vast majority of information that comes in through our senses. This presumably allows us to make sense of the world and also has survival value. Our awareness seems to work much like a sentry, always scanning for potential danger. We see what we need to see for our survival. And this is a mere fraction of what is actually 'out there'.

When an entheogen is taken, and indeed in a peak experience, it appears that this filter is suspended. The person under the influence is seeing a bigger picture and making bigger connections.

Of course, this all sounds amazing, and many people's experiences often are. However, there are dangers to entheogens: some of them are extremely toxic and hard on the liver, the experiences aren't always good, and a very small number of people, perhaps those who are inherently less stable and have a real 'bad trip', have developed mental illness as a result. (*See also page 48.*)

The vast majority of entheogens are *tryptamines*, chemical cousins of di-methyl tryptamine (DMT), which is itself closely related to the 'happy' neurotransmitter serotonin, as well as melatonin, the neurotransmitter released at night that keeps us in synch with the day/night cycle. (Jet lag is a consequence of melatonin release not adapting fast enough to a rapid change in time zone.)

The core of the DMT molecule is the five and the six ring, the hexagon and pentagon, conjoined. As we will discover in Chapter 10, the hexagon and pentagon are some of the fundamental patterns of life.

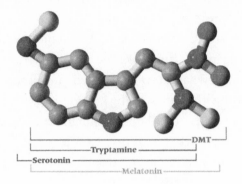

Figure 7: Tryptamines – DMT, serotonin and melatonin molecules. See colour section.

MDMA and mescaline are part of a different, although related, chemical family known as *phenethylamines*, which are also found in chocolate. LSD is unique in that it has the chemical structure of a tryptamine superimposed on a phenethylamine. Two in one.

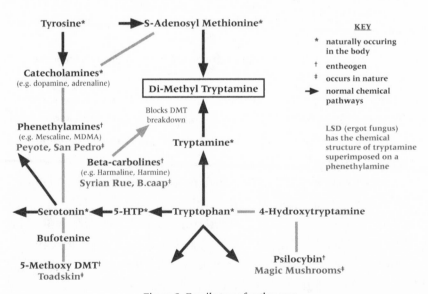

Figure 8: Family tree of entheogens

It seemed to me that DMT was the royal road, as it was the only entheogen actually produced by the brain itself, implying that it had a specific purpose in the architecture of being human. So I set off to Peru to find the Shipibo Indians, whose use of the herbal brew *ayahuasca*, which induces a DMT effect, is central to their culture.

By combining a natural source of DMT, usually the *chacruna* leaf, with the *Banisteriopsis caapi* vine, which grows in a spiral and contains an enzyme inhibitor that stops the body breaking down DMT, the *ayahuascero* shaman creates a brew which, taken in the dark of night in the Amazon jungle, gives a DMT-induced experience that lasts for several hours.

There are plenty of plants that contain DMT, including oranges, but the body's chemistry rapidly breaks it down. Only *ayahuasca*, and Syrian rue, which, as mentioned earlier is reputed to have been an ingredient in the Vedic plant potion *soma*, inhibit the enzyme in the body and allow DMT to remain in circulation for several hours.

The Shipibo do not consider it a drug, and nor do the customs officials. It is a sacrament taken to heal, to connect to a higher source of wisdom or find answers to life's problems. *Ayahuasca* is considered to be, and often experienced as, a living intelligent force. 'She' is not to be taken lightly. She is the Goddess, or Mother Earth. She is represented as a snake, a form that often appears in *ayahuasca*-induced visions.

I flew to Lima, the capital of Peru, then on to Pucalpa, deep in the Amazon, and found a speedboat willing to take me upriver, into the night, to Shipibo territory. The vast river was smooth as silk. All noise was drowned out by the roar of the 40hp engine. I asked my guide if he had ever taken *ayahuasca*. He said he had to find out if his girlfriend was pregnant. In his *ayahuasca* vision he travelled into the womb and saw the foetus of the unborn child!

When I arrived, my guide left me with the shaman and off we went on his motorbike deeper into the jungle to a small community living in open-sided huts with thatched roofs. The shaman's home was made up of a few such dwellings and a communal area with a roof covering a large deck. It was there, he said, that the ceremony would take place that night.

People start to gather as the Sun is setting. Some are going to take part, others are just hanging out. People are hanging up mosquito nets and laying out thin mattresses to sleep on. My understanding of the local dialect is non-existent, but the shaman speaks patchy English, so I learn that some participants have health issues or major problems to resolve. There is one other foreigner, a German artist.

As the Sun sets and the last hints of light fade away, the night fills with sounds of the jungle. The shaman rolls big fat cigars of raw tobacco and, one by one, purifies us by blowing smoke over parts of our body. He blows smoke at my hands, my heart and the crown of my head. He brings out the brew that he has been making throughout the day. He pours the dark brown 'tea' into cups made from a large nut shell, purifies it and chants over it.

I drink my cup. The liquid is strong, foul-tasting. It sends a shiver through me. It tastes like something either poisonous or extremely good for you. Why do things that are good for you taste so bad?

Now I am lying on my back on a deck in the dark, somewhere deep in the Amazon jungle, waiting for the ayahuasca to kick in. I hear the 'ch-ch-ch-ch' of the Icaros, the songs the shaman is singing to the rhythm of the shaking leaves. The air is pregnant with the rich, chaotic sounds of birds, insects and rustling leaves, pierced with the screech of monkeys and other random animal sounds. The jungle canopy is vast, ominous in the dark with patches of sky and stars and the shadows of clouds. Always the chicherero of the cicadas…

Then it starts. I am sinking into the ground. I feel a flash of fear, then I am letting go, overwhelmed by the inevitability of what is happening. My eyes are closed, yet I am seeing kaleidoscopic colours beyond description – ruby reds, emerald greens, liquid silvers and golds, sapphire blues, patterns like cosmic circuitry, evolving, living, unravelling like a Mandelbrot set.

At one point an entity, a vast consciousness, I could say like a snake although I didn't see a snake as such, dived into me, into the very depths of me, into each cell, each strand of DNA, rewiring me like an electric shock in slow motion from the centre to the outside.

Then 'I' am gone, reborn as a vast awareness higher than the trees. The chaos of the jungle is gone. All the sounds are ordered into the lineage of life, from insect to bird to animal. Everything is in order under the command of the benevolent and violent intelligence that conducts the orchestra of life and death.

I am thunder. I am lightning. I am fierce. I am frightening. I am the mother and I am the wife. I am the giver and taker of life.

Everything is exactly as it should be. Everything makes sense.

I open my eyes and try to walk, but it is difficult. Everything seems unreal, made of energy, like a veil. Wow!

Actually, I took *ayahuasca* three nights in a row and then went back for further sessions two years later. To this day it has changed and deepened my relationship to the natural world – and changed me, too. Now I have a stronger intuition and a deeper connection to people and the world around me.

Anyway, back to the chemistry. While working on the *Natural Highs* book, I had an idea. If DMT was the brain's natural entheogen and was helping us tune out of 'Channel Normal' and into other realms of consciousness, a conclusion Dr Rick Strassman had come to, what nutrients would support its natural production? Could taking these nutrients help us to feel more 'connected'? Could they help people suffering from 'disconnection' and depression?

So I mapped it out. Now, I'm not a trained biochemist. In fact, chemistry was one of my weakest subjects at school, but my passion for nutrition had led me to trace the different enzymes and chemical pathways that allow us to create neurotransmitters in the brain from amino acids in the diet. But I needed to check my assumptions were correct, so I got in touch with the grand master of chemistry and consciousness, Alexander Shulgin.

Shulgin, or Sasha as he was known to his friends, was born in Berkeley, California, in 1925 and at the age of 16 won a scholarship to Harvard to study organic chemistry. He later became interested in psychopharmacology. He worked for the Drug Enforcement Agency (DEA) because he, more than any other person, could analyse any new street drug and understand how it was being made. He had a licence to experiment with Schedule 1 drugs and spent decades experimenting with new compounds and trying them out on his fellow scientists and 'psychonauts', who had worked out a system of recording their experiences at different doses. All in all, he invented hundreds and tested thousands of different chemical compounds, some natural, some man-made.

Figure 9: Alexander Shulgin in his laboratory (© Scott Houston/Sygma/Corbis)

Then he published two whopping great tomes, almost 1,000 pages each, called *PIHKAL* and *TIKHAL*, short for 'Phenethylamines I Have Known And Loved' and 'Tryptamines I Have Known And Loved'.

Each compound was described, along with how to make it and what happened to his group of volunteers when they took it. As a consequence, he lost his DEA work and licence. In an enlightened world he would have been given a Nobel Prize. No one has mapped chemistry and consciousness like him. He was a genius chemist and a warm and intelligent man who died in 2014 at the age of 88. He agreed to take a look at my map of the road to DMT, corrected a couple of pathways and very much enjoyed the question.

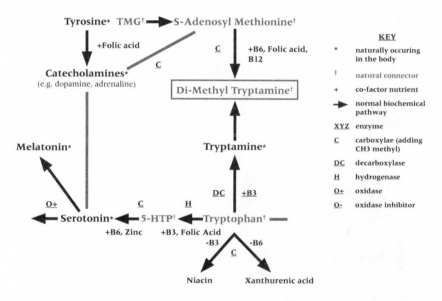

Figure 10: Map of the road to DMT

All this resulted in a nutritional and herbal formula called Connect, which, in a subtle way, seemed to do what it said. We had a great review in London's *Evening Standard* from a journalist who had taken some before going to the theatre with friends and had a great time. It was headed: 'Drink, drugs? No, I'll stick with the natural highs.'

As well as various vitamins and minerals and amino acids, I had included in the formula a San bushman herb, *Sceletium tortuosum*, known as kanna, and kava kava, the Polynesian plant that acts as a mood-enhancing relaxant. All was going very well until kava kava got banned in the EU and *Sceletium* fell foul of new EU herbal medicine regulations prohibiting any herb not in common usage in the EU at that time, despite hundreds of years of safe use. I was pleased to read recently that kava kava's ban has been ruled illegal by the German high courts. In the USA it is making a comeback. It should never have been banned and is very helpful for those suffering from acute anxiety and insomnia.

(By the way, it got banned because an alcoholic woman on several forms of medication couldn't sleep, so added kava kava to the mix and died. On autopsy she had a sclerotic liver. Can you imagine how many medical drugs would be banned if the same criteria were applied to them? Over 100,000 deaths per year in the USA and over 10,000 in the UK are attributed to prescribed medications.)

The Connect formula still exists, but sadly without these herbs.

Awakenings

Shulgin's awakening to the power of entheogens came in the late 1950s, after taking mescaline, the active compound in *peyote*. He recalled:

The most compelling insight of that day was that this awesome recall had been brought about by a fraction of a gram of a white solid, but that in no way whatsoever could it be argued that these memories had been contained within the white solid. Everything I had recognised came from the depths of my memory and my psyche. I understood that our entire Universe is contained in the mind and the spirit. We may choose not to find access to it, we may even deny its existence, but it is indeed there inside us, and there are chemicals that can catalyse its availability.

He is now most renowned for putting MDMA, Ecstasy, back on the map, although it was originally discovered in 1912 by a Merck chemist. It's a phenethylamine. Shulgin's entry in *PIKHAL* when he tried MDMA reads:

I feel absolutely clean inside, and there is nothing but pure euphoria. I have never felt so great or believed this to be possible. I am overcome by the profundity of the experience.

He believed that MDMA could be profoundly useful in psychotherapy, helping people overcome trauma or debilitating guilt, which has been confirmed in a recent clinical trial.[4] It has also been shown to help relieve fearful memories in animals.[5] Shulgin liked to quote a psychiatrist who described MDMA as 'penicillin for the soul'.

I took MDMA once on a ridge above Big Sur, California, the home of Linus Pauling, on a visit in the 1980s, and, like Shulgin and many others, had an illuminating and heart-opening experience.

Ragged Ridge

Today I breathed in the universe,
sitting high on a ragged ridge,
a blanket of clouds below
and vibrant blue above.

I felt the ecstasy of love
fill me like the endless wind
blowing off the sea
and come to rest in my heart as gently
as a butterfly settling on a leaf.

As I dropped from the heights
to the valley below,
riding on a wave through the mountain forest,
I knew that it was time to see the world
from a different point of view.

I was well aware of *peyote* and its sister cactus *achuma* or San Pedro, because my mentor Dr Abram Hoffer, the only man I know who has helped thousands of schizophrenics recover, had extensively researched them and had been the first to identify that the active ingredient in them was mescaline. He made the extraordinary discovery that during *peyote* ceremonies Native Americans were excreting a chemical in their urine that was also found in the urine of many schizophrenics. He discovered that the schizophrenics were producing a hallucinogen, the cause of their hallucinations, from adrenalin, and worked out that the antidote was B vitamins. He ran the first ever double-blind controlled trial in the history of psychiatry, showing that auditory and visual hallucinations stopped in many schizophrenics when given high doses of B vitamins, initially niacin (B3). I read this research at university in the late 1970s, when I was studying the biochemistry of schizophrenia. That was my first exposure to the potential of vitamin therapy.

The great writer and revolutionary thinker Aldous Huxley heard of Hoffer's work and wanted to try mescaline in its pure form. He wrote of his experience in his classic book *The Doors of Perception*, so-named from William Blake's quote: 'If the doors of perception were cleansed, every Thing would appear to man as it is, Infinite.' That book kick-started the 1960s revolution, which was fuelled by LSD. Jim Morrison read it and named his band the Doors.

The discovery of LSD in 1943, by Albert Hoffman, a brilliant chemist working for the Sandoz Pharmaceutical Company in Basel, Switzerland, has to be one of the most extraordinary discoveries of the last century. Just as humanity was really suffering in the final years of World War II, along came this substance, a few micrograms of which puts you in touch with a whole different reality. It opened up the West to Eastern mysticism and also helped kick-start the technological age, which was pioneered by young students in the San Francisco Bay area, the epicentre of both the acid and the digital revolutions. Among them was Steve Jobs, who said that taking LSD was 'one of the most important things' to influence his ideas. I'm sure that LSD also helped a generation of children to break away from the patterns of fear passed on from their parents, who had witnessed the horrors of World War II.

My teacher Abram Hoffer was also part of the first wave of psychiatrists using entheogens to help patients process traumatic experiences. He wasn't happy when the hippies 'turned on, tuned in and dropped out', not least because it led to a ban on all research into LSD. Similarly, Shulgin saw the real potential for MDMA in psychotherapy, but all research into psychedelics became impossible as the authorities clamped down – that is, until relatively recently.

Another tremendous pioneer with a new vision for psychiatry was Dr Stanislav Grof, one of the founders of transpersonal psychology. After extensive years of research using LSD therapeutically, he became convinced that there was an inner wisdom that could be accessed in non-ordinary states of consciousness to resolve the deep psycho-spiritual issues that fuelled mental illness and fed into the ever-present self-destructive trends of modern humanity. (These days he uses different approaches for accessing that wisdom, involving 'holotropic' breathing to resolve the deep pre-verbal traumas we all hold from birth. I'll be exploring this in Chapter 5.)

On my trip to Peru I wanted to experience San Pedro within the context of the Quechuan tradition. If *ayahuasca* was a gateway to the Goddess, the creative power of the Universe, San Pedro was a gateway to God, the Great Consciousness. Both are renowned as benevolent, healing plants, able to release blocks and create a deep connection.

In Cusco I was introduced to Pedro, a San Pedro shaman from the Quechuan tradition. He took me off into the mountains above the city, into a cave looking out across a valley. There he prepared a fire and we made our offerings to the elements (earth, air, fire and water) and the four directions (north, south, east and west) as we imbibed the San Pedro brew.

Figure 11: Shaman Pedro of the Quechuan tradition
(© Atul Banerjee, used with permission)

As the plant started to work, I had the instinct to go walkabout and climbed up a mountain which was flat at the top like an eagle's nest. There I soared like an eagle. The vast space of consciousness expanded and expanded and absorbed me. I cannot describe the ecstasy I experienced – the total connection of everything and the ocean of bliss. It was truly beyond words. And then came visions of the future and guidance. There is no question that this experience fundamentally changed my whole perception of the interconnection and intelligent direction of life.

'I see the future in the present and fly towards it.'

Therapy and Inspiration

There is so much still to learn about the effects of these chemicals on consciousness and the role they can play in opening us up to a fuller experience of life and what it is to be human.

In the same way that previous cultural revolutions involved the use of entheogens I am sure that the use of LSD by the early pioneers in

San Francisco and the Bay Area kick-started the digital revolution that is completely transforming our world today. The fact that an estimated one in four 16- to 24-year-olds have taken MDMA/Ecstasy must have an effect on our evolving culture. Hopefully it is loosening the shackles of our limited thinking.

We are deeply indebted to the great pioneers such as Sasha Shulgin, Abram Hoffer, Aldous Huxley, Stanislav Grof and Lady Amanda Feilding, whose charitable Beckley Foundation in the UK has managed to inspire an intelligent and research-led conversation about entheogens. Thanks to her work and that of brave researchers such as Professor David Nutt, the government's former chief drug advisor, who was sacked for stating the truth that Ecstasy and LSD were less dangerous than alcohol, and Robert Carhart-Harris at Imperial College London, for the first time in 40 years proper research is finally being allowed into the intelligent use of entheogens to help mental health problems and advance our understanding of the brain's chemistry and consciousness.

For example, one study on psilocybin mushrooms investigated personality and behavioural changes after one year in volunteers who had been given psilocybin. It found that 'openness remained significantly higher than baseline more than one year after the session'.[6] Another small study has reported that LSD permanently reduces anxiety in a number of patients.[7] Another, a randomized controlled study, has reported that MDMA is effective for treating post-traumatic stress disorder.[8] We have much to learn and much research is underway and being planned at more than a dozen major universities such as Johns Hopkins University Medical School in Baltimore, Maryland, and London's Imperial College and University College London. As Stan Grof says, 'Psychedelics, used responsibly and with proper caution, would be for psychiatry what the microscope is for biology and medicine, or the telescope is for astronomy.' Watch this space.

I hope that in the not too distant future there will be a reclassification of entheogens for psychotherapeutic use. Many of those discussed here are relatively non-toxic and only capable of inducing adverse effects if used excessively or in the wrong context, without support. Used intelligently, for purposes of insight rather than purely for recreation, they have real therapeutic potential.

However, they are not for everyone – and that is why they are best taken with a reliable guide or experienced psychotherapist. In South America this is the role of the shaman, although there are as many fakes as masters. A true shaman always asks the plant if the person is ready. Many are not. Those who are too attached to their rational mind can have trouble letting go.

The shaman will work with the plant to release blocks in the initiate to bring them into a more connected state. Trauma therapist Luciana, originally from Brazil, is a case in point. Her experience of *ayahuasca* began in her twenties, mainly in the context of ritualized ceremonies in the established Brazilian traditions of the UDV and Santo Daime churches. These early experiences were meaningful, but it wasn't until her early thirties, when she had completed her psychotherapeutic training with an emphasis on trauma, that she had a deeper breakthrough in her own healing with *ayahuasca*. Here's how she describes it:

> *It was in the well-held, carefully structured ceremonies of a Brazilian group that combined Daime traditions with principles of Western psychology and incorporated elements of ancient Eastern traditions that I experienced the healing, or integration, of some deep personal issues. One has little control over what happens in an ayahuasca session, of course, but feeling safe in the group and having a deep trust in the people guiding it are crucial factors in how productive and healing it may turn out to be.*

> *There's no question that the ayahuasca experience has been transformative for me; I have been able to access early traumas and release blocked feelings that I hadn't been able to work with in any other way (conventional psychotherapy, holotropic breathwork, psychodrama, bodywork, psychoanalysis). And it made it possible for me, after and*

outside the experience, to access this material and to continue to deepen my own healing process. I have discovered that the crucial element that allows for the healing of trauma is love. It is the essential ingredient to process trauma. If trauma is seen as a shock (or series of shocks) that involve the absence of love and the profound loss of connection to oneself and to others, then the healing process relies on the presence of love, support and connection.

...Part of the power of ayahuasca lies in a 'magic realm' and is beyond my understanding ... although I have deep trust in it. However, there is an element which is widely accepted by experienced ayahuasca users: it can help us to bypass the defence mechanisms of the conscious mind, therefore releasing 'charged' material from the unconscious, which then becomes available to us. Our unconscious contains many difficult experiences and feelings we may not remember or be able to access, as well as containing much of our creativity, positive qualities and sources of inspiration. Ayahuasca opens the doorway to much of this shadow and this light, sometimes at the same time. It helps us to see ourselves better, all of ourselves, and that's why it's considered a powerful tool for self-knowledge.

These plants have been used for thousands of years without adverse effects, withdrawal or dependency, other than bringing people's fears and neuroses to the surface to be expunged. On the other hand, modern psychiatric drugs have been used for a couple of decades at most – with a growing list of adverse effects, including addiction and akasthisia, a severe inner agitation that can lead to suicide and homicide, especially in the young and old, often as a side effect of drug withdrawal. It is no coincidence that virtually every school killer in the USA has been on, or withdrawing from, psychiatric medication.

The meaning in life is the slightest shift,
like driving a car round a corner into a panoramic view
or breaking through fathoms of dim water into the light.
Nothing is different, nothing is the same.

What once was your life is now only a game.
Like breathing air for the very first time,
it feels so natural. It feels so right
to be bathing in this radiant light.

I hope we will see the re-emergence of a more enlightened form of psychiatry along the lines of Stanislav Grof's vision, which is that the psychiatrist's job is to enable a person to enter a non-ordinary state of consciousness in a safe, supportive environment and help them integrate the healing and learning that take place.

Unlike some who are opposed to psychiatric medicine, I do believe that mental illness can be the result of biochemical imbalances as well as present-day stresses and the pressure of unexpressed past traumas. Most mental breakdowns are a 'perfect storm' of these three contributors. So, much can be achieved with nutritional medicine and really good psychotherapy, including recognition of the transpersonal or spiritual domain (for more on nutritional medicine for mental illness, see www.foodforthebrain.org).

The trouble is that none of these natural plant medicines or nutrients or psychotherapeutic techniques can be patented – they already exist in nature – so there's no money to be made. The money is in man-made, patentable drugs.

A Word of Caution

While there is much debate about the potential dangers of the frequent use of MDMA and LSD, it is certainly clear that some people, while not physically overdosing, have psychologically lost it or done things that have led to their injury or death while under the influence of these drugs. The most widely reported effect is the dehydration of people on drugs sold as Ecstasy (which is often not pure MDMA) dancing all night at raves and, in some tragic cases, overhydration, for fear of the latter. Also, 'street' drugs are often not pure and, in many cases, it is the impurities that cause adverse effects. Frequent use of MDMA also depletes serotonin and could, therefore, exacerbate depression in the long term. It is thus perhaps more therapeutically useful for resolving trauma-related anxiety and depression.

I have not heard of similar cases with plant medicines such as *peyote*, San Pedro or *ayahuasca*, although that too may be possible. These are certainly not addictive and in fact often help people to break harmful addictions to alcohol and other drugs.

These mind-altering substances are, in my opinion, sacred and best taken in that context with an experienced guide or companion. I do not believe they are for everyone but, used intelligently, they can speed up one's personal development. If psychological traumas do occur under the influence, it is important that these are explored further with a therapist, as they represent an opportunity for transformation. The Chinese ideogram for 'crisis' has two images, one meaning 'danger', the other 'opportunity'.

Most drugs consume energy, which is experienced as the 'down' the next day. However, in my experience, there are two exceptions, namely *ayahuasca* and *peyote* or San Pedro. They give you energy.

Also, although some of the plant medicines are legal, or at least tolerated, in countries with a history of their shamanic use, most of these substances are illegal in most countries. Whether it is wise to class all hallucinogens as 'Class A', along with highly destructive drugs such as heroin and cocaine, is highly debatable. They are not addictive and are certainly less harmful than alcohol. I welcome the move to create a new classification that would allow entheogens to be used in a psychotherapeutic context.

Hopefully, with the 'war on drugs' strategy having proven a dismal failure everywhere, a more intelligent approach to drugs, including entheogens, will emerge in our culture. If there is a need for a 'war on drugs' it should be on psychiatric drugs, as the next chapter explores.

Yet despite this, the Psychoactive Drugs Bill that came into effect in the UK in April 2016 makes illegal anything that is in any way mind-altering. As George Bernard Shaw said, 'Those who cannot change their minds cannot change anything.'

Chapter 4

Say No to Drugs

In an enlightened world, pharmaceutical drugs would play a minor part in medicine, being reserved for emergency use – antibiotics for life-threatening infections; tranquillizers for breakdowns; anti-inflammatories for acute pain; anti-coagulants for immediate protection post-heart attack – that sort of thing. Instead, we have got to the point where one in five people in the USA have been prescribed pharmaceutical drugs for depression, insomnia, anxiety, psychosis and memory problems. Such is the widespread state of our disconnection.

Hypnotized

In the UK over 80 million prescriptions are written out every year for psychiatric drugs, including addictive benzodiazepines, sleeping pills, mood stabilizers and anti-psychotic drugs.[1] Most of these are numbing or hypnotizing drugs, suppressing emotions in a way not dissimilar to Aldous Huxley's 'soma' in *Brave New World*.

Malcolm Stewart, having returned from his enlightening comas, was immediately prescribed antidepressants.

They made me very depressed. They were an absolute nightmare. We couldn't get the doctor to take me off them. Maybe that might have helped to get me back into the body. It is very difficult to know. Once I had them I was crying a lot, while before that I was in bliss.

According to his wife, Nora:

When he was put on the antidepressants, it was terrible. He started to shake, his blood pressure went up, he stopped talking, he was angry, depressed and crying. It was really bad and all the nurses could see it, but the doctor refused to take him off them.

Pharmaceutical drugs, by their nature, have to interfere with the body's natural and multi-connected chemistry. If you give a nutrient, that is part of the body's design, so it knows what to do with it. Drugs, to be patentable, have to interfere with a natural process, often by blocking an enzyme, as in the case of cholesterol-lowering statins, or blocking a receptor, as in the case of most antidepressants, which block the recycling channel or re-uptake channel for serotonin, or stimulant drugs for ADHD, which block the dopamine receptor, thus mimicking slow-acting cocaine. The result can be a short-term boost in serotonin or dopamine, but a long-term depletion, leading to terrible withdrawal symptoms, including depression and hyperactivity – the very symptoms the drug was supposedly taken to cure.

Antidepressants are undeniably linked to increased risk of suicidal thoughts, among other adverse effects, including sexual dysfunction. Countries who prescribe the most have the most suicides. There have been cases of teenagers on medication who find they can't get an erection during their first sex act and some feel so bad about this they attempt or commit suicide, not knowing that there is nothing wrong with them – it is a side effect of the drug.

Antidepressants are especially dangerous for older people such as Malcolm, as their less resilient chemistry is less able to deal with the drug. In a study published in the *British Medical Journal* involving over 60,000 people over 65 diagnosed with depression, among those given antidepressants there was one more death for every 28 people every year, compared to depressed patients not given antidepressants, and five times as many suicides.[2] A review of 70 trials, also published in the *British Medical Journal*, found antidepressants double the risk of suicide and aggressive behaviour in under-18-year-olds.[3] The risk of suicide is especially strong when withdrawing from these drugs. The World Health Organization (WHO) rates three selective serotonin re-uptake inhibitors (SSRIs) as among the top 30 drugs for which dependence has been reported.

It is very difficult to get off most antidepressants, due to horrendous withdrawal effects. Approximately four in 10 people have withdrawal symptoms, which can include depression. Doctors have no training in how to get people off the drugs they prescribe and tend to deny the seriousness of the situation. Among the most addictive are benzodiazepines and sleeping pills. Yet every year in the UK there are 16.5 million prescriptions for these drugs, and many for more than four weeks, which is the time needed to develop dependency. We have probably in the order of 4 million prescription drug addicts or dependents in the UK out of a population of some 60 million. Of course, all this is good for business.

Big Pharma

Big Pharma has become a trillion-dollar industry, built on 'blockbuster' drugs with obscene marketing budgets, not only financially underpinning the whole medical industry, from medical training to journals, research and media, but the whole financial world of investments and stock market trading. Despite tens of billions of dollars of fines for illegal and fraudulent activities, ranging from hiding drug-induced deaths to fraudulent marketing and paying off doctors, the mega-industry gravy train rolls relentlessly on. With an estimated 30,000 deaths per year from drugs given and taken in the right dose in the UK (the conservative published estimate is in excess of 10,000 deaths per year[4] but many drug-related deaths are hidden and unreported in hospitals) and hundreds of thousands of annual deaths in the USA, prescribed drugs have joined the top five causes of death.[5] Medical error, much of which is related to inappropriate drug prescription, is the third leading cause of death in the USA, after cancer and heart disease, according to the *British Medical Journal*.[6] To put this into context, this is 10 times more deaths than from road traffic accidents (1,713) and illegal drugs (1,957), using the latest 2013 figures, and more than double the number of deaths from breast cancer. In 2012, there were 11,716 deaths from breast cancer in the UK.

Much of the marketing for psychiatric drugs is based on highly suspect research. For example, a seminal study in 2001, known as Study 329, concluded that antidepressants were both effective and safe for adolescents. Following the study, the UK's biggest drug company, GlaxoSmithKline (GSK)'s sales of Paxil (paroxetine) rose to bestseller status in the USA, with sales of $340 million in the same year.

However, in 2004 GSK was fined $2.5 million for mismatches between their marketing claims and the data. The terms of the settlement included a requirement for GSK to post study results on the company website, including Study 329. In 2012 they were fined again, this time $3 billion – the biggest-ever fine in corporate history. The next year paroxetine sales increased by 3 per cent.

Recently Study 329 has been shown to be nothing close to the truth. Using exactly the same data as the original study (obtained through an arduous process), an intrepid band of researchers came to exactly the *opposite* conclusion, namely that: 'Neither paroxetine nor high-dose imipramine demonstrated efficacy for major depression in adolescents, and there was an increase in harms with both drugs.' This re-analysis was published in the *British Medical Journal*.[7]

GSK is now planning to beef up vaccine sales as patents run out on profitable blockbuster drugs. Vaccination is just another drug delivery system. How can we trust Big Pharma-funded drug *or* vaccine trials?

But beware if you try to rock the boat. I've been there several times. The first time I criticized a major profitable drug I was burgled, followed and photographed. On one occasion an intruder forced his way into my institute and I literally had to fight him to get him out! The second time, coinciding with the publication of *Food is Better Medicine than Drugs*, was limited to verbal abuse, vilification and attempts at character and career assassination. This included immense pressure to remove me from my visiting professorship at a UK university and a campaign to vilify my reputation with any professors or leading scientists with whom I worked.

The funniest incident, if you can call it that, happened in the lead-up to the media tour for the book in South Africa. A carefully orchestrated media campaign was set up to trash me on arrival. An organization was even set up in my honour, called the Campaign Against Fraudulent Claims on Medicine (I called it CAC, which is the Afrikaans word for s**t), by a bunch of pharmacologists and pharmacists and medical people in the paystream of Big Pharma, who then contacted all mainstream media with a series of 'anti-Holford' demands. But it all went terribly wrong for them. As a joke I set up the Campaign for Ridiculing Atrocious Press-mongering (CRAP) and sent out a release headed 'CRAP on CAC'. I had a nonstop series of interviews with all the main publications and admittedly there were some pretty sceptical journalists to start with, but the stories came out positively and the book went to number 2 on the bestseller list. Most journalists could smell a rat in the form of Big Pharma trying to squash the truth.

It is extraordinary that in the UK there is not one public pressure group tackling this industry's relentless pursuit of profits before lives. We have campaigns for animal rights, gay rights, civil rights and eco-rights and against war and tax-dodgers, but not one tackling the industry that is fined more than any other for illegal and immoral activities. In the UK, where Big Pharma's influence goes deep into the Medicines & Healthcare products Regulatory Agency (MHRA), the government agency responsible for protecting us, no significant fines have been issued, despite the very same violations being rampant as elsewhere in the world.

I am pleased to say, however, that there is a new professional group, the Council for Evidence-based Psychiatry,[8] which at least has psychiatric drugs under the spotlight.

I also have a campaign on avaaz.org[9] with almost 5,000 signatures to date. At least that's a start. It's still rolling, so feel free to sign up. It calls for five reforms:

1. Investigate and act against pharmaceutical companies employing illegal marketing activities by appointing an independent watchdog, not funded by the drug industry, which can be freely contacted by patients and by doctors witnessing bribery and encouragement to prescribe a drug 'off label' – for a condition it has no licence to treat – by pharmaceutical representatives.

2. Tighten up requirements for licensing new drugs to include a thorough assessment of benefits versus risks, as well as withdrawal effects.

3. Record and minute meetings to be made publicly available, including representation from consumer groups.

4. Enforce pharmaceutical companies to publish their trial data, without hiding adverse effects, on their website for free access.

5. Take patient-reported adverse reactions seriously and encourage patients who have had adverse effects to share them on the website rxisk.org (see below) so other patients and doctors are informed.

Psychiatrist Dr David Healey, who first blew the whistle on the now established links between antidepressants and suicide, has done the most with his website rxisk.org, where patients and doctors can report and see adverse effects from drugs.

Professor Peter Gotzche, one of the key investigators for the independent Cochrane Collaboration, an international body that assesses medical research, calculates, in his book *Deadly Psychiatry and Organised Denial*,[10] that deaths from psychiatric drugs are the third major killer after heart disease and cancer. Before you consider taking an antidepressant, I strongly recommend you watch his lecture on YouTube entitled 'Why Few Patients Benefit and Many are Harmed'.[11]

Whatever happened to 'First do no harm'? Doctors no longer have to swear this Hippocratic Oath and, with that, an important moral obligation has been lost. Hippocrates is known as the father of medicine because he wanted to know the true cause of disease. Today's medicine, which covers up the symptoms and ignores the causes, is a hypocrisy.

My advice is to do your best to stay away from psychiatric drugs. If you are having a really difficult time in life, a skilled psychotherapist and nutritional therapist should be your first port of call. Be very suspicious of psychiatric drugs.

Big Pharma Man

Who gives a damn? What really changes?
The media espouse fashionable opinions to the hypnotized masses,
homogenized by minions, afraid of their bosses.

The outspoken, despising the power of advertising,
Are banished and vanish down social crevasses
To suppress the uprising.

The greedy manipulations of so-called science
Purporting life-saving treatment for man-made diseases
Are a clever disguise to make share prices rise.

They get fined for doctor bribing and data hiding
Downsides and deaths and off-label prescribing,
Nod it off with a sorry, then next time same old story.

The brave new world of zero risk. That's the pitch.
Except there's a twist: drug-resistant superbugs
And a hidden generation of vaccine-damaged kids.

Blockbusters off-patent, nothing in the pipeline.
Vaccines the future, from flu to cancer. Vitamin C works,
but there's no profit, so it's not cool.
Two dozen jabs before school. That's the vampire's goldmine.

What do you call someone who targets vulnerable teenagers
And gets them hooked on addictive tranquillizers?
A psychiatrist – who doesn't think about the downsides
Going crazy when you try to quit – and the suicides.

Do you call it medicine when one in three are dying from psychiatry?
Can't the docs see the wood from the tree?
When all the kid needs is some TLC.

Is this medicine when one in eight have been astatinated
And drugs for heartburn make your brain 'n' bones shrink?
And for diabetes you're given pills so you can still eat sugar 'n' bread
and end up dying from heart disease instead?

All this obscene money is not really funny,
When you see the harm done, the lives lost,
Written off as a cost, to feed Big Pharma man.
But who gives a damn?

In the name of the pharma it's a grand scam.
Big Pharma man – he don't give a damn.

The Alzheimer's Gravy Train

As a case in point, I've been watching the shenanigans on the biggest potential cash cow of all – Alzheimer's disease. Alzheimer's is now the most prevalent example of a breakdown in the brain's ability to function in a connected way. Starting in the centre of the brain, the medial temporal lobe, brain cells (neurons) die off, leading to a progressive loss of cognitive function and, consequently, depression, confusion and frustration. Families struggle to cope with relatives who are affected. Most sufferers end up in care homes.

Already the healthcare cost of Alzheimer's is more than that of cancer and heart disease combined. Left unchecked, Alzheimer's will bankrupt our already failing healthcare system. So, the hunt for the miracle drug is relentless. Charities seek our money, pretending there is a drug cure is just around the corner. Political spokesmen make lame, unfounded predictions that by 2020 we will have it solved. Big Pharma has poured an estimated $50 billion to date into failed drug trials.

Yet no one is talking seriously about the 'p' word: prevention. The charity www.foodforthebrain.org has been campaigning for prevention to be taken seriously, given that half the risk for dementia is caused by things we can change, according to a consortium of 111 leading experts from 36 countries.[12] Researchers at the US National Institutes of Health attribute almost a quarter (22 per cent) of Alzheimer's cases to high homocysteine levels, principally caused by a lack of B vitamins, and another 22 per cent to low seafood/omega-3 intake.[13] (Our blood homocysteine levels reflect a vital process called methylation. I explain exactly how this works in Chapter 7.)

Demented

What's it all about?
All these people checking out.
Years of memories erased.
Whole lives dematerialized.
A one-way ticket out of here
filled with anxiety and fear.
Nothing left worth living for.
Empty shells upon the shore.

The achievement of a dying race,
Rich in wealth, but lost in space?
Or a race for profit – what a disgrace.

Food for the Brain has raised over £80,000 for non-drug dementia prevention research and education. That is over half the total spend, £156,000, by all UK research councils from 2006 up to the end of 2013![14] The charity needs more funds! Please give generously.

To put this into context, the 'best' drug to date is Solanezub. The best non-drug treatment to date is B vitamins, given to those with raised homocysteine. B vitamins are especially effective in those with sufficient omega-3 – you need both to keep your brain healthy *(see page 101 for more on this)*. The chart below shows you the comparative efficacy in the three critical aspects of Alzheimer's: the rate of brain shrinkage, performance on cognitive tests, and clinical symptoms used for diagnosis.

	SOLANEZUB VS PLACEBO	B VITAMINS VS PLACEBO
Reduced brain shrinkage	2% (not significant)	53–73% (high)
Further memory loss	Small difference on 3 tests (1/10, 2/90, 2/56)	Virtual cessation in those with high homocysteine
Clinical dementia rating change	No change	30% more revert to normal
Length of study	18 months	24 months

Figure 12: Comparison of best drug versus B vitamins on memory performance and brain shrinkage

Prevention, however, is more likely to be given lip service until Big Pharma comes up with a drug to give to people under the guise of preventing dementia. The returns could be huge. So, they'd better bury this whole homocysteine and omega-3 story before it's taken seriously. That's how the game is played.

Burying the Cure for Schizophrenia

Another devastating disconnecting disease is schizophrenia, suffered by one in 100 people. Food for the Brain's outpatient clinic, the Brain Bio Centre *(see Resources)*, treats people suffering with schizophrenia not with drugs but by exploring their brain's chemical imbalances and correcting them.

High homocysteine and a lack of B vitamins is a very common finding. We have over 50 years of research on the positive effects of B vitamins – niacin (B3), B12, folic acid, B6 and also zinc and magnesium – often in high doses, thanks to the pioneering work of the late doctors Carl Pfeiffer and Abram Hoffer, who successfully treated thousands of schizophrenic patients. Other common contributors to the disease are a lack of omega-3 fats and antioxidants, and also food intolerances.[15] Some patients have neurotransmitter imbalances that can be made better with the right amino acids.

Many mental health concerns can be resolved by finding out what is out of balance and correcting it with nutritional medicine. This is the subject of my book *Optimum Nutrition for the Mind*. According to a recent article in the *Lancet* medical journal, 'Now is time for the recognition of the importance of nutrition and nutrient supplementation in psychiatry. Nutritional medicine should now be considered as a mainstream element of psychiatric practice.'[16]

Instead, mainstream practice gives mind-numbing, usually patented and profitable drugs which, at best, stop a person harming themselves or others, but do not cure the disease. These drugs are ineffective in one third of patients and their side effects can be severe and debilitating. They rarely improve the negative symptoms of the disease and long-term studies show better outcomes for those not medicated.

Eddie is a case in point. Here's his story:

I'm 26 and from Northern Ireland, and three years ago I was diagnosed with paranoid schizophrenia. I was really suspicious and paranoid of other people, to the point where I couldn't work any longer and I couldn't interact with my family and friends at all. I became really socially withdrawn. My quality of life was just at the bottom, I couldn't do anything I wanted to do and therefore they put me on a lot of psychiatric medication – like Aripiprazole, the anti-psychotic, Escitalopram, the antidepressant, and also Buspirone, for anti-anxiety, and Diazepam, for sleeping, and some medication to treat the side effects of the medication, like Procyclidine. I was on that as well.

None of these drugs worked for me in any way: I felt worse, I was more anxious and I was more physically ill. I put on a lot of weight – about 10 stone (64kg) in the period of a year and a half – and then I came

across Patrick's work and I started to adapt my lifestyle accordingly. I took
an interest in nutrition, I bettered my diet and lifestyle and I am now
medication free.

I have a really good quality of life now. I've lost about 8 stone (51kg)
in the last 14 months. I'm doing a business course to help myself set up
exercise classes so that I can help people in the same situation as me, and
a lot of that is down to understanding better how nutrition affects both
my body and brain and not being on the medications that were affecting
me so negatively. I have been given a new lease of life and I'm really
thankful for that.

Eddie told me that he'd noticed that when the doctor was prescribing him one of the drugs, the name of the drug was written on the pen he was prescribing it with! Now I would call that astute observation, not paranoia.

The sad truth is that most family members and people with schizophrenia do not know there are alternatives to drugs because the research has been buried, their psychiatrist doesn't know either, and they haven't taken their health into their own hands as Eddie did. That's a hard and a brave thing to do when your mind is in a mess.

Abram Hoffer dedicated his life to making a nutrition-based approach available. But his treatment, which was highly effective on recently diagnosed schizophrenics, was then given, by other researchers hellbent on stopping this approach becoming popular, to those who had been on heavy-duty medication for several years, and found to be ineffective. The vitamins couldn't make enough difference in a drug-addled brain. Thus, once again, drug medicine stayed dominant.

Most psychiatrists are blissfully unaware of the power of this approach to schizophrenia, or the enlightening approach of Dr Stanislav Grof, which is focused not on numbing down symptoms but getting to the root cause, be it psychological traumas locked in the psyche or biochemical imbalances correctable with nutrients rather than drugs. Short-term use of tranquillizers if a person is in complete meltdown, plus good nutritional medicine and psychiatric support, could help so many avoid relatively ineffective long-term medication.

Addicted to Prescribing Drugs

The knee-jerk reaction of most doctors when presented with a patient in a state of disconnection – be it an inability to sleep, extreme anxiety, depression or psychosis – is to prescribe sleeping pills, tranquillizers, antidepressants, mood stabilizers and anti-psychotics. These are often addictive because they mimic the natural neurotransmitters that switch off adrenalin or promote sleep or a good mood. The more often a person uses these drugs, the fewer natural neurotransmitters the brain produces, until the person becomes dependent on the drug and experiences terrible and sometimes life-threatening withdrawal effects. This is a subject I explore in detail in my book *How to Quit without Feeling S**t*, co-authored with Dr James Braly and Dr David Miller.

'Doctor, I seem to have become addicted to prescribing drugs.'

© Chris Quayle

There is a better way, which combines enlightened psychotherapy and nutritional medicine. If there is a place for psychiatric drugs, it is as 'holding' drugs to suppress overwhelming emotions when dealing with short-term crises, as one would do by getting drunk when overwhelmed with grief. However, this is best avoided except for very short-term use, as all such numbing substances carry the risk of addiction if taken beyond a couple of weeks.

Too many people have become hooked on antidepressants after being prescribed them for depression brought on by grief, losing a job or a marital breakdown. These are not good reasons to take drugs. There is no substitute for feeling and working through these deep emotions with the support of friends and a good therapist. In the following chapters, I will give you some tools for this.

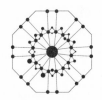

Chapter 5

Doors
to Enlightenment

One of the questions I asked the 100 people who had scored the highest in my 100% Health questionnaire was: 'Have you had a peak experience or profound experience of unity?' Another was: 'Do you believe in God, a higher power or consciousness?'

In total, 47 per cent said they had had a peak experience or profound experience of unity. A quarter of these people said they had had many. Twenty-eight per cent weren't sure if they had had one – that's 75 per cent (so far) – and 25 per cent said they hadn't. Similarly, 57 per cent said they believed in God or a higher power or consciousness, 25 per cent said they believed to an extent – that's 82 per cent (so far) – and 18 per cent said they didn't. Not surprisingly, those who had had profound experiences of unity believed in a higher power, while those who hadn't generally didn't.

So, most people base their 'belief' on their experience, which makes sense. I doubt that I would believe in a higher power or intelligent consciousness if I had not had the experience of it as such.

If you haven't had an experience like this, you may be wondering how it happens. Is it something that can be facilitated?

Beyond the Thinking Mind

First, it is important to recognize and respect that some people do not want this kind of profound connection. It challenges their concepts of how the world is. That is the last thing they want, at least consciously.

Often we become cut-off as a defence mechanism, which is usually triggered by traumatic experiences of profound disconnection. We learn not to trust and take refuge in hard-nosed science. But, as Einstein said, 'Not everything that counts can be counted, and not everything that can be counted counts.' Behind every cynic, it is said, is a mystic.

It is also important to say that although these experiences represent a peak moment of connection, day-to-day connections – stroking the cat, admiring the view, being moved by a piece of music – are also valuable. These are not intellectual experiences – they are deeply emotional and/or spiritual.

Mysteries

Where does the light come from when you dream?
How can you know that which is unseen?
Where do I go between waking and dreams?
From where do ideas appear and thoughts arise?
Where do I go when my body dies?

The fact that they are not intellectual is important, because the rational mind, while a great tool for self-enquiry and functioning in the world, is often an obstacle to connection. The ability to sense and feel, rather than to think, and to be completely present, almost transparent, is an essential quality for those seeking a deeper understanding of life. Remember, everything is energy. Everything is happening in consciousness. Everything *is* consciousness. And the ability to *experience* this, not just intellectually understand it, requires an intelligence beyond thought – beyond the thinking mind.

Swami Muktananda, author of *The Play of Consciousness*, one of the classic autobiographies mapping the higher levels of spiritual development, was once asked, 'Does your mind think?'

He replied, 'Only when I want it to.'

Are you a master of your thinking mind or is it a master of you? If you pause for a moment without thought, does your monkey mind chatter with random thoughts, judgements, projections, ideas, opinions and fantasies?

If you are strongly identified as your mind – as in Descartes's famous quote: 'I think, therefore I am' – it is hard to let go of thoughts. But it is the struggle of the mind to let go of control, to stop intellectualizing, that is often the greatest obstacle to an awakening and connecting experience.

'Empty' meditation approaches, such as Zen, Advaita or Vipassana, bring to the surface the endless chattering of the mind as a means of going beyond it. I once asked a monk what meditation was about. He said, 'You put a cow in a field of grass. It eats and eats and eats and eventually falls asleep.'

What he meant was that after some time in meditation the mind quietens down. In time thoughts cease to arise or, at least, have little impact on the meditator's immersion in the field of consciousness. Not everyone wants this, as the cessation of 'mind' control feels like a mini-death if you are identified completely with the thinking mind. However, it is in this silence, this empty space between thoughts, that insights, ideas and solutions arise.

Gurus, Masters and Mysteries

This brings to mind the experience of Jessica, a student of mine who accompanied me on a field trip in India when I was involved in a charitable mobile hospital project tackling nutritional deficiencies in the state of Maharashtra. We were staying at Ganeshpuri, in the Gurudev ashram of Gurumayi, the current head of the Siddha Yoga lineage and the disciple of Muktananda, who was the disciple of Nityananda before him.

Every morning we would meditate early then chant a beautiful prayer, the Guru Gita, as the Sun rose. Except for Jessica (and some other of my students). She had no interest in this and was just there for the nutrition project.

One afternoon I took her for a walk up to a hilltop where a *sadhu*, a holy man, had done his spiritual practices for years. It was a beautiful spot and we sat there to enjoy the sunset before heading back.

At one point I turned to look at Jessica and realized that her eyes were closed and tears were tumbling down her face, which was full of serenity.

After quite a while, she opened her eyes and I asked, 'What happened?'

'There were these eyes, so full of love. And then the next, and the next.'

She had met the lineage of the Siddha masters as a direct vision and experience. Now she was buzzing. Everything looked amazing to her. She commented on the vibrant light, the green fields, the majesty of the visible world around her. When we returned to eat the usual plain dinner of lentils, rice and salad, she said it was the best food she had ever tasted!

The next day she was angry. Really angry. She had not wanted this experience and could not absorb it. She pushed it away, denied it.

Several years later, by which time a major health issue of hers had remarkably resolved itself, she recontacted me to thank me and to let me know that it had been a positive life-changing experience, even though she'd not really been able to take it on at the time.

Gurumayi, and Muktananda before her, is said to be a 'Shaktipat' guru. That is, she can give people an awakening just with a thought, a glance or a touch. For those who don't believe in such things, I can assure you it has happened to thousands. In fact, Malcolm Stewart, my friend who spent three months in a coma, filmed Muktananda giving Shaktipat to many people for a BBC documentary called *The Guru's Touch* back in the 1970s.

There are, no doubt, many others who can initiate an awakening. My first direct experience of this was through the instruction of Oscar Ichazo, an American philosopher and founder of the Arica School®, a School of Wisdom and Knowledge. Being a 'non-believer', I liked Oscar's proposition that there are laws of consciousness and that the expansion and awakening to a full state of consciousness does not require 'faith or belief as such'. He is profoundly knowledgeable on the science of transcendence.

So I signed up for a course called 'Three Days to *Kenshō*™'. *Kenshō* is a Japanese term from the Zen tradition. *Ken* means 'seeing', *shō* means 'nature, essence'. *Kenshō* is an initial insight or awakening.

In truth, I didn't know what I was doing when I went on the course. I just knew I wanted to do it. The trainers took us through a series of exercises, some physical, involving specific breathing patterns, and various meditations, some repeating mantras and looking at *yantras*, which are geometric patterns – the visual equivalent of mantras. Oscar himself was not there, although we watched filmed lectures from him over the three-day period. Then it happened.

In one of the meditations suddenly a tsunami of love was pouring into me from above. Just before it hit I remember a feeling of unworthiness, but that was totally annihilated as I drowned in an ocean of profound love. In the centre of my inner field of vision was a beautiful, mesmerizing pearl-shaped blue flame, about a centimetre high. Each millimetre of my breath, flowing in and then out, was exquisite, like sipping the best wine you can ever imagine, very slowly.

I don't know how long I was in this meditation – perhaps half an hour. But I had clearly been *kenshōed*! And so had the others on the training. Trainings offered by the Arica Institute have catalysed awakenings in many people (*see Resources*).

So, it is clear that there are some mystics, and mystical exercises, perhaps not that many, than can deliver these kinds of profound and undeniable awakenings.

Of course, there are others, including the Tibetan Buddhist Dzogchen traditions and masters. Some people have a transformational experience with Christ or Allah, or within the context of another religion. Others occur spontaneously under the strangest circumstances, sometimes at moments of crisis. I am simply describing the ones that did it for me.

When I was in an ashram once I met a lovely Zen Buddhist priest and also a Franciscan monk in his robe, belted with a cord, and sandals. He asked the guru, 'Is there any difference between a living master and a dead master?', obviously referring to Christ.

She said, 'No.'

'So,' said the monk, 'why have a living master?'

She replied, 'Because she can tell you things.'

'What sort of things?'

'You're too fat. You need to see Patrick.'

Plant Medicine

Many people have their first awakenings through the use of entheogenic substances, as I described in Chapter 3. I have no problem with this, and have had awakenings this way myself. However, I do believe that the use of entheogens within a respectful context, rather than as 'party' drugs, is the right way to go for those seeking profound awakening. These drugs and plants are powerful, and there can be downsides. For those who grip tightly to their view of reality and can't let go, these experiences can be fraught. There is no doubt that many people have had a profound awakening with LSD, for example, but there are also a few who have had horrible experiences, or couldn't handle it or even went crazy. This is certainly not a road to travel lightly, or without guidance.

According to Luciana, the trauma therapist whose transformation in *ayahuasca* ceremonies was described earlier (*page 46*):

> *People tend to over-focus on the plant, forgetting that the ritual is what enables the profound experience. Without proper structure, entering*

the realms of the unconscious may be too chaotic and potentially overwhelming. Non-ordinary states of consciousness may lead us, potentially, to profound transformation, both psychologically and spiritually; we are given a glimpse of what may lie beyond our ordinary realms of consciousness, and that is no small thing.

To feel love for others and for oneself, to feel grateful and in awe of the magic of life, to feel touched by profound beauty, to open our hearts and truly connect – this is what the experience of a non-ordinary state of consciousness can open us to. It may also take us, of course, to our inner hell, the suppressed emotions, those dark sides of ourselves that we would rather not see; our ego may take an expected bashing. But this is a necessary stage in paving the way towards greater authenticity and connection, both to ourselves and others.

Walkabout

I have also had profound experiences in nature. This is part of the 'walkabout' tradition of the Aboriginal people. Several years ago, after the bust-up of a significant relationship, I was working hard and living alone and, despite a fair amount of outward 'success', I was uncomfortably aware that in essence I felt lonely, and I wasn't happy with this almost permanent, nagging, 'empty' and 'incomplete' feeling. I knew that the answer lay on the inside, but I didn't know the way in.

So I decided to confront the fear of being alone by going to a part of the world where I didn't speak the language and to a region where there wasn't anybody there, and just be by myself.

I booked a flight to Santiago in Chile, hired a jeep and headed off into a remote region in the high plains of the Andes with the intention of reaching the top of Volcan Copiapo, a dormant volcano at 6,052m (18,500ft).

After two days' driving I headed inland and civilization soon disappeared. I drove along a deserted mining track, rising higher and higher until I came over a ridge and saw a vast deserted plain and a turquoise lake, home to hundreds of bright pink flamingos, surrounded by snow-capped volcanos.

The next day I left my jeep and headed off on foot up Volcan Copiapo. Soon there were no signs of life. There was only me.

Figure 14: Volcan Copiapo, Chile. See colour section.

At night, as I camped, the eastern horizon lit up with lightning and I heard the sound of distant thunder. The sky was sprinkled with millions of stars.

In the day, I walked like an ant, ever uphill, in this vast deserted space. Being by myself, with no distractions, I became acutely aware of the voice inside my head. Do you know the one? That inner judge that says things like 'What if I get lost? Why on Earth am I doing this? I'm a failure. I'm a fraud. What if someone steals my jeep? I shouldn't have come this way. I should have saved that snack bar for later.' Or the inner show-off: 'Wow, this looks great – I must take a picture to show people how brave I am in the middle of nowhere.' Or the endless cacophony of sub-personalities.

Instead of listening to these voices and buying into their fears and fantasies, I started to repeat the mantra 'Om Namah Shivaya' internally. The meaning of this mantra is best described as 'I bow to the inner self/Shiva' affirming that 'Nothing exists which is not Consciousness,' including my self.

After two days in this solitude, repeating the mantra, the voices in my head stopped and silence began to take their place. I started to just be present – to make a choice and get on with it.

I also started to feel a kind of connection with the Earth. My senses became more acute. I could hear the sound of water under the earth, although there was no sign of running water in any direction. I had gone from lonely to alone to all-one.

My simple goal was the top of the volcano, but as I got closer and closer, suffering from lack of oxygen, the ever-steepening icy terrain and my lack of physical strength, I realized I couldn't make the very top, especially without crampons, since it was covered in ice. The view, however, was magnificent in every direction. And my consciousness seemed to expand in this breathtaking vista – not that I had much breath left.

When I finally made it back to 'base camp', my tent in the middle of nowhere (see if you can spot my tent in the photograph below. Clue: it's in the centre line), exhausted but alive, I burst into tears. I'm not sure if they were tears of joy or relief.

Figure 15: Tent at 'base camp', Chile.

Nothing

The sound of nothing moving across still water,
The faint glow at the edge of a dark night,
The sky mauve, blue, black and white,
No movement, no sound, no light.

Hear the wind of a breezeless night,
Feel the beat of a soundless drum,
Absorb the heat although there is no Sun,
Know that you are not alone.

I decided to leave the mountains and be by the ocean, so I drove for two days to a deserted beach and put up my tent. Once again I was alone. I had the basics of food and water and I sat meditating on the ocean roaring up the beach, and wrote the poem on pages 27–28.

It was then that a great love, a tremendous gratitude, welled up inside me. I felt the sacredness of life and all that we take for granted.

Experiences in untouched wildernesses are not to be underestimated as a means for liberation and upliftment. Mountains are sacred places and have an undeniably powerful effect. I have often had insights, and come back to life refreshed, from bold adventures into the unknown. Two such memorable journeys were the pilgrimage to Mount Kailash in Tibet and kayaking in Svalbard, a group of islands near the North Pole (*see colour section*). Both the high plains of Tibet and the vast frosty ice-packed ocean of the Arctic are, in themselves, a profound meditation.

Mount Kailash is considered the home of Shiva for Hindus, and the home of the ultimate Buddha for Buddhists – the mystical battleground of the great Tibetan Buddhist master Milarepa, who defeated the Bon magician Naro Bön-chung. Both Hindus and Buddhists circumambulate the mountain as an act of pilgrimage. No-one is allowed to climb it.

Touching the Transpersonal

There are other powerful tools and processes that make available the wisdom that comes from 'transpersonal' experiences.

Carl Jung was an influential Western psychiatrist who encouraged such experiences and introduced the notion of the collective unconscious. His book *Memories, Dreams and Reflections* is a classic. The Italian psychiatrist Roberto Assagioli then took Jung's work to another level and founded various schools of 'psychosynthesis', a comprehensive theory for human psychological development and integration of all aspects of our being, i.e. 'synthesis'. This is my preferred form of psychotherapy, because it includes the transpersonal and the spiritual aspects of our journey through life. (Therapists and courses are available in many countries; *see Resources*.)

Another much-loved training is the Hoffman Process, a week-long unravelling of the negative behaviour patterns we inevitably inherit from our parents. The work is deep and effective and many people have profound awakenings and access to their inner wisdom. (More on this in Chapter 11.)

Holotropic and Transformational Breathwork and Rebirthing

Another way in is through holotropic breathwork, as originally developed by Stanislav Grof, further developed into transformational breathwork and also used in the process of 'rebirthing'. Through the use of a specific breathing pattern and musical soundtrack, it is possible to induce a shift in consciousness that takes a person back into unexpressed and unprocessed early experiences. These are often pre-verbal and virtually impossible to access in talking therapies. One of the important recognitions that has come through this kind of approach is that unprocessed birth experiences are central to a state of disconnection. (Again, there are trainings available, as well as one-to-one sessions offered by practitioners; *see Resources*).

The use of specific breathing techniques is very old. It is a fundamental part of yogic practices, known as *pranayama*, in which the breath, or spirit, is named *prana*. It is also used in the Sufi practices of *zhikr*, exercises designed to induce a transformational state of union with the divine, and in the Tibetan and Hawaiian practices of the Kahunas, the 'keepers of the secret knowledge'. In almost every mystical tradition the breath and spirit are inextricably entwined.

Certain musical tones and rhythms also help to induce a shift in consciousness and this has been used in every mystical tradition, from the trance-inducing drumming of African tribes to the angelic choirs and Gregorian chants of the Christians, the call to prayer of Islam and vast musical feast of the Hindu *kirtanas* and *bhajans*. Certain of the instruments used, such as the tamboura and the kettledrum and the gong, were created to mimic the sounds heard in deep states of meditation. (There's more on the subject of sound and connection in Chapter 10.)

Spontaneous Awakenings

People also have awakenings quite spontaneously, often at times of crisis. Some so-called psychotic breakdowns are awakenings or opportunities for growth, but without the right guidance and support too many people get labelled as schizophrenic and put on heavy-duty tranquillizers.

Great thoughts can also arise spontaneously, from $E=mc^2$ to that sudden 'Aha!' when a solution to a problem occurs to us or, more often, our perspective changes.

The philosopher Wittgenstein said, 'Thinking is a gift that is given to one who is worthy of it.' He was saying that when you immerse yourself in a problem or an *impasse*, do the groundwork, so to speak, this helps create the space for a breakthrough.

It was Einstein's absolute absorption in studying the nature of light that led to a profound mystical experience out of which he realized $E=mc^2$. Many important discoveries in science have occurred in this way.

The Meaning of Peak Experiences

As important as peak experiences are, because they show us extra dimensions of existence and higher states of consciousness, they are usually temporary and we revert to our contracted state of awareness. As William Blake so aptly said, 'If perception were cleansed every Thing would appear to man as it is, Infinite. For man has closed himself up, till he sees all Things thro' narrow chinks of his cavern.'

One book, *The Mystique of Enlightenment* by U.G. Krishnamurti (not the other, more famous Krishnamurti), is rather enlightening in this context, as well as being quite hilarious in places. Krishnamurti had a complete meltdown, after which people would visit him to learn his 'secret'. But he had nothing to teach.

'The so-called self-realization,' he said, 'is the discovery for yourself and by yourself that there is no self to discover. That will be a very shocking thing because it's going to blast every nerve, every cell, even the cells in the marrow of your bones.'

Peak experiences may be shocking, even unwanted, but if they are understood as giving us a taste of different aspects of our potential, different layers of consciousness, then they can serve to galvanize the real groundwork that is necessary to clear our consciousness so that a fuller and more wonderful experience of life can start to take hold.

This process requires vital energy for transformation, which we can generate by moving our centre of awareness out of, exclusively, the mind and into the centre of the body. The mind–body connection is the focus of the next chapter.

PART II

THE FORM OF CONNECTION

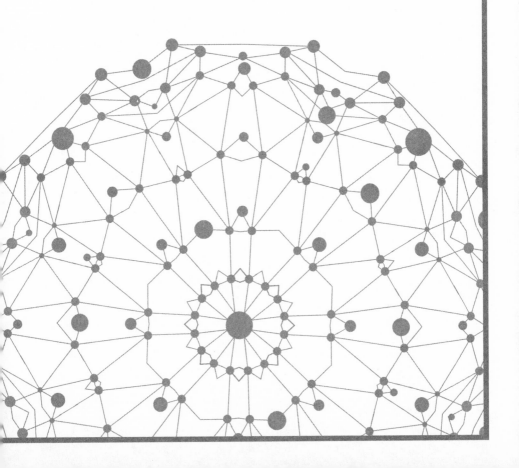

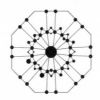

Chapter 6

The Mind–Body Connection

In the early days of holistic medicine I remember a letter in *The Times* newspaper from a National Health Service employee saying that conventional medicine was holistic – 'we have a department for the skin, the bones, the heart, the liver, the mind and so on'. Of course this misses the point that the body is an integral system – each part is not only connected to each other part but the system functions as a whole.

Similarly, not only does every thought and feeling have a corresponding effect on the body's chemistry, but every chemical change, be it a sugary snack, an alcoholic drink or a serving of oily fish, alters how we think and feel. Mind and body is a false dichotomy.

Systems-based Medicine: The New Paradigm

Modern science is often said to emanate from the Age of Reason in the 17th and 18th centuries. Partly as a reaction to the superstitions of medieval Europe, we entered the era of Newton and other scientists who could eloquently show 'cause and effect' in natural phenomena by means of experiments. As important as this scientific revolution has been, it has had a downside. Because many vital parts of life, such as emotions and spirituality, can't be measured in a scientific way, they have become increasingly less important in Western culture. Intellect has triumphed – science has become dominant over art and God – and today there is a cultural belief that science will solve our ills.

Medically, this approach has clearly failed, with the ever-increasing global incidence of preventable man-made diseases, including cancer, diabetes and Alzheimer's. The belief was (and still is to a large extent) that by running precise experiments on, for example, small pieces of our biology, we'd discover the secret of health. This is called reductionism, in that you reduce a complex system to tiny pieces, which you then examine in detail, in the belief that you'll understand the whole by putting all the pieces back together. But we need a different way of thinking, one that is systems-based. As Einstein said, 'The significant problems we have cannot be solved at the same level of thinking with which we created them.'

Fundamental to systems thinking is the concept of 'resilience', which we can think of as the amount of money we have in our health deposit account. One common finding coming out of systems-based studies of complex adaptive systems, whether applied to economies, ecologies or health (our body's ecology), is that there are only half a dozen critical factors that keep the system healthy. Small changes in these factors can 'tip' a system into ill-health. (For further reading, read *Resilience Thinking* by Brian Walker and David Salt.)

The vast majority of the health problems we suffer from are a consequence of losing our resilience in one or more of only six core biological processes (*shown opposite*): digesting and absorbing the right nutrients, because these provide all the ingredients for a healthy body; balancing our blood sugar, because that is our fuel supply; having enough lipids (fats), as fats keep the water part of the body inside the cells; ensuring we have sufficient hydration; optimizing oxidation with clean air and antioxidants, which detoxify the body's exhaust; and methylation, which is the subject of Chapter 8.

Another finding in systems-based science is that we need much more extreme changes to 'tip' ourselves back into health. For example, we all need about 50 micrograms (mcg) of the essential mineral chromium a

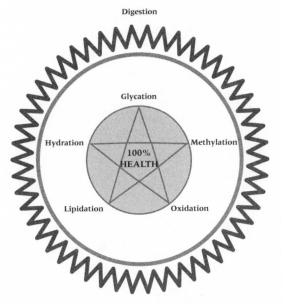

Figure 16: The six fundamental processes that determine our health

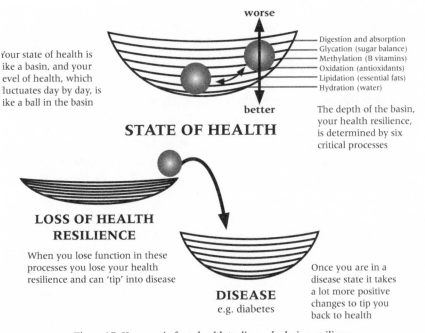

Figure 17: How we tip from health to disease by losing resilience

day to keep blood sugar levels stable. However, if we've developed diabetes, we'll probably need 500mcg a day – 10 times the usual amount – to help reverse it. Simply eating a well-balanced diet may prevent it, but it won't reverse it. Another example is vitamin C. I eat about 200mg (milligrams) a day and supplement an additional 900mg twice a day, giving myself a total daily intake of 2,000mg. However, if I get the first signs of a cold or flu, I take 1,000mg an hour until the symptoms are gone. When we're sick, we need more to return to health.

Mind over Body

As important as good nutrition, exercise, reducing stress, not smoking and creating a toxin-free environment are, our state of mind and spirit also have an enormous effect on our ability to recover our health. This should not be underestimated. Everyone knows someone who has beaten the odds of a life-threatening disease with amazing focus and willpower.

A case in point is that of Sophie Sabbage. Over a year ago Sophie was diagnosed with terminal cancer. She had lung cancer that had already spread to her bones and brain and her doctors agreed she didn't have long to live.

My turning point was shortly after being diagnosed with multiple metastases in my brain, a devastating day and my darkest hour by far. That was the day I nearly gave up and actually prayed for God to take me fast rather than let me lose my lucidity and clarity of mind. I knew I could do this cancer journey if I had my mind. But without it I was done. I have never known such despair.

But then they told me I had to take steroids and have my whole brain irradiated. And something shifted. A force of will? Courage? Utter stubbornness? Perhaps even blind stupidity? But it rose up my tumour-ridden spine like an electric charge and the fog cleared. I knew I needed to say no. I knew steroids would take me downhill faster than a teenager on a skateboard – that I would get fat (and depressed), not sleep well (when we heal) and increase my blood sugar (which cancer loves). It made no sense to me. I also knew people said, 'I'm not the same person,' after whole-brain radiation. And, above all, I knew I needed to trust my own intuition above anything any expert was telling me to do.

That was the day I took charge of my treatment and my choices. I had more lesions in my brain than they could count. Five months later my brain was cancer free. I never took a steroid and they never irradiated it! The radiologist still talks about it at the hospital. He had never seen a result like it. The chemo helped. And other stuff I do. But refusing those treatments was the way I boldly empowered myself and the despair left me. I haven't felt it since.

She is clearly beating the odds, having written an inspiring book, *The Cancer Whisperer*, about how to work creatively and constructively with a cancer diagnosis and how to let cancer heal your life. Her approach includes many of the aspects we explore in this book: feeling your feelings; asking for help; establishing your boundaries; knowing your purpose; and clearing your mind of negative beliefs. Of course, there is also a need to face the facts about your health, learn about your illness and take the right course of treatment, but Sophie's story illustrates the power of taking control of your life and working with your body, not against it.

Sophie now helps others navigate the course of their treatment and recovery by offering workshops, online courses and coaching (*see Resources*). Her 'compass' for navigating through the process of a life-threatening illness and its treatment is described overleaf.

Sophie Sabbage's Compass for Navigating Diseases

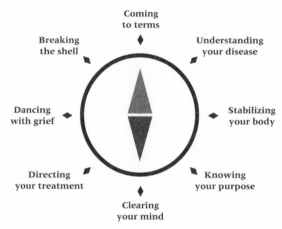

Figure 18: The compass (© Sophie Sabbage, The Cancer Whisperer, 2015; see www.sophiesabbage.com. Used with permission.)

1. Coming to Terms

This is an important phase to engage in fully from the beginning. It is about getting through the shock of your diagnosis, while laying some firm foundations for the journey ahead.

2. Understanding Your Disease

Educating yourself about your particular disease is one of the most important and empowering things you can do after you've received your diagnosis. Either you can leave this to your doctors and do what they say, or you can find out exactly what you're dealing with and what treatments are available (or not). Then you can partner with your doctor and any other practitioners you find with more confidence, intelligence and freedom to choose your own path.

3. Knowing Your Purpose

Faith is the wind in your sails and purpose is the rudder on your boat. Purpose is a powerful force when consciously chosen and deeply committed to. It will guide all your choices and decisions on this journey, so it's important to get hold of it as early as you can. To survive or to thrive? To hold on or let go? To take charge or be taken care of? To get through this or grow through this? To live or to die? There are no right answers. Just choices. Yours. Boldly and bravely made.

4. Stabilising Your Body
This phase will depend on the nature of your diagnosis. If you catch your disease early your body may be stable enough to make more progress with the other phases. This phase includes changing your diet, detoxifying your body and your environment.

5. Clearing Your Mind
This phase is all about coming to terms with your humanity, accepting your vulnerability and doing battle with the inevitable fear that grips you when you are diagnosed with a serious disease, such as cancer. It is also about looking at the fears, feelings and limiting beliefs you may have been carrying for many years but not paid attention to. Many diseases have emotional and psychological roots as well as physical and environmental ones.

6. Directing Your Treatment
This is all about taking charge of your treatment plan by feeling informed enough and clear-headed enough to do so. It is well documented that patients who direct their own treatment fare better than patients who don't.

7. Dancing with Grief
This is an invitation to completely redefine your relationship with grief and embrace it as a profoundly healing force in your life. It is not meant to be held at bay until the end is inevitable or preserved by your loved ones for after you have gone. Nor is it exclusively reserved for patients labeled 'terminal'. Grief is likely to flood your life as much as terror will stalk it when you are told you

have cancer. But unlike terror, which tears you apart and shreds your sanity, grief restores your right mind and makes you whole.

8. Breaking the Shell

This is where your work with the previous parts of the compass can take you to a new horizon in your relationship with your disease, by inviting you into a radically different dialogue with your disease, one in which you can find the pearl in the oyster shell, the concealed and unimagined treasures your disease can offer up when you listen to it very closely and ask what it is inviting you to change in your mind, heart and being. This is an alchemical inquiry that promises a different kind of medicine, the kind that turns fear into gratitude, sorrow into wonder and bitterness into hope –the kind that can provide emotional and spiritual healing on a journey of physical healing that has no guarantees.

A great example of this is Danny, who had spent the best part of 20 years in the Sinai desert, where Moses crossed the Red Sea, taking people on retreat and helping them take charge of their lives, when he started to get sick. He was helping to build a school for the local community at the time:

My health was deteriorating, but I carried on regardless. I refused to acknowledge that something was wrong with me. I had always been healthy. I was fighting, almost with rage, denying that my health was deteriorating. I worked with Dr Ahmed, a Bedouin herbalist. People travel from far and wide to see him. He is a serious doctor and healer, taking care of his tribe. People come with serious diseases and they get better. I knew he had some real power, but he tried everything he knew, yet nothing was working for me. I was getting worse, so I flew back to the UK.

I thought I just would get better if I rested. But I was getting worse – something was really wrong.

I went to the local farmers' baling festival, where they bring in the last of the bales. Ironically, I was just picking up the last straw bale when I collapsed and fell unconscious. For me, it was literally the last straw.

I was taken to the Gloucestershire Royal Hospital, where they connected me to equipment to monitor my liver. They said I had broken the NHS record for liver inflammation and they needed to take me immediately to Birmingham for a liver transplant. I was drifting in and out of awareness, but this news was a turning point. It didn't match my state of mind.

It didn't generate any anxiety, fear or panic. I just sat up and said, 'We need to have a conversation. We need to make a decision. I don't think this is what we are going to do.'

They probably thought I was a nutcase. I asked to speak to the doctor in charge. He arrived and informed me that this was serious, a life-or-death situation, and that a liver transplant was no small deal. He was a very charismatic person and we made a connection immediately. He wanted to know where I was coming from.

I told him, 'With respect to all of you, I am the CEO of my body, and we need to have a discussion together. There is something that I need to do for myself.'

I needed to take charge of this. Energetically, this was a massive turning point for me – to take leadership.

I told him, 'I need 24 hours to think about it, to do some work, to meditate, and I need a quiet room, and we'll have another conversation about this tomorrow. I'd appreciate it if you would disconnect me from all this equipment.'

There were six people around me with clipboards at that point and there was a long moment of silence.

The doctor asked me all sorts of questions to see if I was clear in my mind and then said, 'I get you and I'll support you – but on one condition, which is that we will come every half an hour and check in on you and we need to keep monitoring your liver function.'

I had to sign papers to confirm that it was my choice not to have the operation.

After that I sat upright in my bed for several hours. I wasn't drifting – it felt as though my life was dependent on staying present. I could not go to sleep. It reminded me of that Rumi poem 'Don't go back to sleep!'

> The breezes at dawn have secrets to tell you.
> Don't go back to sleep!
> You must ask for what you really want.
> Don't go back to sleep!
> People are going back and forth
> across the doorsill where the two worlds touch.
> The door is round and open.
> Don't go back to sleep!

There was a certain urgency in my body and its intelligence took over. I knew that I had a lot of health in my body. My focus was on my body community of billions of cells supporting this crisis. I don't remember doing anything calculated or controlled. I cannot really name what I was doing or what was happening. I felt completely peaceful. I was not in my mind. I had no fear. I was confident that I could cross this 'Red Sea'. This was my challenge.

There was a turning point after seven hours. The room became very busy with quite a few medical staff. The doctor came back in and said, 'I don't know what you're doing, but keep doing it. The blood flow is improving.'

The liver inflammation had gone right down. My liver had made a completely unexpected turnaround.

They kept me in another two days and then I left. I went completely yellow and had a long recovery rebuilding my liver. The first two months were very painful as my body detoxified. It was the first time that I had put myself at the top of my own list of priorities. I needed to heal, grow vegetables, cook, eat well, read and walk. It took me about two years to get back to full health.

Danny's and Sophie's transformations have in common a positive attitude and clear intention. Both fully owned and took charge of their life situation.

The idea that our state of mind has a profound effect on our body is further illustrated by a study by Professor Ellen Langer, who took a group of men aged 75–80 on a country retreat. Half were asked to think about the past. The other half were invited to stay in a house that had all the artefacts from the year 1959. These men listened to music, watched films and ate food from that era. Within five days, several of their signs of ageing had improved: they had more joint flexibility, better vision, better breathing and better cognitive function.[1]

The Power of Positive Intention and Creative Visualization

First championed by Carl Simonton in the 1970s, the power of positive and creative visualization in promoting health, and especially in boosting the body's immune system, is now well established. Wikipedia's entry for 'creative visualization' cites numerous studies showing that it can help with 'the healing of wounds to the body, minimizing physical pain, alleviating psychological pain including anxiety, sadness, and low mood, improving self-esteem or self-confidence, and enhancing the capacity to cope when interacting with others'.[2] This has given rise to the field of psycho-neuro-immunology (PNI), a perfect example of the mind–body connection.

Later in this book we will use creative visualization to enhance feelings of connection, be it with ourselves, others and our community, such as the HeartMath® exercises (*see page 168*); with nature (*page 127*); and with the divine (*page 238*). If you are dealing with a health issue, there is a creative visualization process in the Exercise Appendix that you can adapt according to your circumstances to help yourself recover. This kind of exercise can also be done for others, to help them heal.

This is really the basis for distance healing and prayer, the evidence for which is becoming increasing well established.[3] This certainly warrants further research. However, it is being actively resisted, since it challenges fundamental beliefs about how we can affect others at a distance and how we are connected in ways beyond the conventional senses.

Activating Our Blueprint for Health

Biologists are especially interested in morpho-genesis (the body coming into being), for example how egg cells turns into animals. In case you think that all this is done by genes, it isn't. Genes simply assemble amino acids into proteins, i.e. make building materials. They don't organize those building materials into body parts. Biologists have considered that there is some kind of organizing field, which they call a *morphogenetic field*, which acts like a blueprint. Rupert Sheldrake describes it like this:

> *In systems organised by fields, the parts all interact through the field of the whole system. First, morphogenetic fields work by imposing patterns or structures on otherwise random or indeterminate processes in the systems under their control. Second, they contain attractors, which draw systems under their influence toward future goals. Third, they evolve, along with living organisms themselves.*

This means that there is a healthy blueprint for our body and an 'attractor' – a force that attracts it into health if we give it the right conditions. It is also consistent with the way we can heal ourselves and others with positive intentions, and explains the 'phantom limb' phenomenon, where people who have lost limbs still sense them. For some, the 'phantom' fades with time, but this doesn't usually happen when an artificial limb is worn. As one researcher expressed it, 'The lifeless phantom is animated by the living phantom.'[4] Sheldrake proposes that the phantoms are the fields of the missing limbs.

He also proposes that our mind and body have a *morphic field* which includes and is more than the brain and the physical body. Patterns of activity across this field, *morphic resonances*, contain memory, not only of our personal history but the history of our species:

> *The morphic fields of all species have history and contain inherent memory by the process I call 'morphic resonance'. This resonance occurs between patterns of activity in self-organising systems on the basis of similarity, irrespective of their distance apart. Morphic resonance works across space and across time, from the past to the present. Through morphic resonance, each member of the species both draws upon and contributes to the collective memory of the species.*

This could explain how the beheaded flatworms (*see page 10*) could remember what they had learned when their heads grew back and how caterpillars could pass on their learning to moths. Sheldrake describes it as follows:

> *Morphic resonance is a process whereby self-organising systems inherit a memory from previous similar systems. In its most general formulation, morphic resonance means that the so-called laws of nature are more like habits. The hypothesis of morphic resonance also leads to a radically new interpretation of memory storage in the brain and of biological inheritance. Memory need not be stored in material traces inside brains, which are more like TV receivers than video recorders, tuning in to influences from the past. Thus each individual inherits a collective memory from past members of the species, and also contributes to the collective memory, affecting other members of the species in the future.*[5]

It's a bit like the iCloud, with individual storage facilities, but we can all access it, and it shapes our collective knowledge in much the same way that Carl Jung proposed the collective unconscious did back in 1916.

The theory of memory as resonances is explored in Rupert Sheldrake's *The Science Delusion*. It fits in perfectly with Malcolm Stewart's experience (*page 14*) and consequent beliefs.

Don't Worry, Be Happy

As science evolves, it becomes ever clearer that our intention and attitude have a profound effect on our body and life. For example, in one study, those with a high level of optimism had a 55 per cent lower risk of death from all causes and a 23 per cent lower risk of cardiovascular death.[6] Another study found that the risk of dying in the next two years was halved in those with a positive attitude.[7] A study on Catholic nuns found that the happiest nuns lived an extra nine and a half years.[8]

The most extensive study of the effects of psychological profile on health and ageing is the Longevity Project, which was begun by Dr Lewis Terman in the 1920s and written up in a book called *The Longevity Project* by Howard Friedman and Leslie Martin. Terman selected 1,500 bright boys and girls, all born around 1920, and his researchers studied their lives in meticulous detail at 10-year intervals right up to their deaths. The main findings were that conscientious, purposeful and hard-working people lived longer. Other key factors were doing something you loved and having a high level of social connectedness, with stable relationships, frequent contact, and interactions that cared for others. The emotions associated with a longer, healthier life were positivity, optimism, resilience, self-esteem, happiness, life satisfaction, love, friendship and hope. (Interestingly, though, the researchers found that individuals who were too optimistic, perhaps as a result of not learning from the difficult times in life, didn't live longer.)

Cynicism is Bad for You

The worst emotional state for health and longevity is not depression or stress – it's cynicism. Cynicism is a shut-down state of being, a negative outlook on life. It comes from a lack of trust in life, rather than a background of optimism and openness. It has become a way of being in this age where science, for some, has replaced God as a major belief system. Part of the scientific maxim is 'Prove it to me': people feel that nothing is real until it is proven. The trouble with this kind of thinking is that a cynic is more likely not to engage emotionally in activities, and, through questioning everything, to close down opportunities for new experiences.

Cynicism also raises inflammatory markers in the body, and the more cynical a person is, the more those markers are raised. A study has shown that being stressed is worse than being depressed, but being cynical is the worst of all.[9]

Cynicism also shortens our telomeres.[10] What are telomeres? They are rather like the hard bit at the end of a shoelace, in this case the end of your DNA containing chromosomes, copied to build a new cell. They become shorter each time a new cell is made until they are too short and cells stop dividing and hence replacing themselves. This initiates rapid ageing. The length of our telomeres is a very good predictor of our healthy lifespan.

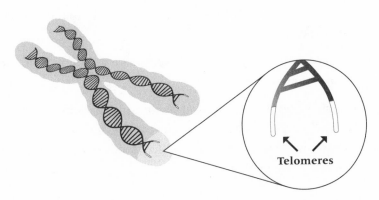

Figure 19: Telomeres: structures at the end of our chromosomes

Many studies have found that people in prolonged stress situations, such as caring for a sick child or parent with dementia, have shorter telomere length. So do those who have suffered childhood trauma and chronic depression. And those with 'hostile' cynicism have not only shorter telomeres, but also an increased level of inflammation in the body.[11] Conversely, studies that show that meditation is associated with longer telomeres.[12] The more open our heart and the more open we are to life, the more likely we are to live longer.

SUMMARY

In summary, the mind has a profound effect on the body. In truth, the two cannot be separated. By recognizing this connection, you can develop a way of life that is good for you and your body. Here's how:

- Respect your body and treat it well, with good nutrition, exercise and enough rest and sleep.

- Develop a positive attitude towards your own health and stay open to new ideas.

- Live conscientiously with good intentions, both for yourself and others.

- Engage in life, enjoy yourself and make a difference to the world around you.

- If you do get sick, use it as an opportunity to examine where you are mentally, emotionally, spiritually and physically. Do what you need to resolve conflicts, take charge and align yourself with getting well.

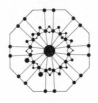

Chapter 7

Methyl Magic and the Brain-Makers

People wax lyrical about the amazing cosmos, plants and stars, but there is something equally amazing and a lot closer, and that is your body. Every second of every day it's adjusting your inner chemistry to keep the fundamental processes running smoothly, from making insulin because your blood sugar just went up, to making adrenalin so you can react quickly when crossing the road, building a new dendritic connection between your brain cells as you hardwire something you've learned and strengthening a stressed bone with new cells after a long walk. Every one of these micro-adjustments happens because of methylation.

A methyl unit is very simple. It is one carbon atom attached to three hydrogen atoms – CH_3. Adrenalin, for example, is made by attaching one of these methyl molecules onto noradrenalin, its precursor.

Genes, the programs for building new proteins and enzymes, hormones and cells, are turned on and off by methylation. If a gene becomes damaged, it is also repaired by methylation. Methylation is also a vital way in which the liver detoxifies and breaks down toxic material. There are a billion methylation reactions every couple of seconds and healthy methylation is the key to the body and brain's adaptability and connectivity.

So vital is methylation that if you measure whether or not a person is good at it, which involves a blood test for homocysteine, it predicts everything imaginable, from a child's school grades to an adult's risk of Alzheimer's to how long a person is going to live. (Having a low homocysteine level is associated with having longer telomeres; *see page 95*.)

Knowing your homocysteine level is, in my opinion, the single most important health statistic you need to know, more so that your weight, blood pressure or cholesterol level. (If you find it hard to remember, just think of 'gay chapel' – homo-cysteine.) A homocysteine level of more than 10μmol/l (micromoles/litre) means an increased risk of dementia, heart disease, stroke, osteoporosis and probably cancer. A homocysteine score (H score) below seven is ideal.

Healthy methylation depends on having enough B vitamins, specifically B2, B6, B12 and folic acid. So if your homocysteine score is high, it means you're not getting enough of one or more of these nutrients. Also, homocysteine is formed from the amino acid methionine and the liver can break down this toxic amino acid with an enzyme dependent on zinc and trimethylglycine (TMG). N-acetyl cysteine (NAC), a potent antioxidant, also helps lower homocysteine. So these are the nutrients that support healthy methylation:

- vitamin B2

- vitamin B6

- vitamin B12

- folate and folic acid

- trimethylglycine (TMG)

- zinc

- n-acetyl cysteine (NAC)

SAM-e: The Master Tuner

With all these nutrients, homocysteine turns into S-Adenosyl-Methionine, or SAMe for short, also known as the master tuner, because it is SAMe that does all this methylating. It's an energizing and mood-boosting nutrient with all sorts of magical healing properties in its own right and it is vital for healthy methylation.

You can buy SAMe over the counter in the USA but not in Europe since it fell foul of the EU medicines directive. This states that anything that cures, treats or prevents a disease is deemed a medicine. SAMe was thus anointed. Any medicine must have a licence, which costs a fortune by the time you've fulfilled all the requirements and is therefore way beyond worth doing unless you have a patent and therefore no one can compete with you. This law was set up to protect the interests of Big Pharma. Since SAMe is non-patentable, being a natural substance, it has vanished, at least in Europe, down a legislative hole.

Methylation Support Supplements

The alternative, which, quite frankly, is usually just as good if not better, is to supplement the nutrients above. How much do you need to take? The answer to that is whatever is necessary to keep your homocysteine level low.

Many people start to absorb vitamin B12 badly as they get older, so have to supplement a lot to get a little more in. To put this into context, the RDA (ridiculous dietary arbitrary) for B12 is 2 micrograms (mcg). It should be 10mcg, which is what I take daily in my multivitamin as well as eating fish and eggs. (B12 is found in fish, meat, eggs and dairy products.) But the level needed to bring down a person's homocysteine if it is high and they are over 60 is usually 500mcg – that is 250 times the RDA! Fortunately there is no toxicity with B12 and the amount is very small (there are 1,000 micrograms in a milligram and 1,000 milligrams in a gram).

The levels I recommend are shown in the chart overleaf.

Nutrient	No risk Below 7	Low risk 7–9	High risk 10–15	Very high risk Above 15
Folate	200mcg	400mcg	800mcg	800mcg
B12	10mcg	250mcg	500mcg	1,000mcg
B2	25mg	50mg	75mg	100mcg
B6	10mg	15mg	20mg	50mg
Zinc	5mg	10mg	15mg	20mg
TMG		500mg	1.5–3g	3–6g
NAC		250mg	500mg	750mg

Figure 20: Nutrients and levels to supplement, depending on your homocysteine score

If your homocysteine level is ideal, below seven, a good multivitamin should give you the basic nutrient levels. If your level is above 10, which is the level that correlates with accelerated brain shrinkage and later risk for Alzheimer's, you need to supplement a homocysteine-lowering formula to achieve the amounts above. This will probably mean taking two pills a day. (*See Resources for a list of methylation support formulas.*)

But the first step is to measure your homocysteine level. This can be done through your doctor, but a) they need to be switched on and b) they need a good reason to do it, such as memory concerns or cardiovascular disease. There are private labs that do it, but some need a doctor's referral or signature on the request form. There is also, however, a home test kit that you can buy from www.yorktest.com. You prick your finger, collect the blood as described, send it off to the lab and get your result a few days later in the post.

Methyl Magic

So many disconnection diseases are both linked to high homocysteine levels and made better by supplementing with the nutrients shown above. The list is growing, but includes Alzheimer's disease, ADHD, autistic spectrum disorders, bipolar disorder, cerebrovascular dementia, depression, heart disease, multiple sclerosis, osteoporosis, Parkinson's disease, rheumatoid arthritis, schizophrenia and stroke.

I have written a book called *The Homocysteine Solution* with Dr James Braly which also explains the diet and lifestyle habits that improve methylation.

People with raised homocysteine levels who supplement these nutrients and make the necessary dietary changes report instantaneous improvements. One man, Chris K, felt very unwell, with constant tiredness, worsening memory and concentration and little zest for life. He felt depressed and had no sex drive, even though he had no diagnosed disease as such. His homocysteine score was 119! One year on, his homocysteine level was nine and his failing memory and concentration had been completely restored. 'I feel very healthy,' he said. 'I feel really, really good. You have saved my life, or at least made it worth living again.'

To make this real, the figure below show the difference in the rate of brain shrinkage in people with pre-dementia given either placebos or B vitamins. They are split into three groups: low, medium and high omega-3 fat levels in the blood. Those both given B vitamins and with sufficient omega-3 levels had 73% less brain shrinkage over the next year, compared to those on placebo.[1]

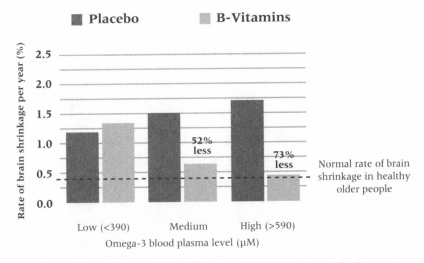

Figure 21: Graph showing rates of brain shrinkage in a study of pre-dementia patients taking a placebo vs B vitamins.

Amanda-Jane W., aged 33, was suffering with chronic fatigue and low mood. She was shocked to find her homocysteine level was 25.9. She followed my homocysteine-lowering diet and supplement recommendations. Almost immediately her sleep improved, and within four weeks she had much more energy. Two months later she retested her homocysteine level and found it had dropped to 9.4 units. That's a 64 per cent decrease. Here's what she told me:

> *I feel much better. I'm very busy right now, and in the past I'd feel overwhelmed and not able to cope, both mentally and physically, but now I feel great. My mood is very positive – no panic or depression. I feel buoyant, energetic and enthusiastic. I haven't had any colds or infections. I'm sleeping much better and my PMS has disappeared – I experienced no breast tenderness, mood swings or tearfulness in my last period. I am really delighted.*

But what if you have no disease as such? In an uncontrolled experiment I decided to try out these nutrients on a group of experienced meditators. Many reported deepened meditation. Other feedback I've received concerns dreaming. One person said that they had started dreaming, or recalling dreams, for the first time. Another said, 'For the first time I'm dreaming in colour.' Many others who had some kind of mental fussiness or discombobulation reported feeling much more 'connected'.

The Brain-Makers

There are, of course, other vitally important nutrients that help brain function and connection. The dry weight of the brain is 60 per cent fat. The trillions of brain cells are largely made out of essential fats bound to phospholipids. The binding depends on methylation nutrients. These three families of nutrients – essential fats, phospholipids and methylation nutrients – are the 'brain-makers'. Achieving an optimal supply of them is central not only to intelligence and memory, but also to mood and sense of connection.

Brain-Maker no. 1: Essential Brain Fats

As far as essential fats are concerned, the most abundant in the brain is DHA (docosahexaenoic acid). It makes up a quarter of the brain's cerebral cortex. Oily fish contain roughly equal amounts of DHA and EPA (eicosapentaenoic acid, an omega-3 fat). Only 'DHA, alone or combined with EPA, contributes to improved memory function in older adults (45+) with mild memory complaints', concludes a meta-analysis published in the *Public Library of Services* journal.[2] The benefit is apparently driven by DHA at a daily level between 500 and 1,000mg. There is also evidence of benefit for schoolchildren.[3]

EPA, meanwhile, has strong antidepressant effects. Last year a meta-analysis concluded that 'the use of omega-3 is effective in patients with diagnosis of depression'.[4] A similar dose is needed for an effect.

To achieve at least 500mg of both EPA and DHA does mean supplementing them, as well as eating fish. I take a twice-daily capsule, giving myself 250mg of each, and eat oily fish three times a week, plus a tub of taramasalata – fish roe is a great source. I also eat chia seeds, the highest vegetarian source of omega-3.

Brain-Maker no. 2: Phospholipids

All fish, not just oily fish, are excellent sources of the next brain-maker, phospholipids, as are eggs. Phospholipids are the backbone of brain cells – the essential fats literally hang off them, creating the intelligent membrane that not only holds neurons together but also contains the receptor sites for neurotransmitters, the brain's communication molecules. They are semi-essential, meaning that the body can make them, but growing evidence shows that we just don't make enough and need to get a direct source from our diet or supplements.

The most abundant phospholipid in the brain is phosphatidyl choline (PC). Also important are phosphatidyl serine (PS) and phosphatidyl dimethylethanolamine (DMAE). Both PC and PS[5] have been shown to improve memory, concentration and speed of thinking and to protect those with mental illness.[6] One study gave students a large dose of

PC and reported memory improvement within 90 minutes.[7] Lecithin granules or capsules are a direct source of PC. I supplement all three in a brain food formula, as well as making a point of eating six eggs a week, plus five servings of fish, three of which are oily fish.

Brain-Maker no. 3: Methylation Nutrients

As we saw earlier, several B vitamins are important methylation nutrients, but we also need methyl groups. Greens contain the natural 'methyl'-folate vitamin, but it is in an unstable form. That's why most supplements contain the stable form called folic acid, but it has to be converted back into methylfolate to work properly, and not everyone is good at doing this. Recently, stable forms of methylfolate have become available and are preferable in lowering high homocysteine levels and thus improving methylation. I use these in my methyl support supplement (*see Resources*). Lentils, beans, nuts and seeds are also important sources of folates.

So, for a healthy brain and optimal connection, you want to eat fish, eggs, greens, beans, nuts and chia seeds and supplement with extra omega-3 fish oil high in DHA and EPA, plus phospholipids and methylation nutrients – B6, B12 and folate, plus zinc and TMG. The ideal dose will depend on your homocysteine level.

It is especially important for vegans to supplement these nutrients, including a seaweed-derived source of EPA and DHA and plenty of chia or flax seeds and their oil. Chia oil is also available in capsules. B12 is also found in shiitake mushrooms and nori seaweed.

Methylation is the subtle way in which our system is micro-adjusted to stay in balance, or be homeodynamic, since balance implies something too static. This is of course happening within a world of energy that is cycling the Sun's energy and intelligence from algae to plankton to fish to essential omegas and vitamin D. The next chapter explores how we can tap into and generate vital energy, beyond the delivery mechanism of optimum nutrition.

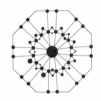

Chapter 8

Generating Vital Energy

Vital energy is often described as the energy we draw in from the Universe and, depending on how receptive we are, it has the power to nourish us at a fundamental level. It is the hidden ingredient that connects us with each other and the world around us.

It has been embraced by Eastern philosophies for generations. Buddhists and Hindus call it *prana*; the Chinese refer to it as *chi*; the Japanese traditions call it *ki*. Each term translates to mean 'life force' and there are entire medical systems based on generating and distributing this vital energy. It's what makes us feel vibrant and alive.

Yoga, *tai chi, qigong* ('chi gung') and other Oriental exercise systems and martial arts are all designed to make us more receptive to vital energy; so too is acupuncture, which works by unblocking channels of energy called 'meridians' through which the energy is said to flow.

According to traditional Chinese medicine, vital energy comes to us from the food we eat and the air we breathe. I am convinced that this is more than just the sum of the nutrients in our food and the effects of oxygen or negative ions. Fresh organic food, prepared consciously, has a profoundly different effect than processed fast food such as a hamburger, made from grossly mistreated animals, and reconstituted fries, made from pesticide-laden potatoes. Making food with love and receiving it with gratitude may make a real difference to our energy levels. Vitamins, minerals and essential fats all have their own *chi* factor too. Eating well and supplementing the right nutrients are also part of the energy equation.

Similarly, it isn't just what we breathe but how we breathe it that nourishes us. Breathing 'from the heart', as in HeartMath's Quick Coherence technique (*see page 168*), helps us interact with the world around us in a more open-hearted way. Alternatively, breathing 'from the belly' allows us to feel more centred, less caught up in the mind or feelings and consequently more aware of what is going on.

Learning how to generate energy at every level, and not expend too much, not only helps us feel energized but also gives us the energy to deal with life's inevitable stresses and challenges.

Expending Energy

Just as we generate energy, we also dissipate or expend energy. This is easy to understand at a physical level, as it equates to exercise – think of calories in and calories out. However, we also expend psychological energy by thinking too much and reacting stressfully and emotionally to situations or thoughts. Physically, this leads to energy being 'trapped' in our body as muscular tension. In his book *Mindbody Prescription*, Dr John Sarno describes trapped psychological energy and unexpressed feelings as a primary source of chronic back pain and explains how to release this.

As well as trapping energy, we often use drugs such as alcohol and cannabis to numb ourselves from stress and pain, and this also leads to a loss of energy. Many psychiatric drugs, such as tranquillizers, mood stabilizers, anti-psychotics and antidepressants, are also numbing. They may have a short-term use in a crisis situation, but long term we have to deal with our experiences in order to prevent them fuelling negative patterns.

Caffeine and nicotine don't exactly numb us, but in releasing short-term energy they can also lead to long-term energy depletion.

The 'high' of drugs leads to depletion in much the same way that a wave, when it breaks, releases energy. That is why there is a 'down' after the up.

The most energy-depleting drugs are, in order: alcohol, heroin and opiates, tobacco, cocaine, barbiturates, antidepressants, amphetamines, marijuana, sugar and caffeine. However, the plant entheogens *ayahuasca* and *peyote* or *San Pedro* (*discussed in Chapter 3*) give us energy. They do not deplete it.

On the one hand, the ideal is to live in a naturally energized state as a consequence of good nutrition, vital energy-generating exercise and a clear mind. On the other hand, there are times when we react with a negative emotion, be it frustration, depression or aggression, and this generates so much pressure in our psyche that we have to let off steam. Occasional use of alcohol, sugar, caffeine and nicotine to help deal with and dissipate the energy created by traumatic reactions is not a problem, but if you have become a habitual consumer and, for example, turn to the bottle whenever anything is troubling you, I recommend you read my book *How to Quit without Feeling S**t*, co-authored with Dr James Braly and Dr David Miller.

There are also other ways we dissipate energy, for example by being cruel and abusive, or going into fear reactions such as panicking or having phobias, or over-exerting ourselves by becoming a workaholic or exercising to the point of exhaustion. Overeating is another way we dissipate energy. Which of these examples do you tend towards?

All of this is important for connection, because by generating energy and reducing our expenditure of energy we have more energy available to jump a level of consciousness to a more connected state. Many mystical traditions and transformational processes require this by stipulating special sugar-free diets, the avoidance of alcohol and other drugs, no sex or TV and so on. However we do it, by consciously avoiding our habitual ways of dissipating energy, our potential energy for transformation increases.

How to Increase Vital Energy

There are many ways for us to increase our vital energy, the most popular of which are yoga, *tai chi* and *qigong* (*chi gung*). They all include focusing on specific ways of breathing, which can also form the foundation for meditation, which can, again, generate vital energy. So can chanting or singing spiritually uplifting songs. There are many ways of using the breath.

The Breath of Life

Breathing is something we take for granted and yet for thousands of years ancient traditions have used breathing exercises to evoke conscious, healthful changes in the body. The breath is the link between mind and body. Each emotional state has its own distinct breathing pattern. For example, when we are anxious or afraid, our breathing becomes rapid and shallow. Conversely, when we are happy and at ease, our breathing is naturally slow and deep. So the breath is the key to calming the mind and relaxing the body.

Slowing and deepening the breath may also result in living longer. Numerous theories abound about delaying the ageing process, yet only one statistic remains consistent among animals: all animal species have, on average, 2.5 to 3.5 billion heartbeats in a lifetime.[1] For humans, with an average heart rate of 72 beats per minute, lifespan averages 70 to 80 years. By this equation, slowing the heart rate to 60 beats per minute could add seven years more life.

Although not proven, breathing more fully to slow your heart rate certainly seems sensible. Deeper breathing and a slow pulse are both recognized signs of health. The stronger your heart, the less often it needs to beat, and the deeper the breath, the more tissues can be oxygenated.

There is also a need to balance the in-breath and the out-breath. That is how we balance oxygen, which we inhale, and carbon dioxide, which we exhale. Breathing in and out through the nose helps this.

People at altitude live longer, perhaps due to the relative lack of oxygen. This also improves the blood's oxygen-carrying capacity.

Many people overbreathe, taking in too much oxygen, often through the mouth. This is linked to anxiety, asthma, insomnia, snoring, fatigue and heart disease. There's a whole book, *The Oxygen Advantage* by Patrick McKeown, which goes into optimizing breathing patterns using Buteyko breathing, both for athletes wanting to improve their performance and for those suffering from the conditions above.

There's More to Air than Oxygen

But there may be more to breathing than that. As well as containing oxygen, in yoga philosophy the air we breathe contains *prana* – the vital energy we talked about earlier. By doing conscious breathing exercises, we can accumulate this energy and revitalize our body and mind.

Science is ever closer to measuring this invisible energy. Some scientists think it's connected with charged particles in the air, called ions. When these particles are negatively charged, they have positive effects on us – and vice versa. This is what ionizers are all about: they generate negative ions.

High levels of positive ions, the bad guys, are found during strong winds, such as the Mistral that blows along the Rhone Valley in France. With it comes the equivalent of PMT (pre-mistral tension), as the wind is rumoured to make people grumpy and irritable.

After a thunderstorm, or close to a waterfall, the air is charged with negative ions, the good guys. These may literally help us to accumulate vital energy. We feel more alive when we spend time in natural surroundings – walking by the sea, relaxing in a park or strolling through a forest, for example. According to research by Dr Aaron Michelfelder, Professor of Family Medicine at Loyola University Chicago Stritch School of Medicine in America, walking in a forest or park reduces levels of the stress hormone cortisol and lowers pulse rate and blood pressure.[2] It also increases levels of white blood cells, so orchestrating an immune-boosting effect.

Another way of accumulating vital energy is with specific breathing exercises such as Diakath Breathing™.

Diakath Breathing™

Diakath Breathing directly generates vital *chi* energy and is also an excellent way to enter a meditative state. It uses the *Kath Point™*. Although not an anatomical point as such, this is the body's centre of gravity, and by placing our awareness here, rather than in the head, as we most often do, it is possible to become aware of the whole body.

All the martial arts, in their pure form, are practised with this awareness, which gives us a more complete and grounded experience of ourselves. You can experience this for yourself by practising this simple breathing exercise:

Exercise: Diakath Breathing™

This breathing exercise (reproduced with the kind permission of Oscar Ichazo) connects the *Kath Point™* – the body's centre of equilibrium – with the diaphragm muscle, so that deep breathing becomes natural and effortless. You can practise this exercise at any time, while sitting, standing or lying down, and for as long as you like. You can also practise it unobtrusively during moments of stress. It is an excellent natural relaxant and energy-booster, helping you to feel more connected and in tune.

The diaphragm is a dome-shaped muscle attached to the bottom of the ribcage. The Kath Point is located three finger-widths below the belly button and 2.5cm (1 inch) inside the core area of the body. If you place your index finger just below your navel, your ring finger will be at the level of the Kath Point. When you put your awareness in this point, it becomes easy to be aware of your entire body.

Ideally, find somewhere quiet first thing in the morning. When breathing, inhale and exhale through your nose. As you inhale, you will expand your lower belly from the Kath and your diaphragm muscle. This allows the lungs to fill with air from the bottom to the top. As you exhale, the belly and the diaphragm muscle relax, allowing the lungs to empty from top to bottom.

1. Sit comfortably in a quiet place with your spine straight.

2. As you inhale and exhale slowly through your nose, focus your attention on your Kath point.

3. Let your belly expand from your Kath point as you inhale slowly, deeply and effortlessly. Feel your diaphragm being pulled towards the Kath as your lungs fill with air from the bottom to the top. On the exhale, relax both your belly and your diaphragm, emptying your lungs from top to bottom.

4. Repeat at your own pace.

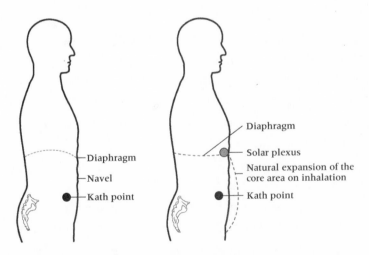

Figure 22: Diakath Breathing
(© 1972, 2016 by Oscar Ichazo. Used with permission. All rights reserved. Diakath, Diakath Breathing, Diakath Breathing illustration, Kath and Kath Point are trademarks of Oscar Ichazo.)

Exercise for Vital Energy

Exercise is often thought of as simple physical training, but it should be about more than that. Scientific research into yoga, *tai chi* and *qigong* have found a positive health effect that doesn't follow on from aerobics classes or running around the park. While excessive aerobic exercise can actually depress the immune system and overstress the body, *tai chi* and *qigong* can boost wellbeing, mood and immunity,[3] and yoga has been shown to have positive effects on pulse, blood pressure,[4] mental[5] and physical performance beyond those expected by physical exercise alone.

In addition to helping us to keep fit, these ancient systems of exercise were designed to generate vitality. The underlying philosophy of the ancient Indian traditions and the martial arts of the East is that tension blocks the flow of vital energy and stops us being rejuvenated. Therefore the purpose of doing yoga, *tai chi* or *qigong* is to release the blocks, unlock the tension and allow us to return to a state of equilibrium and connection. Unlike body-building, whose aim is to build strong, tight muscles, the emphasis is on increasing flexibility and suppleness to allow the *chi* or *prana* to flow.

Certainly, a growing body of research supports the stress-relieving benefits of these types of exercise. Studies have found that *tai chi* and *qigong* can reduce levels of stress hormones and decrease heart-rate,[6] for example. Doctors at the Boston University Medical Centre have found that yoga is especially beneficial for those suffering from stress-related conditions, as it can stimulate the parasympathetic nervous system (the opposite to the sympathetic nervous system, which is triggered by stress) and increase levels of the calming neurotransmitter gamma amino-butyric acid (GABA).[7] Low levels of GABA are common in those with anxiety disorders, depression, epilepsy and chronic pain.

Doing yoga, *tai chi* or *qigong* usually requires you to attend a class (*see Resources*). If you live in a remote location with a lack of good local teachers, or you simply struggle to find the time to attend regular sessions, this can be difficult. However, there are many great DVDs and online instructors as well.

All over the world yoga is becoming widely practised, but sometimes it seems, at its lowest level, to be oriented towards goals such as weight loss and a tight belly, rather than its true purpose, which is to become aware of our deepest nature. Bhole Prabhu, a yoga expert, says:

The goal of seeking to experience this deepest potential is not part of a religious process, but an experiential science of self-study. The most important teaching of yoga has to do with our nature as human beings. It states that our 'true nature' goes far beyond the limits of the human mind and personality – that instead, our human potential is infinite and transcends our individual minds and our sense of self. The very word 'yoga' makes reference to this. The root, yuj, meaning 'unity' or 'yoke', indicates that the purpose of yoga is to connect or unite ourselves with our highest nature.

So, when choosing your yoga teacher, it is best to find one who is well plugged in to the deeper goal of this practice.

If you're looking for a quick and extremely effective form of vital energy-generating exercise that you can do at home, I recommend Psychocalisthenics®.

Psychocalisthenics®: The Holistic Workout

This contemporary exercise system was developed by Oscar Ichazo, founder of the Arica School®, a School of Wisdom and Knowledge. *Psychocalisthenics* means strength (*sthenia*) and beauty (*cali*) through the breath (*psyche*). It encompasses a routine of 23 exercises that can be done in less than 20 minutes. The breath is the driving force, as each of the exercises is guided by a precise deep-breathing pattern.

The combination of movement and breathing exercises is what makes Psychocalisthenics (shortened to P-Cals®) a perfect combination of revitalization and regeneration. At first glance, it looks like a hybrid of yoga, dance, *tai chi* and martial arts, which is hardly surprising, as Ichazo is a master of both the martial arts and yoga. 'In the same way that we have an everyday need for food and nourishment,' he says, 'we have to promote the circulation of our vital energy as an everyday business.'

He first developed Psychocalisthenics in 1958 and it has since been taken up by thousands of people all over the world. Advocates give it glowing reports. 'This is exercise pared to perfection. I wasn't sweating buckets as I would be after an aerobics class, but I could feel I had exercised far more muscles. I was feeling clear-headed and bright rather than wiped out,' said natural health expert Jane Alexander, when she reviewed the routine for the *Daily Mail*.

One of the things I like most about P-Cals is that you don't have to go anywhere, wear special clothes or buy equipment. Once you've learned the routine, you can do it in around 16 minutes in your own home, accompanied either by the DVD or a talk-through music recording.

The best way to learn it is to do the one-day training, which is usually held in London (*see www.patrickholford.com for details or www. pcals.com for worldwide trainings*). You can also learn it from the DVD, but there's nothing like having someone there to give feedback on your movements and offer hands-on assistance. There's also a fascinating book called *P-Cals/Psychocalisthenics: Exercises to Awaken your Core Fire*, and a DVD, CD and Wallchart (*available from www.holfordirect.com in the UK and www.pcals.com*), which explains the basis behind P-Cals and how each exercise revitalizes different parts of the body and mind.

Fasting

Fasting for a number of days, which relieves the body of the need to spend energy digesting, is increasingly being recognized for its health-restoring effects. This is another way to generate vital energy and also helps break addictive eating patterns. Try my three-day fast routine at www.patrickholford.com/3dayfast. (This is not suitable for diabetics or those with medical conditions that require frequent food intake.)

In summary, to maximize your overall energy for transformation, stress resilience and connectedness:

- Become aware of how you dissipate energy when stressed, especially those ways that have become habitual, and, in doing so, deal with the issues that are leading you to lose energy in this way.

- Spend as much time as you can in clean air. If you are a city-dweller, take regular trips out to the countryside and choose holidays in the mountains or by the sea.

- Be conscious of your breath and give yourself the opportunity to breathe more deeply, either by regular energy-generating exercise and/or through breathing exercises such as Diakath Breathing.

- Include some form of vital energy-generating exercise, such as yoga, *tai chi*, *qigong* or P-Cals in your weekly routine.

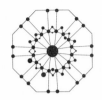

Chapter 9

The Earth Connection

How do you wake up? Today, I am up at 5 a.m., watching the Sun rise over London as I write. Petrol blue emerges at the horizon out of the dark night, with the peachy pink hints of the Sun soon to follow. Tomorrow it is full moon. When did you last sleep under the stars? How easy is it to forget these things?

Half the world's population is currently urbanized. By 2029 two-thirds, estimated to be 8.3 billion, are expected to live in cities. The end result of this mass urbanization is that we end up being disconnected from each other, from our true self, from our miraculous body and from the incredible Earth we inhabit.

In our infinite stupidity, partly through organized religion attempting to control our relationship with the divine, partly through the arrogance and ignorance of atheistic scientism and the belief in humanity's superiority, any animistic idea of a consciousness or intelligence in nature is often considered heresy, a bygone belief of pagan simpletons. Yet there was a time not so long ago when it was a capital offence to cut the bark of an oak tree. Worship of the planets, the Sun and the moon, now so *passé*, was central to life.

Life still depends on that glorious Sun and the oceans that sway with the pull of the moon. Yet any attribute of intelligence or majesty to these celestial objects is liable to attract accusations of lunacy.

This has to change, because with this limited thinking we lose our connection with nature.

Food for Thought

This disconnection has led to factory farming (intensive animal-rearing with little to no respect of the life of the chicken, cow or pig), GM crops, pesticides and chemical fertilizers. The 'sell' is that this is the only way to feed the masses, but it isn't true. This is the way for Big Farmer to own food production and make more profit.

Quality, nutrition and compassion have been sacrificed along the way. We have destroyed the topsoil, ignored the carbon cycle and suppressed the small-scale local growing of food in order to own and control food from the seed to the plate.

Living in cities, where water comes out of a tap and garbage is simply removed, we have little desire to recycle and to preserve water and power. But water will become the most valuable commodity in the not-so-distant future.

In the meantime we have become so alienated from the Earth that misshapen food is discarded and everything is over-sanitized. We are germ phobic, not realizing that a far greater danger is created from chemicals designed to kill nature's pests and weeds. For example, glyphosate (Roundup), one of the most widely used herbicides, has recently been classified as 'probably carcinogenic to humans'.[1]

We are bug phobic too. When essential life-giving bacteria were first cultured from human faeces, the denigrating newspaper headline read: 'Let them eat shit.' But the point is that our sterile environments have disrupted the complex microbiome. Many urban children no longer have the resilience and the gut intelligence to know how to react to foods, so are becoming increasingly allergic and asthmatic. For them, the modern world has become toxic.

Most children don't even know where food comes from, let alone how to grow it. But there is something wonderful about growing our own food and eating it – the miracle of seeds turning into food on the

The Hadron Collider, the world's largest particle accelerator. CERN, Switzerland
(© Maximilien Brice, CERN/Science Photo Library)

It is ironic that atheistic scientists say that out of nothing everything came into existence with the Big Bang, while the religious say that God created everything out of nothing. At least they agree on something.

Pilgrims gather at the Ka'aba, Mecca, the most sacred Muslim site in the world.
(Shutterstock/Zurijeta)

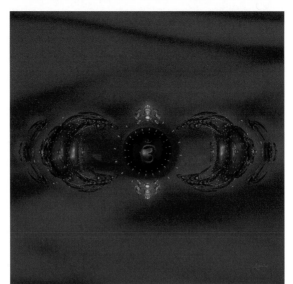

Ajna, the energy centre between the eyebrows, is blue.

Anahata, the heart centre, is green.

The *hara*, the energy centre below the navel is yellow/orange.

Posters of all five, and individual prints, are available
from www.patrickholford.com/connection

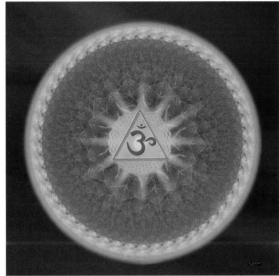

Sahasrara, the
spiritual centre
at the top of the
head, is violet.

Muladhara,
at the base of
the spine and
perineum, is red.

We are physical, chemical, psychological and spiritual beings, living in an environment. Our health depends on each of these realms being in harmony. When this is achieved we are naturally full of energy, free of pain, happy, alert and purposeful.

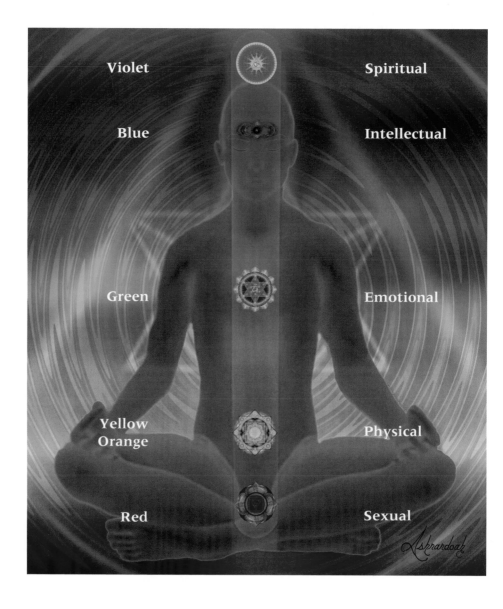

Violet — Spiritual

Blue — Intellectual

Green — Emotional

Yellow Orange — Physical

Red — Sexual

The five energy centres and their zones of connection.
(© Ashnandoah)

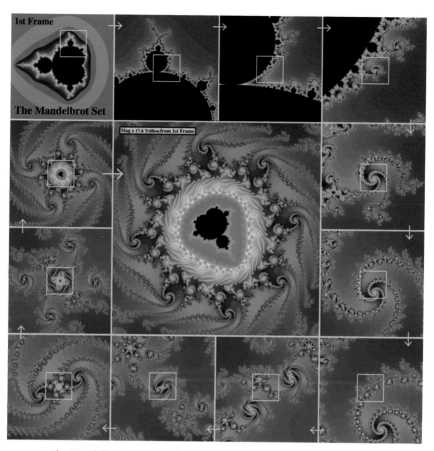

The Mandelbrot set, a simple reiterating mathematical formula, creates unique but similar patterns as it unfolds. The central image is magnified 17.6 trillion times from the first frame (top left). (© Greg Sams)

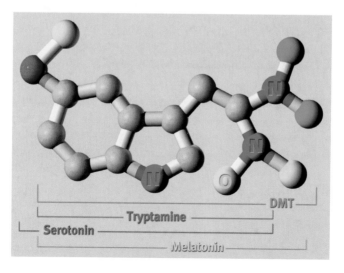

DMT, serotonin and melatonin molecules.
At the core of the DMT molecule are the conjoined hexagon and pentagon.

Volcan Copiapo, Chile

My body is from the Earth. The Earth is from the Stars.
The Stars are made of Light. My body is made of Light.

Mount Kailash, Tibet
(© Ian Baker)

Kayaking with Tim Lawrence in Svalbard.

Our valley in the Black Mountains, Wales.
(© Steve Flood)

This sand dollar, a type of sea urchin, displays the geometry of five in nature (Thinkstock/SaundersFineArts).

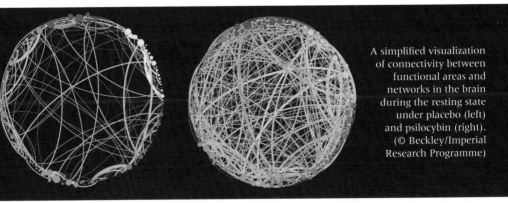

A simplified visualization of connectivity between functional areas and networks in the brain during the resting state under placebo (left) and psilocybin (right). (© Beckley/Imperial Research Programme)

Four upwards triangles and five down-facing triangles make nine interlocking triangles, and create smaller 43 triangles which each represent a particular aspect of existence, and the journey to the centre a pilgrimage to enlightenment.

The Shree Yantra, used in tantra yoga traditions to represent the energies of the cosmos. (Malcolm Stewart from *Patterns of Eternity*.)

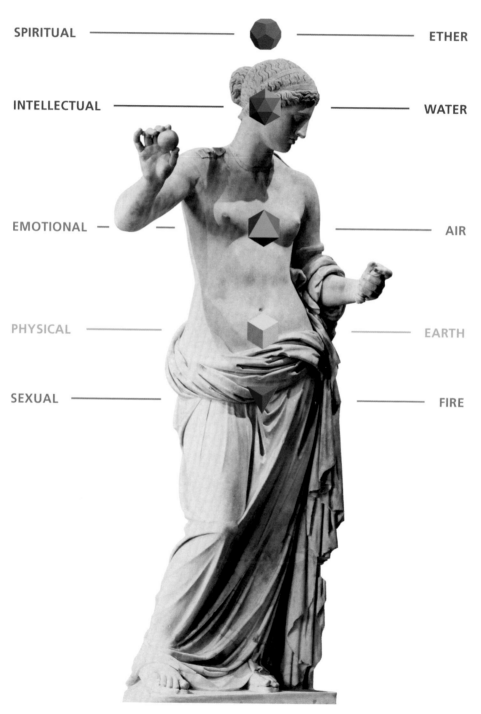

ZONE		ELEMENT
SPIRITUAL		ETHER
INTELLECTUAL		WATER
EMOTIONAL		AIR
PHYSICAL		EARTH
SEXUAL		FIRE

The five zones of connection.
(Malcolm Stewart from *Symbols of Eternity*.)

table. It is a simple and important way to connect with the Earth and should be taught in all schools. That is, if health and safety will allow it, as Dudley Sutton's poem illustrates:

Forbidden Fruit

One day a gusty autumn breeze
Was shaking apples from the trees
When just as I was bending down
To pick one up from off the ground
A fellow bellowed: 'Leave that there
You really ought to have a care –

What of safety, what of health?
That apple should be on a shelf
Checked and washed and sanitized
Waxed and wrapped and rightly sized:
Think what danger there could be
If we ate apples from the tree!'

This wretched health and safety bore
Was pointing to a superstore,
A blot upon the countryside
Where apples came from far and wide

Though they, despite the salesman's hype,
Were seldom tasty, never ripe.

Home to earwig, wasp and spider,
Rotting apples brewing cider
For the lusty swains romancing
Busty dames at harvest dancing,
Prancing through the superstore
Pissing scrumpy on the floor.

O, if there had been a superstore
In paradise in days of yore
And Eve had stuck her pretty neck out

To bring that apple to the check-out
Where handsome Adam manned the till:
Might we not be in Eden still?

© *Dudley Sutton, 2015*

Another simple way to connect with the Earth and the food it produces is to say grace, however you choose to do it. It also connects you with the people you dine with. Research from the HeartMath Institute[2] shows that extending a positive feeling, such as gratitude to your food, the Earth and/or the Creator, improves a coherent and connected heart state as measured by heart rate variability (HRV). This, in turn, switches off the adrenal hormones that suppress digestion and allows you to enjoy your food more fully. Whether you are vegetarian, 'fishitarian' or an omnivore, be grateful for the sacrifice of your food.

Meat or Veg?

Animals are grossly mistreated in modern farming and considered simply as a food factory. That mentality has allowed appalling mass production and exploitation of them. So I have great respect for anyone who chooses not to eat meat. I eat fish and a couple of times a year I eat meat. However, I am especially conscious, as far as I can be in the circumstances, that the life of the fish or animal that I eat becomes my life. Wherever I can, I choose animals that have had a good life and a quick death, and make sure nothing is wasted. My son, who runs a smallholding in Wales, raises turkeys, chickens and pigs in very humane conditions. At Christmas he slaughters a turkey and prepares it carefully. Nothing is wasted.

I don't think it is strictly necessary to be vegan or vegetarian from a health or nutrition point of view, however. There are unhealthy meat-eaters *and* vegans.

If vegan, it is especially important to understand nutrition and why a vegan diet alone is unlikely to provide enough vitamin D, omega-3 fats and vitamin B12. Of course, all of these can be supplemented, and Sun exposure is more important for vitamin D levels than any food. As mentioned earlier, omega-3 fats are also available in chia and flax seeds, so they have to be a daily food for a vegan. Also, I'm not convinced you can get enough of the most potent omega-3 fats (EPA and DHA), which help build the brain, from vegetarian sources alone if pregnant. That's why I recommend pregnant and breastfeeding vegans supplement their diet with omega-3 fish oils. But then again we have the issue of overfishing to consider.

B12, which is only found in foods of an animal origin – meat, fish, eggs, milk – is an interesting one. Actually, there is B12 in shiitake mushrooms and laver seaweed, which the Japanese call nori and wrap their sushi in. The Welsh also make laverbread.

I remember an exchange with Robert Cohen, who runs the 'notmilk.com' campaign. While I agree that milk is not part of our evolutionary design – our ancestors weren't milking buffaloes – and is not an essential for a healthy diet, if you are strictly vegan, the question remains, where do you get B12 from? I pointed out to Robert that there were many surveys and studies that showed vegans to have low B12, high homocysteine and worse cognition as a result. I asked him if he supplemented B12. He said he did not and was perfectly healthy. I asked him where he got his B12 from. He said, 'Oral sex.'

Interesting. He's got a point. Both semen and vaginal fluids are very rich in B12. It can be stored to some extent as well, so maybe a daily dose is not so important. However, if a person has no dietary source of B12, does that deplete seminal/vaginal B12? I don't think this study has ever been done. Theoretically, a vegan would run out of B12, but Robert, having been a non-supplementing vegan for many years, assures me this is not the case.

B12 is synthesized in the large intestine by bacteria, but it is said not to be absorbed that far down the alimentary tract. It is also present in bacteria and other micro-organisms, so eating food that is not pristinely clean might be another potential source. The odd weevil might be useful! Heaven help you if you're a celibate, germ-phobic vegan who doesn't believe in supplements!

Anyway, leaving the B12 issue aside, it is perfectly possible to be super-healthy if you are vegan *and* if you include some fish and meat in your diet.

Another issue to consider is protein. Back in the 1970s, when I was practising various meditations, I was advised to eat more protein. Be it from a vegetarian source such as quinoa or chia seeds, or via meat, fish and eggs, protein is grounding and it is said that if you are doing lots of meditation it is a good idea to make sure you eat enough protein to keep yourself 'grounded'. *Chi*-generating exercises that focus on the Kath Point, such as Diakath Breathing (*see page 110*) are also 'grounding' or centering.

I have met quite a few 'transcendental mystic' types, often vegan, who are barely 'on the Earth'. They live in lofty realms, often disconnected from what we might call 'reality'. Such people don't always want to be here at all, let alone be here now. Although often pitched in the guise of being connected to higher realms, this can be another way of being disconnected. We are not just spiritual beings. The physical realm exists too and we all need to deal with life in this world. Men are from Earth. Women are from Earth. Deal with it.

The Importance of Earthing

Accumulating evidence shows that we actually need 'earthing'. That is, to 'plug in' to the Earth itself.

If you think about it, all electrical devices are 'earthed', which allows an exchange of electrical charge in the form of charged particles, known as negative ions or electrons, with the Earth. We need this connection too. Every day the Earth receives something like 50,000 lightning strikes and consequently has a supply of 'free' electrons that will change the electrical charge of our body if we make contact with it for long enough.

Our ancestors would have been 'grounded' naturally all day long, because they would have either walked barefoot or worn leather shoes, and both allow the exchange of charged particles. Today we wear shoes with rubber or plastic soles, neither of which allow this exchange to happen.

The Earth is a rich source of negative ions, while we, especially in disease states, have more positive ions. So, could it be that the exchange of ions that takes place when we are connected to the Earth has a direct effect on health?

Earthing Changes Physiological Measures of Health

Consider these experiments, published in the *Journal of Alternative and Complementary Medicine*.[3] Each experiment involved 'grounding' people, usually overnight, by means of a copper plate connected to the Earth. Some were 'earthed', others were not, thus acted as controls, without knowing which group they were in. So these were 'double-blind' trials that set out to measure if earthing produced any biological changes.

The first group of 12 people all had diabetes. Their blood sugar levels were measured at the start, after 24 hours and after 72 hours. There was no change in the control group, but the glucose levels of the earthed participants dropped from 10.6mmol/l (millimoles/litre) down to 8.8 after 24 hours and 7.4 after 72 hours. (A healthy blood sugar level is below 6.)

The next group of 12 had their thyroid hormone level measured. The earthed participants had an increase in the active thyroxine (t4) hormone compared to the controls. This shift is consistent with better thyroid function.

The experimenters also found that earthing changed the balance of electrolytes (charged mineral particles) in the blood.

Another experiment has revealed that red blood cells don't clump together so much when people are earthed, because earthing changes the electrical potential of cells, which helps to keep the red blood cells apart and 'free flowing', which is associated with better circulation and less risk of blood clots.[4]

Earthing Improves Sleep and Reduces Pain

In another experiment, researchers studied the effect of earthing on sleep in 61 people.[5] Those 'earthed' reported taking less time to fall asleep, having better-quality sleep, feeling more rested and having less muscle stiffness, back or joint pain or pain overall. For example, 74 per cent of those 'earthed' reported less back or joint pain compared to none in the control group.

Another study measured levels of the stress hormone cortisol and melatonin, which is not only vital for sleep and keeps us in synch with the Sun cycle, but is also a powerful antioxidant.[6] Earthing normalized cortisol levels, which should be low at night and increase as we wake, and also raised melatonin levels.

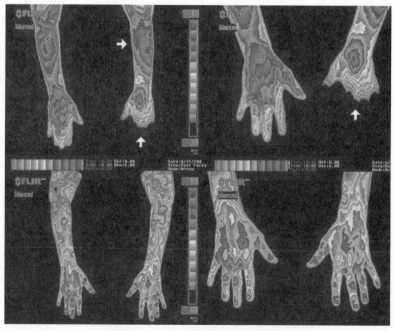

Figure 23: Poor circulation thermographs
(Image used with permission of Martin Zucker, co-author of Earthing)

Case histories have demonstrated rapid reduction in inflammation and pain when patients are earthed overnight. For example, consider the thermographs opposite taken of a 49-year-old woman with chronic neck and upper back pain, restless legs during the night and stiffness and soreness on waking. The arrows in the thermographs indicate areas of poor circulation. In the top right image, the fingers appear to be missing because their temperature has become the same as the room.

After four nights of earthing she reported a 65 per cent reduction in pain, a 75 per cent reduction in restless legs during sleep and an 80 per cent reduction in waking stiff and sore. As the bottom row of thermographs show, her circulation has dramatically improved.

There's a good book, *Earthing*, by Clinton Ober, Stephen Sinatra and Martin Zucker, which goes through this kind of research.

Earthing Protects Us from Electromagnetic Fields

In urban environments we are exposed to many electromagnetic fields from mobile phones and other devices and unavoidable wireless signals, and there is growing evidence that this is not so good for our health. (To read more, see my report on my website 'Are you being electrified?'[7])

For example, electronic magnetic radiation, which is perceived by the brain as light, suppresses melatonin production. So, don't sleep with your mobile phone switched on or next to the base station of a digital phone, which is transmitting a signal 24/7. How many of us live in a permanent bath of electromagnetic radiation? It is better to limit this while you sleep, especially if you find it hard to.

At a basic level, we don't want our body to be electrically charged, and earthing has been shown to help with this. In one study, the voltage of 12 people was measured before and after earthing. Before, the average voltage was 3.27 volts. After, it was 0.007 volts. This demonstrates the benefit of spending some time getting earthed every day.

How to Earth Yourself

So how do you do it? There are a few basics you need to know. Certain materials allow the flow of charged particles. These are called *conductive* materials. Some do it really well, such as copper, while others are half as good and are called *semi-conductive*. Concrete is conductive, while wood is not. Asphalt is not conductive, being made of petrochemicals. Any vinyl, plastic or rubber surface is not. If you paint concrete or put down carpet it is unlikely to retain any conductivity, although a wool carpet will be better than a synthetic carpet. Water is conductive, even more so if it's salt water, since the mineral particles allow for the rapid flow of ions. Sea water is therefore several hundred times more conductive than tap water. Walking barefoot on wet grass or swimming in the ocean would be two excellent ways to get yourself earthed.

If you live in a city and don't have the opportunity, the best way to earth yourself is during the night by using an 'earthing sheet'. I have one and wouldn't be without it. It's actually a half-sheet that goes across the bottom half of my bed. It looks like an ordinary sheet but has a fine mesh of conductive threads in it and plugs into a regular wall socket that you leave turned off (provided you live in a country where the mains is earthed by means of the third plug point). It earths you all night long. These sheets are available online (*see Resources*).

I also like to go for walks barefoot, connecting with the Earth and recognizing that it, like me, is made of the elements that originated from the stars – from light itself. With my awareness in the Kath Point, just below the belly button, I repeat internally:

> *My body is from the Earth.*
> *The Earth is from the stars.*
> *The stars are made of light.*
> *My body is made of light.*

Synchronizing with the Earth

The Earth also has a natural frequency, that is, an electromagnetic vibration, to which our body naturally synchronizes if we spend enough time earthed in a natural environment.

In a deeply relaxed, or meditative state, our body literally vibrates at about 8 cycles per second (known as Hertz, or Hz). At the same time, our brainwaves shift from their everyday beta range (13 to 40Hz) into the same 8Hz deep alpha range. When this occurs, it creates an electromagnetic field around the head and the heart. The heart's electromagnetic field actually extends for several metres.

The Earth's electromagnetic field also has a frequency of around 8Hz. When we are in nature, without any other interfering signal and hopefully no phone signal, it changes our brainwave pattern. We become in sync with the Earth, crossing into the theta brainwave spectrum, from 8Hz to 3Hz. The theta state is particularly interesting and occurs in profound states of meditation and creativity.

Opening Up to Nature

A simple way of connecting with nature is by opening your senses and mind to it. You can do this as a meditation, either when you are in a natural environment or by imagining yourself in a beautiful natural place.

Exercise: At One with Nature

1. Close your eyes, and imagine you are sitting on a mountain, or in a green valley or meadow, or by the ocean or under a starry sky. Feel the beauty and the presence of the natural world around you in whatever form you find most powerful or lovely.

2. Now become aware of the life force that runs through everything in nature. Consider the ways in which the Earth nourishes all of life; how trees and plants grow and offer their gifts to the Earth and to us; how the tides flow…

3. Consider the vastness and magnificence of the ocean, the awe-inspiring vastness of the sky with its stars, the life-giving power of the Sun, the cycles of the seasons and the profusion of insect and animal life.

4. Become aware of the Divine Intelligence that runs through nature. Become aware of how you are part of that Divine Intelligence – the exquisite design of your body, the beat of your heart, the ebb and flow of the breath…

~

Protecting the Earth

The Earth is our most precious resource. Life depends on it, and unconscious over-exploitation, overdevelopment and overpopulation are threatening our very existence. From fracking to intensive farming, unsustainable energy production to global warming, there is much to be concerned about.

Our food production depends on a very thin layer of topsoil. To put this into context, imagine the Earth as an apple. Three-quarters of its surface is covered in water. Of the remaining quarter, half is uninhabitable and unable to grow crops because it is polar regions, deserts, swamps and mountains. So that leaves one eighth. Only one quarter of this is suitable for growing food. That's 1/32th of the Earth's surface, and only a tiny fraction of this, the topsoil, can grow food. That is why we cannot afford to lose arable land to more buildings, or destroy the topsoil with unsustainable farming methods.

Also, with 7 billion people to feed, we need to grow more productive sources of nutrients, such as beans, rather than meat, as well as controlling world population growth, otherwise there will be big food shortages, especially if weather patterns go astray with global warming and sea levels rise, flooding arable land. That's why it is vital to stop burning fossil fuels.

Cut Carbon for Health and Happiness

Mukti Mitchell, a campaigner for low-carbon living, points out that 80 per cent of the energy we use is wasted. A typical UK citizen's carbon footprint is 10 tonnes of CO_2 (carbon dioxide) per year. This can be divided into five main lifestyle areas – heating, transport, food, holidays and shopping, each emitting around two tonnes.

We can greatly cut down our carbon footprint by good house insulation; using public transport; cycling; sharing car transport or choosing a hybrid or electric car; buying local and seasonal food; wasting less; avoiding imported foods with a high water content as these have a high carbon footprint in proportion to their nutritional value; eating less meat; reducing the frequency of long flights; buying better-quality appliances that last longer and fixing things when they break down. For more on this, and how to calculate your own carbon footprint, read Mukti Mitchell's online article 'Cut Carbon for Health and Happiness'.[8]

Fortunately, we can generate more than enough power from sustainable sources – the Sun, wind and tides. Cars and public transport can run on electricity instead of ever-diminishing oil, which only forces more destructive methods of extraction. So much is possible if we put our relationship with the Earth higher up our list of priorities.

Make Less Waste

A simple way we can reduce the burden on the Earth is to make less waste. In the UK we make 100 million tons (1 ton is about the weight of a small car) of rubbish a year. That's about 1 ton per household, with the rest coming from business. We each throw away, on average, six trees' worth of paper every year. Glass takes thousands of years to break down. Plastic takes hundreds of years. Nationally, we get through 50 billion fizzy drinks a year. That's a lot of cans and bottles. In addition, the average UK household throws away edible food worth about £400.

We are getting better. Back in 1995 we recycled 7.5 per cent of waste. Now we recycle 45 per cent and are well on target for the EU's goal of 50 per cent by 2020.

The game is to make your non-recyclable rubbish less and less. If you have a small garden, compost food waste. Buy fewer goods and food in unnecessary packaging, especially plastic. Don't accept a shopping bag if you don't need it. Take a bag or two with you when you go out. Recycle bottles and jars. Fix things rather than buying new appliances every time something breaks down. Buy stuff made out of recycled materials. These are simple steps to take to reduce the load on the Earth. Do what you can.

We need more green policies and commitment at every level, otherwise we may end up with catastrophic circumstances.

I was there when the ice cap melted

The blazing Sun. You really felt it.

The glaciers grumbled and then they crumbled.

Did we cause it, or was it fate?

The year the Arctic became prime real estate.

SUMMARY

In summary, to improve your connection to the Earth:

- Spend more time in natural and wild environments.

- Swim in the ocean and walk barefoot on the land.

- If you live in an urban environment, invest in an earthing sheet so you're earthed while you sleep.

- Don't bombard yourself all day long with electromagnetic radiation. Turn off your cell phone while you sleep and don't sleep next to the digital phone base-station.

- Choose the food you eat carefully and be grateful for what you eat. Grow your own food where you can. Eat less meat and only sustainable fish.

- Be mindful of the Earth's resources and, where you can, choose more sustainable methods of energy production.

- Make less waste, recycle, fix things and buy things made from recycled materials.

- Respect the Earth and nature and get involved in campaigns to protect it. Your life, and the life of your children, depends on it.

Chapter 10

The Shape and Sound of Connection

There is a beauty and an order to life. Shapes, sounds and measurements make a myriad of intricate connections. The word 'geo-metry' literally means 'the measure of the Earth'.

Two of the most common geometrical patterns of living forms are fives and sixes – pentagons and hexagons. We saw the pentagon and hexagon in tryptamines *(see page 34)* but they are also in the building blocks of DNA, such as guanine, shown overleaf. Pythagoras is said to have started his teaching by cutting an apple transversally through its core, revealing a pentagram.

Figure 24: Pythagoras used an apple in teaching. (Thinkstock/Martin Muránsky)

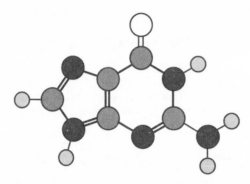

Figure 25: Guanine, one of four building blocks of DNA code. (Thinkstock/chromatos)

My interest in the geometrical patterns of life, specifically in DNA, arrived with Linus Pauling, the genius chemist and grandfather of modern chemistry who, as mentioned earlier, won one Nobel Prize for his discoveries about the nature of the chemical bond and another for his successful campaigning for a ban on nuclear weapons testing. This was all during the oppressive McCarthy era in his homeland, the USA, where he was accused of being a Communist.

Meanwhile, back in the UK, in Cambridge, fearing that Pauling would beat them to it, James Watson and Francis Crick were working around the clock to produce a model of DNA structure. Pauling wanted to visit the UK to see the X-ray photographs of another key researcher, Rosalind Franklin at King's College London, but was grounded in the United States, his passport confiscated due to his peace activism. But for that missing piece, he probably would have been first to define the structure of DNA, for which Watson and Crick were awarded the Nobel Prize. Crick, by the way, was on LSD at the time he cracked the structure.

Crick, a great admirer of Pauling, wasn't convinced that DNA had evolved on Earth. He proposed that it had come from space and 'seeded' life on Earth. Others think it could have been formed before life began or evolved out of ribonucleic acid (RNA).[1] This is one of those hot questions – how DNA evolved and, with that, life on Earth.

Researcher Graham Hancock's book *Supernatural* explores the origins of humanity and proposes one radical theory that DNA, 95 per cent of which we do not understand and used to call 'junk' DNA, encode our evolution, with 'downloads' becoming available as we evolve. It's a thought-provoking read for those interested in exploring such heretical ideas.

The Geometry of Five

Figure 26: This sand dollar, a type of sea urchin, displays the geometry of five in nature. (Thinkstock/SaundersFineArts) See colour section.

Five is a very interesting number. On a physical level, the body is anatomically divided into five main cavities[2] – the pelvic, abdominal, thoracic, cranial and dorsal cavities of the spine.

In Malcolm Stewart's book *Patterns of Eternity* (only available from www.holfordirect.com), he fathoms the depths of the 'starcut', a simple geometrical pattern that has remarkable depth and mathematical mysteries relating to the number five. It is made simply by drawing a square, then drawing a line from each corner that cuts the sides of the two opposite sides of the square in half. The starcut contains all sorts of mysteries and mathematical relations. It is full of life. The eye cannot settle on this intriguing diagram.

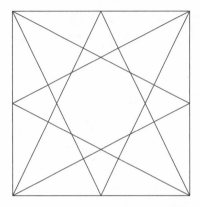 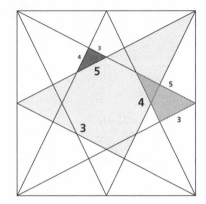

Figure 27: The starcut

Mathematically, the starcut introduces the number five in its 32 3-4-5 triangles. (One elegant geometrical fact is that if one side of a right-angled triangle measures three and the other four, the diagonal is five.) The diagram above shows three of them, but see if you can find the other 29 hidden in the starcut.

The starcut underlies many significant patterns and proportions that appear in a variety of forms across the world: in China, in the shaman's dance; in Egypt, in the Great Pyramid; in Europe, in a Raphael fresco; in Asia, in the Vedic fire altar. It may also be the secret of the success of the Spanish swordsmen. All this and more is revealed in the book *Patterns of Eternity*.

The starcut is also a much more interesting board across which to play games than that used for chess and checkers. In my house I have a coffee table with the starcut engraved in it. Sometimes, for example, we play 3-4-5, the equivalent of noughts and crosses where the winner is the one who creates a 3-4-5 triangle first, while the opponent places beads in the way to stop them. (A portable starcut game set, with instructions for a variety of games, is available from www.holfordirect.com.)

Figure 28: The starcut coffee-table

Phi: The Golden Number

'The quality of five is integral to the immense productivity of the starcut because five – with its relations to the "square root" of five and the golden number phi – has the quality of life,' says Malcolm Stewart. 'Many authors have written on the golden number/section/mean, on its connections with the five-sided pentagon, with logarithmic spirals, organic growth patterns and the association between five-ish geometry and life.'

The golden number *phi*, ϕ, which is (√5+1)/2, equals 1.618033989. Like √5, it is an 'irrational number', meaning it never resolves. It was probably also known to the Egyptians. The *sheked*, that is, the height to base ratio of the Great Pyramid, was 7 to 11. If the base of this triangle is 1, the height is √ϕ and the side length ϕ.

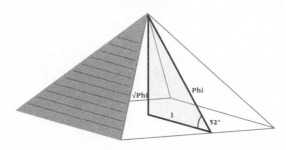

Figure 29: The Egyptian pyramids use ϕ, the golden number

The golden number exists throughout the natural world in the proportions of our body, plants, DNA, the solar system, mathematics, geometry and fractals. It is a fundamental to creating spirals – remember, energy moves in waves or spirals, creating what we think of as matter.

The thing about ϕ is that it defines proportions and allows a number to multiply infinitely big or divide small while remaining in proportion.

As an example, you can see this in the Fibonacci number series in which each successive number is the sum of the previous two: 1, 2, 3, 5, 8, 13, 21, 34, 55, 89, etc. (1 + 2 = 3; 2 + 3 = 5 and so on). When you divide 5 into 8, 8 into 13, 13 into 21, and so on, you approach closer and closer to the golden number (also known as the golden section) which is 1 divided by ϕ (e.g. 1/1.61). Try dividing 5/8 or 8/13 or 21/34 or 55/89. They all get closer and closer to 1/ϕ.

Figure 30: Phi exists in the natural world. Top left: Hubble Space Telescope image of the gigantic Pinwheel galaxy (© European Space Agency & NASA); top right: hurricane approaching Southeast Asia (Shutterstock/Harvepino); bottom left: nautilus shell (Thinkstock/AdrianHancu); bottom left: Romanesco broccoli (Thinkstock/pavolga)

We see φ in spiral phyllotaxis, which is the way the vast majority of all plants grow, with their leaves radiating out in a spiral from the stem, as beautifully illustrated in Romanesco broccoli. It is inherent in the angles of a pentagon (*see Figure 34*), and in the motion of the planet Venus, with its five close approaches to Earth every eight Earth years and 13 Venus years.

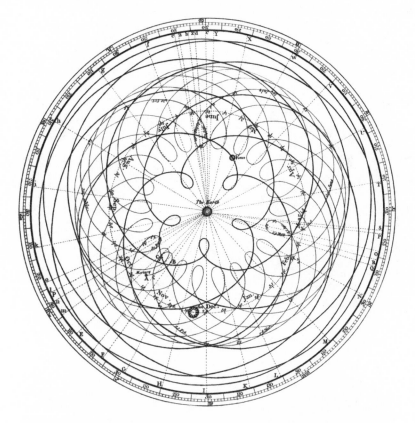

Figure 31: Published in 1756 by the Scottish astronomer and instrument maker James Ferguson, this diagram shows the Earth in the centre, with the orbits of Mercury and Venus forming a series of complex epicycles which replicate the perfect symmetry we know as the golden number. (Royal Astronomical Society/Science Photo Library)

Wherever you look, big or small, you find these proportional relationships. The lesser is in proportion to the greater, which is in proportion to the whole.

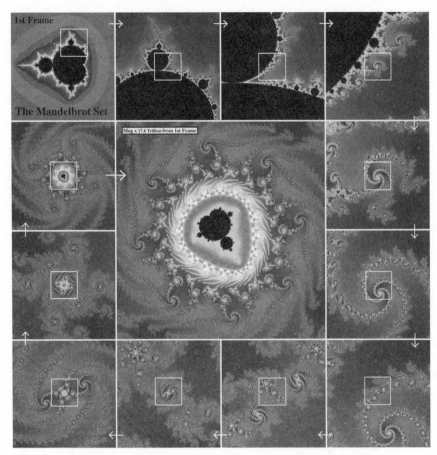

Figure 32: The Mandelbrot set, a simple reiterating mathematical formula, creates unique but similar patterns as it unfolds magnified 17.6 trillion times, in the centre, from the first frame (top left). (© Greg Sams, used with permission from TheStateIsOutOfDate.com) See colour section.

The whole field of fractal mathematics, made popular by the extraordinary Mandelbrot set seen above, has opened up some of the simplest formulas that create the most complex and self-repeating but never the same patterns that also occur in our natural world. If you are new to the Mandelbrot set and 'fractal' geometry and mathematics, Arthur C. Clarke made a very good documentary on this called *Fractals: The Colors of Infinity*, free for view on YouTube[3]. Also see the 'deepest ever Mandelbrot set' on YouTube.[4]

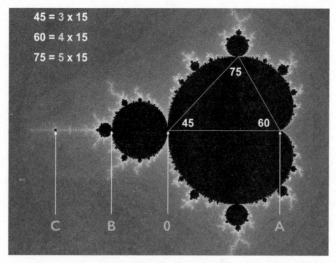

Figure 33: The Mandelbrot set
(Reproduced with kind permission of Malcolm Stewart from Patterns of Eternity)

In Malcolm Stewart's second book, *Symbols of Eternity* (also available from www.holfordirect.com), he explores this further and points out that the 3-4-5 relationship exists in the Mandelbrot set and that the sections of the Mandelbrot set – that is, A to B to C to D – are also in the golden proportion of ϕ.

Another place where ϕ emerges is in the five-sided pentagon. The pentagon is fundamental to the Chinese healing arts, which are based on five elements.

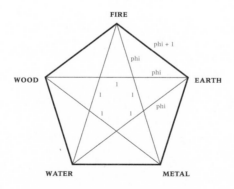

Figure 34: The five elements of the pentagon

Another influential work on the numerical patterns of life and the Universe is *God's Secret Formula* by Peter Plichta. He has multiple PhDs and scientific credentials in chemistry, biology, physics and mathematics and has made major discoveries in chemistry. He proposes that all mathematical phenomena – if you like, how God counts – can be explained with prime numbers – that is, numbers greater than one that are not divisible by any number other than one – and fractal mathematics. For example, three is a prime number and there are three dimensions of space, three kinds of chemical bond (ionic, covalent and metallic), three components of atoms (protons, neutrons and electrons), three components of DNA (sugar, base and phosphate), three states of matter (solid, liquid and gas), three aspects to time (past, present and future) and three forms of life (plants, animals and humans). Not everyone agrees with Plichta's theories, but his book is well worth a read if you wish to dive deeper into the mathematical patterns of life.

The Shape of God

In *Symbols of Eternity*, Malcolm Stewart explores the question: 'What is the shape of God?'

> ...the Hadron Collider, making a vast circle nearly thirty kilometres long, is what it takes to make the smallest tube in the world. The tube is formed by magnetic fields so narrow that two protons bulleting around in opposite directions have no room to do anything but collide. The detritus of the collision is recorded and analysed so as to find out what matter the Universe is, finally, made of.
>
> So, why do we spend so much effort, money and brainpower smashing matter into smaller and smaller smithereens while meanwhile we pretty much ignore the overwhelmingly huge space of existence? 'Well, there's nothing there,' some may say. But this is not true – what is there is dimension and geometry.

Figure 35: The Large Hadron Collider particle accelerator at CERN, Geneva, Switzerland. (© Maximilien Brice, CERN/Science Photo Library) See colour section.

Even though some mathematical theories have proposed that there are 11 dimensions (so far), even the Hadron Collider, costing US$13.25 billion, is built out of just three: front to back; side to side; above and below and 'right here' – the centre.

This is also my experience, and Malcolm's, in non-ordinary states of consciousness, including out-of-body experiences. There is still a very clear sense of left–right, up–down, front–back and centre. While the colours, sense of time and space may be altered, the fundamental dimensions remain the same. I have yet to meet anyone who has had a non-ordinary state of consciousness or near-death experience who doesn't describe the same dimensions. Are these the dimensions of the Universe?

The shape that really defines these dimensions is the cube. It is perhaps no surprise to find that it is fundamental to the design of temples in many religions, not just as the 'home' of God, but the shape of God, and no more so than the Ka'aba in Mecca, to which millions of Muslims go on Hajj pilgrimage every year, circumambulating seven times[5] anti-clockwise round it. *Ka'aba* means 'cube'.

Figure 36: Pilgrims at Ka'aba, Mecca, Saudi Arabia.
(Shutterstock/ Zurijeta) See colour section.

Key to the Ka'aba is its eastern cornerstone, a black stone, a lingam, almost certainly of meteoric origin. Malcolm points out that according to Indian legend, Mecca (previously known as Mocsha or Moca) 'was the site where the great Mahadeva ("the great Spirit" = Shiva) conferred illumination and liberation (Mocsha). The place was a temple of BRHM: Brahma? Abraham? One can hardly miss the shared syllabic roots. Also, the place housed one of the great Siva Lingam stones.' It should be pointed out, he says, 'that the "liberation" involved seems to have been the experience of being immolated in a conflagration probably caused by the arrival of a meteor!'

The significance of the cube is not unique to Islam. The *tefillin* (phylactery) worn each day as part of a religious practice by the Children of Israel in the Jewish tradition is also a black cube.

Figure 37: The tefillin, *used in Judaism
(above right © David Alpert)*

Billy Phillips,[6] a scholar of the Kabbalah, the key mystical teaching within Judaism, explains that:

> *...we wrap the* tefillin *around our left arm* seven times, counter-clockwise, *to bind and weaken our negative desire and ego.*

> *Each of us is required to sacrifice our ego for the sake of sharing with others. The* tefillin *acts like an antenna that draws down a powerful spiritual force that negates and sacrifices the influence of our selfish nature and ugly ego. Ninety-nine per cent of Jews have no clue that this is why we bind* tefillin *on our left arm. We use the left arm as the left connotes our ego and the negative (Isaac) and the right refers to the soul and the positive (Abraham).*

> *Each year, Muslims go on a pilgrimage (Hajj) to walk around the Ka'ba in Mecca* counter-clockwise, seven times. *This is exactly how we wrap and bind our* tefillin — counter-clockwise, seven times.

> *The purpose of Hajj for Muslims is to connect to the* same *event of Abraham binding Isaac (Muslims relate this to Abraham binding his son Ishmael). The connection is profound. Perhaps this is why the Ka'ba in Mecca is known as the* House of Allah. Ka'ba *and* Allah, *as we know, spells* Kaballah.

The Platonic Solids

The Greek philosopher Plato placed great emphasis on the cube, and other forms, which have since been known as the Platonic solids. He wrote about them *c*.360BCE in the dialogue *Timaeus*, in which he associated each of the five classical elements (earth, air, water, and fire and ether) with one of the regular solids.

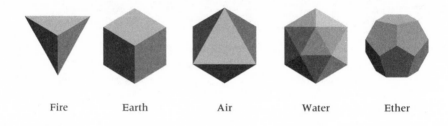

| Fire | Earth | Air | Water | Ether |

Figure 38: The Platonic solids and elements

Writing about the Platonic solids in *Symbols of Eternity*, Malcolm Stewart says:

> *They all signify the Divine manifest in creation, as five fundamental aspects or states of being. For as long as such symbolic equivalences have been made, the red tetrahedron has been associated with fire, the plasmic and radiant form. The yellow cube is the symbol here of the materiality of Earth, the solid form of matter nourishing us and our actual social experience of life. The green octahedron is for the air we breathe, circulating in the blood and alive in us as emotion. The icosahedron has always been associated with water, the fluid state of matter; here a figure for our mental realm, constantly adapting to both our perceptions and to our own thoughts in their endless flows and eddies. Space itself transcending physical form is symbolised by the dodecahedron – the spheric that Plato, in his description of creation in* Timaeus, *omitted to name directly. Its presence is union.*

The Science of *Yantras*

Yantras are specific diagrams used during meditation practice, often with mantras, to produce specific transformational effects.

One of the best known is the Shree Yantra, formed from nine interlocking triangles – four pointing up and five pointing down. It is, at a basic level, a map representing all forms of energy, with the male Shiva principle going up and the female Shakti principle going down, creating 43 triangles representative of the entire cosmos. Reverence of the Shree Yantra is central to the Shri Vidya system of Hindu worship and whole books have been written about it.

The connection between the male and female principle – between Shiva and Shakti – is the foundation of the alchemical tantra yoga traditions, creating the ultimate connection – the union of these two principles. (*More on this in Chapter 14.*)

Figure 39: The Shree Yantra, used in tantra yoga traditions to represent the energies of the cosmos. (Reproduced with kind permission of Malcolm Stewart from Patterns of Eternity) *See colour section.*

The Sound of Connection

In the same way that there are *yantras* that resonate and connect with our essential nature, and *forms*, such as the Platonic solids, that have an effect upon the psyche, so there are sounds, or mantras.

So far we have touched on the primordial sound 'Om'. There are many other mantras and tunes that have a direct heart-opening effect on us. 'Hare Krishna, Hare Rama' is an obvious example known to many, and musicians such as Krishna Das have immersed themselves in the transforming and connecting power of chants such as this. His chant 'Namah Shivaya', based on the ancient mantra 'Om Namah Shivaya', is most uplifting. (That was the mantra I repeated on my way up Volcan Copiapo.) The Siddha Yoga tradition have this as their mantra and have some powerful and magical versions of this chant.

In every mystical tradition the act of singing has a connecting effect, be it the haunting sound of Gregorian chants, the call to prayer in Islam, the overtone *sutra* chants of Buddhists, the Indian *pujas* such as 'Pasayadan' – a prayer for grace, written in the 13th century by Dnyaneshwar (my favourite version is the Siddha Yoga version) – or the Calling, played on a bamboo flute, at the start of a Sufi *zhikr* or Sema ceremony. There is also a group 'choir' effect, when well tuned, which creates overtones and harmonics that raise the atmosphere and open the heart and elevate the spirit. The silence at the end is particularly important, leaving a feeling of centredness and presence.

There are also those songs that just touch you – personal to all and dependent to some extent on one's culture. I'm thinking of Louis Armstrong's 'Wonderful World', Captain Beefheart's 'Bluejeans and Moonbeams' or Bob Marley's 'Three Little Birds'.

Then there is uplifting and mystical music, such as Elgar's 'Nimrod' or Parry's 'Jerusalem' or Arvo Part's 'Spiegel im Spiegel' or the great Kuali singer Nusrat Fateh Ali Khan's 'Allah Hoo'.

Some music is just so perfect it gives you that ascension. Radiohead's 'Creep', King Crimson's 'Starless', Van Morrison's 'In the

Garden', Leonard Cohen's 'If It Be Your Will' sung by the Webb Sisters are examples that do it for me. But we all have our own favourites.

Some songs are imbued with the context of the words, or the film story, for example 'Calling You', the theme song for the wonderful film *Bagdad Café*, sung by Jevetta Steele.

Some songs help during periods of despair and transition, identifying with the space we're in and providing insight. Two of my favourites, at times of great despair, have been Neil Young's 'Don't Let It Bring You Down' sung by Annie Lennox, and the Pogues' version of 'Dirty Old Town', as well many great blues songs. You can find links to these songs at www.patrickholford.com/connection/music.

I'm sure there are pieces of music that touch you deeply. But what is it about particular sounds, notes, chords and musical sequences that have a transformational, uplifting and connecting quality?

Notes, Number and Harmonies

Sound is vibration – compressions of air – that not only affects us through hearing but also affects the body itself. We get a sense of this compression when our ears pop at different altitudes.

The Earth, too, has vibrations, known as Schumann resonances. These are global electromagnetic resonances excited by lightning discharges in the cavity formed by the Earth's surface and the ionosphere and starting in the range of 7.8 to 8Hz. This is also the frequency of the double helix in DNA replication.

The effect of music is dependent on having the right tuning. Musicians will tell you that 'perfect' tuning is when A is at 432Hz. If you start with 8Hz and go up by five octaves – by seven notes in the musical scale five times[7] – you arrive at 256Hz for middle C, in whose scale A has the frequency of 432Hz. This is slightly different from the conventional tuning of A as 440Hz *(see Figure 40 overleaf)*.

Figure 40: The extended Tetraktys
(Reproduced with kind permission of Malcolm Stewart from Patterns of Eternity*)*

Malcolm Stewart noticed that this was in complete accordance with the number patterns of the Tetraktys as taught by Pythagoras. This figure starts with 10 (let us say) pebbles placed in a triangle. The top one is 'one', then, going left, each number multiplies by two, while, going right, each number multiplies by three.

Thinking of these numbers as vibrations or frequencies, Malcolm then extended them to create the 13 musical notes in their different octaves. If you go eight steps down in the C column you arrive at 256Hz, the perfect frequency for middle C, and if you go four steps along the A column, you arrive at the perfect tuning for A, at 432Hz.

He then arranged the 12-note chromatic scale, starting with C at the top, around a 12-pointed star, as a circle.

Figure 41: Circle piano
(Reproduced with kind permission of Malcolm Stewart from Patterns of Eternity)

Now, using the same 3-4-5 triangle that we saw populating the starcut in the last chapter, it contains all the major and minor chords containing C, the combination of notes that has a natural concordance or connection. If you further rotate the triangles it creates other harmonious chords, as you can see in Figure 42 overleaf.

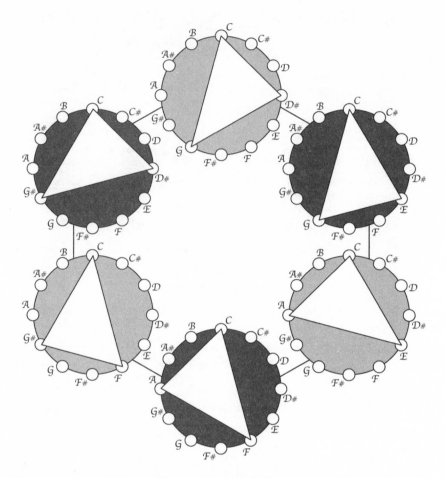

Figure 42: Harmony of spheres
(Reproduced with kind permission of Malcolm Stewart from Patterns of Eternity*)*

The other important connecting relationship in music is that of the 'fifths' – two notes in a 2:3 ratio. Again, that magic number five. If you look again at the Tetraktys, you'll see the second row is two and three – or C and G. This is a fifth. For example, if you play C, then the G above it, you have the first two bugle notes of 'The Last Post'. Go down two more rows and you have A at 27 and, adjacent to it, D at 18: 18/27 = 2/3 – again, D is a fifth of A.

I know these fifths particularly well because I play the tamboura, a fretless sitar with four strings. These are tuned to fifths, for example A, D, D, D, with the last D tuned one octave below the others. This could correspond to the frequencies 432Hz (A), 288Hz (D), 288Hz (D) and 144Hz (lower D). You'll see how this works if you locate these numbers on the extended Tetratkys (*see Figure 40, page 150*).

As mentioned earlier, the tamboura is one of the 'sacred' sounds used in the Hindu tradition. Others include the gong, kettledrum and conch. Other traditions have other sacred instruments, such as the Aborigines' didgeridoo.

There are many other beautiful sounds, frequencies and harmonic relationships that affect us in different ways. It is these kinds of relationships, harmonics and overtones that are key in connecting music.

Primal Music and Rhythms

While much music takes us out of ourselves and acts as a pleasant distraction, some takes us inside and can be used to deepen our inner connection, release blocks and give us energy. For example, Stanislav Grof's holotropic breathing (*see page 75*) and other kinds of transformational breathwork involve a soundtrack that is used during the five consecutive phases of the session: 1) opening music; 2) trance-inducing music; 3) breakthrough music; 4) heart music; and 5) meditative music. This is a great example of using music and sound to create transformation and connection.

Another is having a gong healing. If you've never had one, I highly recommend it. The gong is one of the oldest instruments, dating back to 4000BCE. Today, musicians and healers are using its extraordinarily penetrating sounds in a personalized way to heal, reconnect people with their true sense of self and release negative emotions and fears. The gong master tunes in to where you're at in life and any issues you are working on, then takes you through a sound 'meditation' using different sounds and tones to create a release and move you through to a better place. This recognizes the healing power of sound and music. Often the tuning of gongs is more in line with the ancient primal frequencies that are missed with conventional tuning. If you live in London, check out, for example, www.psychesounds.com.

Certain rhythms and repetitive movements also have the power to create a more connected state. These are used, for example, in the Sufi *zhikrs* and are fundamental in many African and North American tribal ceremonies and initiations. To some extent these also exist in folk cultures closer to home, although many of these traditions are being lost.

Meanwhile in our pop culture, something of music's ability to connect us to a deeper level of awareness is being lost in the quest for a lucrative hit record.

It is also interesting to see that in crowded cities every other person has headphones on as they travel to work. No one connects, says hi, looks other people in the eye. We all just exist in our own bubble. This is a very different experience from that of smaller communities and villages, where it would be rude *not* to say hello. Is it that there are just too many people in cities? Theoretically this should make us more connected, but the opposite seems to be happening.

If you find yourself disconnected, one way through and up is to reconnect with music that touches your soul. Why not treat yourself to an album, a concert or a gong healing? Truly listen and let the sound of music wash through you, knowing that everything is vibration and pausing in the silence to go beyond the mind of thought and into meditation. Check out www.psychesounds.com.

PART III

HEART
CONNECTION

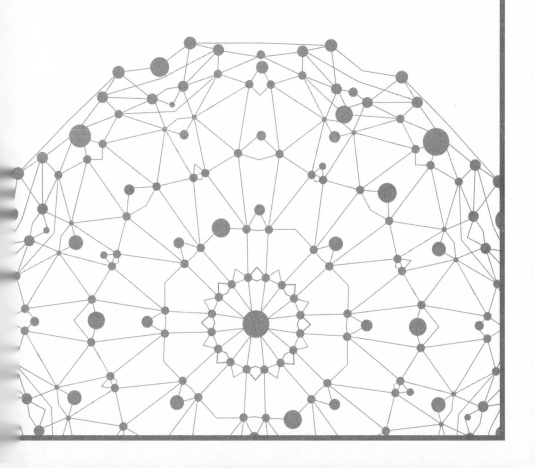

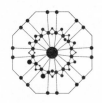

Chapter 11

Opening the Heart

Connecting to a deeper sense of self and self-love (but not in a narcissistic way) is another prerogative for a more connected life. This has a lot to do with the heart.

The heart is about love, and our experience of love tends to go through phases. First, there is experiencing love, or being in love. When we lose love for one reason or another, we experience hurt and fear. Then there is the absence of love, that is, emptiness or loneliness, which is really forgetting love. Then there is longing, the desire for love – the remembering of it. And before long we are back in love. This is the rich and sometimes painful field of the heart.

I am the love, the longing and the emptiness.

Ego and Emotions

Attachment

Consciousness, that is the pure awareness, or the deepest level of 'I' that is always present, is free. It has no thoughts, feelings, judgements, prejudices or limitations. However, our consciousness becomes attached, like light being channelled or limited through distorted glass. We become attached to certain rules or conditions, to ideas about who we are, how others should behave and how the world should be. This is the definition of ego: 'consciousness attached'. As a result, we develop a certain 'ego personality', a particular way of viewing the world, a personalized prescription for our glasses, so to speak. Mine is different from yours and it is this difference between us all that generates conflict. The fundamental for any journey towards a fuller, more connected experience of life is to dissolve these attachments.

Karma

Karma, another loaded and misunderstood word, refers to having an experience, for example falling off your bicycle, being physically hurt and feeling embarrassed, and then having an image stored in your psyche of the bike with the feeling of both the physical pain and the emotional pain of embarrassment attached. This is 'karma' – experiences stored with emotions. Now, when someone offers you a bike ride, you are afraid of being hurt and embarrassed.

The popularized notion of karma implies that there's nothing you can do about it. Stuff happens. It's your karma. That's that. However, the true understanding of karma is that it is *attachment to certain outcomes* that creates karmic reactions. This, in due course, attracts certain experiences. Karma may be created by something as simple as the way we perceive a challenge.

By 'undoing' our store of karmic reactions – that is, memories with negative emotions attached – we can be in control of our own destiny, or at least of how we react to what happens. A big part of the stress of life is not what happens but how we react to it.

Taking the example of the bicycle, this karmic experience will feed into others until you avoid physically challenging situations because you're afraid you'll be no good at them and will end up embarrassed or hurt.

All these follow-on reactions get stored in the same psychic filing cabinet, going all the way back to the first traumatic event. According to psychiatrist Stanislav Grof, who refers to core trauma shocks as 'COEX', an abbreviation for 'condensed experience', they start with the traumatic experiences that occur during the process of being born.

It is a strange thing that in both psychology and neurobiology, it is now well recognized that a newborn infant's neuronal circuitry is extremely pliable and that love actually changes the development of neuronal connections and is thus extremely important from day one. Sue Gerhardt's excellent book *Why Love Matters* makes this very clear. However, given that an unborn infant is also conscious, what is not yet fully recognized is that the process of leaving the contained and secure womb, being forced down the birth canal and squished with each contraction, then thrust out into a whole new world, let alone any other traumas from an extended labour, cord around the neck, forceps delivery or Caesarean, plus the cocktail of adrenalin that is released in vast quantities by both mother and baby even in a normal birth,[1] the blood and the usual screaming, and sometimes traumatized mother, create the karmic experiences that sit right at the back of each drawer in the karmic filing cabinet.

My son was born in the evening and I remember that night he woke up at regular intervals, just like the contractions, screaming. I had the sense he was reliving the experience. Fortunately, his birth was short and uncomplicated. The next night he was fine and slept right through.

Clearing Emotional Charge

All significant consciousness-raising and therefore connecting processes require substantial 'clearing' of the charged events that have shaped the story of who we are and how we see the world. Then we can let go of limited emotional and behavioural patterns and beliefs and truly open our heart. There are several ways to do this.

Deprogramming

One of the first pioneers in such 'deprogramming' technology was the late L. Ron Hubbard, founder of Scientology. He had some pretty weird ideas, but the principle behind one of his devices was actually quite neat. He developed a process of wiring people up to an 'e-meter', which actually measured sympathetic nervous system responses. The sympathetic nervous system is the part of our neurology that is triggered by charged or stressed reactions. The therapist would then work through a series of questions, see if the person reacted, and if so, go deeper: 'So, tell me about your mother...' The goal was, ultimately, to get to the point where there was no residual charge left. Then the person was declared 'clear'. Leonard Cohen wrote about this in his song 'Going Clear'. Whatever views you might have about Scientology – and I want to make it clear (sorry) that I have never been involved in it other than reading the book, nor have any desire to be – this is an example of a way of systematically reducing emotional charge.

Another method, the Imago method, was developed by psychotherapist Harville Hendrix and outlined in his book *Getting the Love You Want*. This is used by some psychotherapists, especially when helping couples to work through issues and reunite.

Sharing and Listening

A exercise I like, called 'Clearing Emotional Charge', is given in the Exercise Appendix (*see page 227*). If you have an emotional charge with a partner or friend, it first establishes your connection with them – that is, the shared basis for love – and then allows each of you to fully share what happened, without adornment, and the feeling that experience generated. It is important that one person shares and the other truly listens and then has an opportunity to respond and equally be heard. It is also important to own your reaction, rather than saying, 'You made me feel...', and to accept that the other person's feelings and perceptions are equally valid for them, even if you don't agree.

If you don't have the opportunity to clear an emotional charge with a person face to face, or you have a charge from a particular event, you can adapt this exercise by having a listening friend who will not interject but truly hear you and then describing exactly what happened, without interpretations. If you do have an interpretation that puts the other person down, see if you can invent a kinder one that does not.

I remember a workshop in which I asked people to recall a charged experience in this way. One woman recalled an incident when, as a young girl, she was sitting in an armchair in the living room when her mother came in and told her that her father had died. Relating it brought up a wave of sadness and a flood of tears – a release of stored emotions.

She went on to explain that more recently, when her mother had died, she and her sister had been deciding who would take what from the house and she had said she didn't want the living-room furniture – she had always hated it, and especially that chair. It was only in doing this exercise that she had realized that that was where she had been sitting when she had heard the news of her father's death. In just this way, we accumulate emotional charge – hatreds, aversions, judgements, beliefs, fears and so on – until our ability to experience life exactly as it is without preconception becomes impossible.

Many psychotherapists and psychoanalysts witness their clients' key formative experiences in a similar way. They may also follow trauma 'tracks' to help relieve a client's negative patterns. Other enlightenment traditions, such as the Toltec tradition in Central America, have a process called 'recapitulation'. The Landmark Forum, another popular self-transformation process, has a similar method for accessing core charged experiences, although it does not systematically work through the whole territory of our psyche.

The Hoffman Process

A very thorough way of clearing emotional charge is the Hoffman Process, a one-week intensive psychotherapeutic 'retreat' that is akin to a psychological detox. The process is well proven, having been done by over 100,000 people. It is based on the understanding that love is what we all need to be happy and that a child will mimic their parents to get that love. The pre-process homework includes making a list of all your mother's negative patterns of behaviour, all your father's and all your own. These could be being critical, non-committal, fussy, grumpy, judgemental, over-caring, stern, rebellious, needy, arrogant, withdrawn, uptight, a drama queen, a killjoy, and so on. Right now, make a list of 10 of your own patterns.

Given that our psyches can take on those patterns from our parents or reject them so that we become the opposite (for example if you had a controlling parent you become the libertine), it soon becomes clear that almost all our 'unique' characteristics appear to originate from either our mother or father and their conditioning effect on us.

The Hoffman Process is very good at unravelling self-destructive habits and discharging the negative emotions held in these karmic experiences or traumatic memories. As well as an immediate sense of liberation, it enables you to recognize when you have become plugged into a negative pattern and gives you the tools to break free. There's a very good book on this called *You Can Change Your Life* by Tim Laurence, who trained with the late Bob Hoffman and founded the Hoffman Process in the UK. This is a very good book to read to become clear on the negative patterns that are running your life; the actual training will help you find a way to break free.

The Hoffman Process have kindly allowed me to reproduce their 'Negative Transference Exercise' (*see page 230*). This is a great way to clear emotional charge and takes the 'Clearing Emotional Charge' exercise one step further by helping you to identify the patterns that the incident has triggered.

Releasing Negative Emotions

If you find yourself stuck in negative emotions about someone in your life, here are two other exercises that you can do to help yourself find peace and resolution. Remember, the opposite of love is not hate, it is indifference. If you have hateful feelings for someone, it is likely that if you can find a way to discharge your negative emotions, there is love underneath.

Exercise: Writing Down the Emotion (1)

1. Take a piece of paper and, without any censorship whatsoever, write down as quickly as you can one of the emotional scenes from your past, written in the first person, in the present tense, as best you can recollect it. State how you felt then and how you are affected now. Make it emotional, specific and powerful.

2. When you have finished, take the piece of paper and burn it. Sense the power of that burning – the power of that negative pattern being destroyed and floating away with the smoke.

Exercise: Writing Down the Emotion (2)

This kind of writing exercise is good for discharging the negative emotions you have in unresolved relationships, perhaps concerning an ex-partner or parent.

1. Make a list of all the people you feel upset with or haven't forgiven. Choose one.

2. Next, write a letter expressing all your negative feelings about that person's attitude or behaviour. Hold nothing back, but tell them that you won't accept their negative projections. Important: *Don't* send it!

3. Now write a letter expressing everything you appreciate about that person and all you have learned from your

interaction with them. Really open your heart to them and forgive them if you can.

This simple exercise will allow you to move on without carrying the weight of the past with you.

$\backsim$

Learning from Others

One way or another, we all have to do the homework to undo the emotional charge we've accumulated in our life. In fact, as lovely as the idea of 'be here now' is, in truth it's impossible without first discharging a large number of the unexpressed emotional reactions that fuel our self-destructive habits and limit our ability to connect.

Sometimes group processes are good, because collectively we process a wider range of karmic experiences. Also, when we read a good life story or watch a film about a life that is perhaps very different from our own, it can broaden our experience and help us develop more compassion for others. Two great examples of films that really show how we are all a consequence of our early karmic experiences are the South African film *Tsotsi*, which won an Oscar, and *Buffalo 66*.

Most negative emotions can be categorized into shades of sadness, anger or fear, originating from early core traumas. A loss of security in infancy can generate a track for sadness, which is then deepened by further losses throughout life. Relationship difficulties often stem back to early traumas of not being heard or understood, or being ignored. This generates anger. As we develop our sense of self, we have to adapt and find our way of functioning in the world. This is a struggle, and the shocks of change, such as moving to a new area, or starting a new school, or our parents splitting up, generate fear. Unexpressed and unresolved, these negative emotions can end up running the show, as happens in the film *Inside Out*, in which fear, anger, disgust and sadness are represented as personalities inside the head of the main character, suppressing her natural joy and enthusiasm for life.

Another great example of this is the epic story *The Wizard of Oz*. As Dorothy walks the path of her life, the yellow brick road, the fact that she is out of balance is represented by the lion who has no courage. The tin man who has no heart represents relating out of balance, while the scarecrow who has no brain represents an inability to function. As Dorothy faces up to her demons, the witches, she becomes more balanced – more connected. Exactly what the dog has to do with it, I haven't quite figured out, but 'dog' is 'God' backwards, and the wizard himself turns out to be a bit of a sham.

Certainly, by working through experiences that generated fear, anger, disgust and sadness, we, like Dorothy, can become freer from the past and open our heart.

The Importance of the Heart

While base Western science and medicine have relegated the heart to a mere muscle or pump, it is clear that it is far more fundamental to our existence on every level, not just as a physical distributor of oxygen and other nutrients.

Heart and Brain Connections

First, on a physical level, there are many neuronal connections between the heart and the brain, and more go from the heart to the brain than the other way round. Thanks to the research of the HeartMath Institute, headquartered in California, we now know that the part of the brain, the limbic system, that produces stressful reactions and hence the release of adrenalin, can be switched off far more effectively by heart-focused activity than head-focused activity. In other words, generating positive and heartfelt emotions, or even just breathing into the heart space or centre of the chest, switches off a stressful reaction far more quickly than 'thinking' your way out of it, which is more the territory of cognitive behavioural therapy (CBT). While CBT can be useful for reframing negative beliefs in a moment of stress, it is not the quickest way to come out of a stressful reaction.

Thanks to a device developed by HeartMath® called the Inner Balance®, a sensor that you clip onto your earlobe and plug into your phone or tablet, you can directly monitor your state of heart 'coherence' or 'stress-free-ness'. You also need to download the free Inner Balance app to your phone or tablet for this to work.

Figure 43: The free, downloadable Inner Balance app (Image courtesy of HeartMath)

This measures what is called the heart rate variability (HRV), which is a pattern of activity to do with the changes *between* each heartbeat, rather than the pulse, which is the total number of heartbeats per minute.

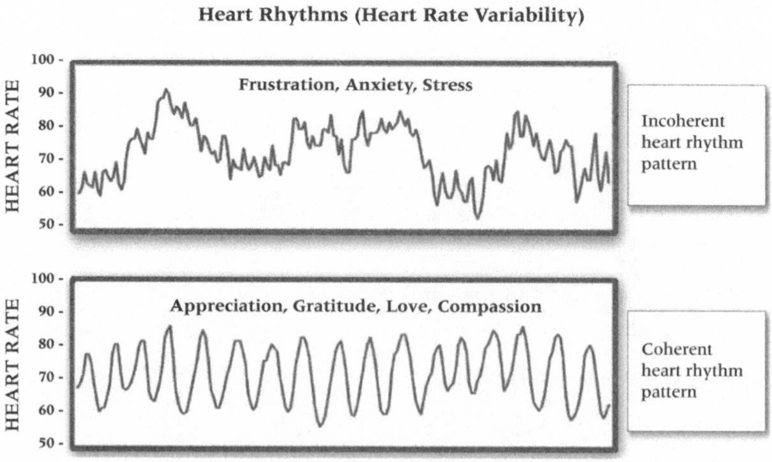

Heart Rhythms (Heart Rate Variability)

HEART RATE

Frustration, Anxiety, Stress

Incoherent heart rhythm pattern

HEART RATE

Appreciation, Gratitude, Love, Compassion

Coherent heart rhythm pattern

Figure 44: Coherent and incoherent HRV patterns. (Image courtesy of HeartMath®)

In Figure 44 you can see the difference between an incoherent HRV, associated with feelings of frustration, anxiety or stress, and a coherent HRV, associated with feelings of love, gratitude, compassion and appreciation. They have the same number of beats a minute but a very different pattern of activity. That pattern is the HRV.

The pattern of HRV also correlates with brainwave patterns as seen in beta-wave activity (more stressed), alpha-wave activity (more relaxed) and theta-wave activity (well connected) recorded in artists and musicians when they were in the flow, as well as advanced meditators.

A coherent HRV is actually to do with the balance between the two patterns of autonomic (think automatic) nervous system activity we have at our disposal. When we are active and alert, the sympathetic nervous system is dominant. When we are relaxed, the parasympathetic nervous system is dominant. Think of these two as a see-saw.

If we are both alert and calm, there is equal activity between the sympathetic and parasympathetic nervous systems. We are in balance, like a lion who is chilling out but briefly scans the surrounding world, listens to the sounds, smells the wind and is able to react in an instant. This is how we are programmed to oscillate between these two nervous-system settings.

Coherence

What is fascinating is that heart-centred focus is what most readily switches us into a 'coherent' or more connected state. John Levine has composed music called 'Silence of the Heart' (available on CD from www.holfordirect.com)which helps put you into a state of coherence and is great to play if you're feeling stressed or depressed. The HeartMath Institute has developed many techniques for encouraging this. Perhaps the simplest and fastest is the Quick Coherence® technique (*see overleaf*), reproduced with the HeartMath Institute's permission.

Exercise: The Quick Coherence® technique

There are two simple steps to practise to get coherent:

Step 1: Heart-Focused Breathing

Focus your attention in the area of the heart. Imagine your breath is flowing in and out of your heart or chest area. Breathe a little slower and deeper than usual.

Step 2: Activate a Positive Feeling

Make a sincere attempt to experience a regenerative feeling such as appreciation or care for someone or something in your life.

The heart, like the brain, generates a powerful electromagnetic field. In fact the heart generates the largest electromagnetic field in the body. The electrical field as measured in an electrocardiogram (ECG) is about 60 times greater in amplitude than the brainwaves recorded in an electroencephalogram (EEG).

In a HeartMath study,[2] researchers set out to determine whether the heart's electromagnetic field, as measured by an electrocardiogram, in one individual could be detected and measured in another person when the pair either were seated within about a metre (three feet) of each other or held hands. The results were positive: the data revealed that when people touch or are in proximity, a transference of the electromagnetic energy produced by the heart occurs.

This is very consistent with the idea of morphic resonance (*see pages 92 and 185*). The idea that our heartfelt feelings have an influence on others, and vice versa, is an important recognition on the road to a more connected experience of life.

Accessing the Heart

Many meditation techniques have focused on the metaphysical or spiritual heart. Simply focusing on the heart space and imagining you are breathing into the heart and out from the heart produces a rapid change towards a more coherent HRV. Evoking a positive regenerative feeling, such as love or care for another, as in HeartMath's Quick Coherence' technique (*see page 168*) or Sally Kempton's heart meditation (*see page 170*), further produces a connected state.

Best of all is to project that positive love, feeling or goodwill to others. We had a great example of this in Chapter 2 when Malcolm described the effect of many people praying for him and sending love when he was in a coma. There are many studies now that prove the power of prayer. We have to understand that there is a lot more going on in the heart space than a simple muscle pumping oxygen.

Pet Power

Pets can help us access a heart space. It is a well-established fact that pet owners live longer and that pets can help people to heal faster. Whether this is all explicable by a person feeling love for their pet or whether the pet has an effect on the person may be the wrong question. Studies do show that pet-owning cardiovascular patients have an improved HRV, which might explain their longer survival.[3] Studies testing the HRV of both pets and their owners show they tend to synchronize. This suggests there is a two-way process. It may be that a pet empathizes with its owner's emotional state. Experiments in which healers have been shown to speed up the healing of wounds in animals[4] suggest some kind of shared energy field.

Most mysterious, and not dependent on an electromagnetic field, is the well-documented phenomenon that pets know when their owners are coming home. Rupert Sheldrake has run experiments proving this, which are detailed in his book *Dogs That Know When Their Owners Are Coming Home*.

One example was of Pam Smart's dog, Jaytee, who appeared to anticipate her return home on 85 per cent of occasions, so an experiment was set up to film the dog continuously, then send Pam out and only allow her to return when sent a randomized text, and always by means of a different taxi to avoid similar car noises. Jaytee was filmed in the window only 4 per cent of the time when she was absent and 55 per cent of the time when she was heading home. The difference was highly statistically significant.[5]

Sheldrake has also recorded 177 accounts of dogs apparently responding to the death or distress of their human companion by howling, whining or whimpering and 62 similar accounts of cats showing distress, and 32 instances where the owner, at a distance, knew that their pet had died or was in dire need.[6]

Whatever is going on here, pets can be a quick route into a more heart-centred and healing space. One woman told me that the quickest way she had for going into a coherent HRV pattern was by stroking her cat.

Heart Meditations

Another way into a heart-focused space is with specific meditations. Sally Kempton, author of *Meditation for the Love of It*, has a simple heart-based meditation exercise that goes like this:

Exercise: Focus on an Experience of Love

1. Close your eyes. Focus on your breathing, following the breath for a few moments to let your mind calm down.

2. Think of someone for whom you feel love or who you have loved in the past. Imagine that you are with this person. Visualize them before you or beside you. To anchor yourself in the memory, you might notice what they are wearing or become aware of the setting. Let yourself feel love for them. Open yourself to the feeling.

3. Once you are fully present with that feeling of love, let go of the thought of the person. Focus entirely on the feeling of love. Allow yourself to rest in it. Feel the energy of love within your body and within your heart.

You may need to repeat this exercise a few times before you get the hang of it. Once you have experienced how the felt sensation of love and happiness remains even after you let go of the idea of the person inspiring it, you will begin to realize that your love is actually independent of anything outside yourself. This is one of those insights that can change your relationship with other people, and certainly with yourself.

Sally also has some brilliant downloadable audio meditation instructions that really take you into a deep and connected meditation. For those wishing to explore further, see www.sallykempton.com.

The HeartMath Institute recommends something similar, which is a daily heart-focused meditation practice called Heart Lock-In® in which you fix on a benevolent feeling, a prayer or wish or just love, and send it out, or extend your heartfelt well-wishing to others, perhaps someone you know, or those you have heard are suffering, or your family or community.

Out of the Head and into the Heart

We are very accustomed to thinking in order to find solutions, rather than feeling for them. What is good about all of these heart-centred exercises is that if you are grappling with a particular situation in your life, rather than trying to 'think' your way through it, having established a heart-based state of awareness, you can bring to mind the situation and ask internally if there is a more beneficial attitude to take. Then, without thinking as such, see if anything else arises.

In the HeartMath range of techniques this is contained within the 'Freeze Frame®' technique taught by HeartMath practitioners and on their trainings. Much like the original use of Hubbard's e-meter, if you have an emWave or Inner Balance device that monitors your HRV you can keep bringing a charged or karmic experience into awareness until you no longer react, having discharged or otherwise resolved the negative feelings attached to the experience.

You can do the same thing after any meditation. Just bring to mind the situation you are dealing with and see if anything emerges, beyond thought.

In day-to-day situations, as well as thinking about the logical approach, check into your heart space and how you feel. This is another important source of wisdom, which is often expressed when people say, 'My head tells me this, but my heart tells me something else.' In situations like this, it's good to listen to the heart.

The Energetic Heart

In the Indian tradition of chakras, or energy centres, of the body, the heart is the centre between the base *muladhara* chakra in the perineum, which connects you to the Earth, and the *sahasrara* chakra, the spiritual centre at the crown of the head. We can think of these two as the material Earth 'Eros' energy, connected to the centre of the Earth and representing the female Shakti 'creative' energy ascending, and a spiritual Heaven energy, connected to the Sun or the centre of the Universe and representing the male Shiva 'unifying' energy descending. They meet in the heart space to form a six-pointed star, known as the *anahata* in Hinduism.[7]

The heart is also the centre between the energy centre three fingerwidths below the navel and a third of the way into the body, which Oscar Ichazo calls the Kath™ (*see his Diakath Breathing, page 110*) and is known as the *hara* in Japanese Zen and *tan t'ien* (sometimes written *dantien*) in Chinese Taoism, and the 'third eye' or *ajna* chakra in the Hindu tradition, in the centre of the head, between the eyebrows.

In Taoism there are actually three *tan t'iens* – upper, middle and lower – also corresponding to the head, heart and belly. The same three centres occur in the Peruvian Quechuan tradition, where the *hara* is the *cusco*, literally meaning the navel stone or navel of the Earth, where energy comes into the body, from Pachamama, Mother Earth, as it is from the mother during foetal development. These three energy centres correspond to our intellectual mind, emotional heart and physical body, and the corresponding energies of wisdom, love and vitality.

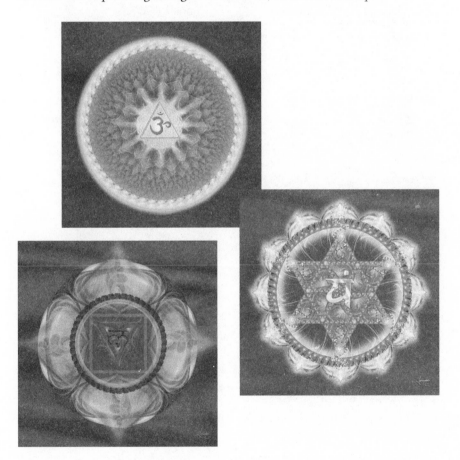

Figure 45: The three energy centres – Sahasrara, *the spiritual centre at the top of the head (top);* Anahata, *the heart centre (above right);* Muladhara, *at the base of the spine (above left). (All images © Ashnandoah) See colour section.*

Each energy centre is associated with a colour. Starting at the top, the *sahasrara* is violet, the *ajna* is blue, the *anahata* in the heart is green, the *hara* is yellow/orange and the *muladhara* is red, corresponding to the visible spectrum of light. (You may recall learning in school that you can make green from mixing yellow and blue.)

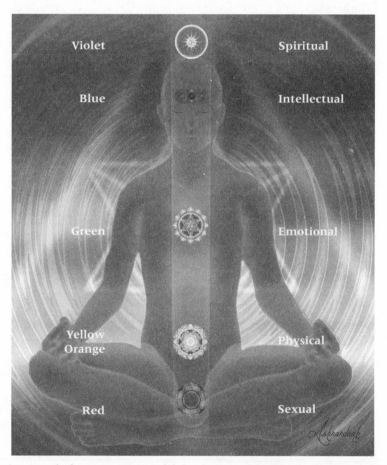

Figure 46: The five energy centres and their colours. (© Ashnandoah) See colour section.

(Apologies to Hindu purists for this simplified variation. In the traditional Hindu system there are seven chakras: crown, brow, throat, heart, solar plexus, sacral and root. The *hara* is not included; it comes, as mentioned, from the Zen and Taoist traditions. Different traditions use different chakras with differing colours and qualities. The key point is that there are energy centres in the body that are part of our subtle energetic anatomy and we can experience them as such. Both yoga and Chinese medicine are based upon restoring the right flow of energy through these centres and subtle energy channels.)

Almost every mystical tradition refers to such centres of energy because they actually exist, not anatomically but energetically, and they are universally experienced by those who have evolved to a level of connectedness that includes awareness of the energy field within and beyond the body.

Often meditations use mantras to bring awareness to these centres. Many yoga classes start and end with three Oms resonating in the heart. Alternatively, remembering that 'Om' is actually made of three syllables, 'A-U-M', we can energize the crown chakra by imagining that 'A' is vibrating in the heart, 'U' is vibrating in the throat and 'M' in the head, from the throat chakra to the crown and out of the top of the head. (In some traditions 'Ah' and 'Om' are used to open the crown chakra.)

I like to bring my awareness to my *hara* to connect with my 'gut instinct' and then, when faced with a choice, I ask which option has the most energy, the most life and is the most attractive. Sometimes the head is ruled by fear and it is good to make choices that have the most 'juice', even if you enter a territory that is less comfortable. 'Feel the fear but do it anyway', so to speak. It is good to live on your edge, rather than avoid all challenging situations. Also, if you are rushing around in a state of anxiety, bringing your awareness to the *hara* can bring you back to the present. Don't be in a hurry, be in your *hara*.

In many ways, awareness of the chakras, with the heart at the pivotal centre, enable us to attain a more profound state of connection.

SUMMARY

In summary, to open the heart:

- Consider undertaking a training or psychotherapeutic process that allows you to work through negatively charged emotional experiences in your past, especially those core experiences that have shaped you.

- Use the exercises given here to discharge negative emotions in unresolved relationships.

- Clear your emotional charges as points of charge arise. Express your emotions and be open to listening to others without judgement.

- Notice your own negative behaviour patterns and beliefs, and what triggers you to feel fearful or shut down.

- Include a regular practice of a heart-centred activity, be it HeartMath's Quick Coherence or Heart Lock-In, Sally Kempton's heart meditation or another meditation involving the heart centre.

- Develop a more heart-centred approach to life, but also listen to your head and your gut instinct. All three centres of awareness make us who we are.

By opening up to your heart space and deepest feelings, as well as being aware of your 'gut' feelings and listening to your more reasoned thoughts, you will connect more fully with life and the challenges that come your way.

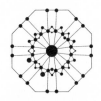

Chapter 12

Community Spirit

Almost half the world's population has an internet connection through the 10 billion internet devices and over 1 billion smartphones in existence. On an average day there are 6 billion Google searches and 1 billion people on Facebook. If Facebook were a country, it would be the second biggest in the world, with 1.3 billion users. As a consequence of this explosion in interconnected digital technology, social media and information, human knowledge is doubling roughly every 12 hours. Compare this to the estimated growth in knowledge in the entire 18th century being equivalent to a week's worth of information in *The New York Times*.

With all this happening, you'd think we'd all feel socially connected. These are, after all, exciting times. But the reverse is also true. The incidence of depression, anxiety, insomnia and stress-related conditions has gone through the roof. The effects of urbanization are isolating people. Major roads are splitting communities. Bad city planning has separated living communities from work communities. Mothers left at home are becoming more isolated. Longer opening hours mean a rota of people staff local shops rather than an individual we can get to know. Online shopping and supermarkets, for all their convenience, further disrupt local community life.

With urbanization, we are disconnecting from our neighbours and creating our own private space. Unlike villages, where everybody knows everybody, for better or worse, and people live and work together and can pop home at lunch from work, in cities we seem to be more separated.

I live for part of the year in London and the other part in a small carless community on an island off Kenya. I know all my neighbours there and word spreads through the village grapevine when anything is going on. If you pass someone it is rude not to say hello, or at least nod in recognition. Despite having been born in Putney, the suburb of London where I live, I only know my neighbours on either side and it is almost considered intrusive to look someone in the eye. My Kenyan friends who come to London feel distinctly uncomfortable in this city 'freeze', where everyone pretends they haven't noticed anyone else. Occasionally I say something or strike up a conversation with someone, but on the whole this is considered strange behaviour. We are all rushing this way and that in parallel Universes.

The Work to Spend Cycle

One thing that has changed in our culture is that we have become habituated to consuming. Despite a big increase in productivity, we still work long hours to accumulate spare cash and spend it on entertainment, clothes and other goods.[1] 'I shop therefore I am.' We have more things, and some have more money, but we have less time to hang out, to socialize, to connect. Social time has a lesser value than stuff. We spend our spare time watching TV, playing computer games, spending hours on Instagram and Facebook and engaging in other (anti-)social media instead of meeting up, taking time, looking others in the eye, exchanging news, ideas and feelings, and processing the inevitable stresses and challenges of life. For a whole new generation, social media is a major part of social connection. One study found that adolescents who self-reported as 'low' internet users (less than one hour per day) had better relationships with friends and family than those who reported 'moderate' (one to two hours per day) and 'high' (more than two hours per day). The authors concluded that excessive internet use could interfere with face-to-face relationships.[2]

These media do allow us to connect with people we have perhaps lost touch with, or make new friends out of common connections or interests. However, we need to be mindful if they become a shallow replacement for real intimacy with close friends to whom we can express our vulnerability. That is the true gateway to connection.

Unfriend my Heart

An example of this is the stress Facebook puts on relationships and the new culture of breaking up on social media. Ilana Gershon, assistant professor of communication and culture at Indiana University, cottoned on to this when she asked her students what constituted a bad break-up. She says, 'I was expecting people to have really dramatic stories. "I caught them in bed together," something like that.' Instead, they all responded with tales of outrage about the medium rather than the message, complaining that they got the bad news by text or by Facebook rather than in person.

This led Gershon to research the nature and effect of social media by interviewing 72 college students and Facebook users.[3] One girl, Rose, told her, 'If people want to maintain a romantic relationship, both members of the couple should get off Facebook.' Why?

> *While my interviewees insisted that Facebook turned them into jealous selves, I argue that the problem was in fact that Facebook encouraged them to be US neoliberal selves—selves that were not conducive to the romantic connections they had or wanted to have. Facebook asks its users to manage themselves as flexible collections of skills, usable traits, and tastes that need to be constantly maintained and enhanced.*

Also, they interpreted Facebook profiles as reliable indications of people's friendships and flirtations, and took others' profiles to be a collection of traces of people's daily social interactions, which my interviewees sometimes saw as consciously collected (and sometimes not). This information often charted too much of another person's life and yet showed too little of the larger contexts. Facebook, my interviewees insisted, encouraged them to care about things that they understood intellectually were inconsequential. Gwen explained to me that she would never have been so anxious about her boyfriend's behavior while she was away on vacation if Facebook hadn't existed.

The very structure of Facebook has people present themselves as a collection of consumer tastes (films, books, music, etc.) and number of friends and alliances, regardless of the quality of those relationships. One student said, 'You have to have the perfect profile picture that you update at least once in a couple of months. If you don't, you're a loser.' Some said that potential employers checked how many Facebook friends a job applicant had (among other things), taking this to be a measure of how effective a networker the person was.

Gershon views the false self of a person's profile as follows:

The problem with Facebook and similar media is that not only do they create only shallow connections, but that they encourage people to treat each other as commodities or businesses: that Facebook takes the logic of viewing the world in terms of consumption, and extends this to the most intimate of relationships. When the self metaphorically becomes a business, it is a compilation of measurable skills and assets that enters into relationships with other selves which may have different arrays of skills. Facebook's interface is constantly suggesting that people add more and more alliances to their profile.

One interviewee explained that his Facebook profile no longer contained information about his birthday:

I took the birthday thing off first because I found it utterly ridiculous that 90 people, 85 of whom I never talk to, wished me a happy birthday. Like they give a damn. The only reason they knew was because Facebook reminded them.

What is missing here is the quality of connection that is present in meaningful relationships. This is what is important, rather than the quantity of so-called Facebook 'friends'.

Loneliness and Vulnerability

But what makes for 'quality' in social relationships? Brené Brown is a professor of social work. Her TED talk, 'The Power of Vulnerability',[4] which has had over 20 million views, explains her research on connection. She found that when she asked about love, people told her about heartbreak. When asked about belonging, they told her about feeling excluded. When she asked about connection, they told her about experiences of disconnection. The breakthrough for her was realizing that shame was the fear of disconnection. 'Is there something about me that if other people know it or see it means I won't be worthy of connection? It's the "I'm not good enough". The idea is that in order for connection to happen we have to allow ourselves to be seen.'

A recent study found that good social connections – friends, family, neighbours or colleagues – improved the odds of survival by 50 per cent. Loneliness, with a lack of such connections, was as harmful as smoking 15 cigarettes a day and twice as harmful as obesity.[5] Persistent loneliness and social isolation should be given the same attention as chronic illness, as a lack of feeling of social connectedness is a major predictor of early mortality.[6]

One of the unfortunate attributes of loneliness is that you think people care about you much less than they do, so there is a danger that you isolate yourself even more.

In Brené Brown's research with thousands of people she found that the big difference between people who had a sense of love and belonging and those who didn't was that those who did believed they were worthy.

Often this sense of unworthiness is rooted in failures in the past. People who have more belief in themselves are more likely to keep trying when the going gets tough. So, if you are in a negative mindset, it is important to treat yourself with compassion, to not give up, to rebuild and reclaim your self-esteem. If you find yourself down in the dumps, just do something distracting and enjoyable for a couple of minutes. Don't bury yourself in a hole of despair. Find a way out of it.

Brené admires her interviewees who did this:

> These people were 'whole hearted'. What they had in common was a sense of courage. The word 'courage' is from the Latin word cur, meaning 'heart'. To tell the whole story from the heart they had the courage to be imperfect, the compassion to be kind to themselves first, then to other people, and as a result they had connection as a result of authenticity. They were willing to let go of who they thought they should be to be who they were.

> The other thing they had in common was that they fully embraced vulnerability. They believed that what made them vulnerable made them beautiful.

Why do we struggle with vulnerability? What makes us feel vulnerable? Uncertainty is a big problem. Instead of living with it, we make everything certain. We 'perfect' our image. On social media we post only those photos, those stories that make us look good. We reinforce a false image of ourselves and, often, our children. And we blame as a way of discharging shame and discomfort. This inevitably leads to even deeper disconnection.

There is another way, Brené says, and that is to 'let ourselves be seen, deeply seen, vulnerably seen. To love with our whole hearts even though there's no guarantee. To practise gratitude and joy in those moments of terror. To believe that we are enough.'

Common Unity: Community and Prejudices

We may be taking small steps towards this. Indeed, some communities and areas are more connected and have more of a community feel. There is also a growing movement toward anti-consumerism. Many companies now offer a four-day week option. Some people are getting their time back and valuing it more than the extra cash to buy more things.

These are the exceptions, however. Also, people are being increasingly forced to migrate and settle in new lands and new cultures. That creates its own isolation, along with the stress of adaptation, plus fears among the locals. One of the great scientific blunders in the world of nutrition was the theory of Ansel Keys that fat was the root of all evil because when immigrants previously eating low-fat diets moved to the USA, they got heart disease. Now we know this was a spurious association and more to do with the increased stress levels of immigration than a change in diet and his own political agenda.

To make a better world, it is vital we all face our vulnerabilities and our prejudices, often towards cultures and people we don't understand. Sometimes this is born out of language, sometimes out of ignorance and lack of understanding.

I am aware, for example, that there are some terrible things going on in the name of Islam. No one with any humanity can watch the ISIS crisis without feeling the horror of these crimes. The same thing happened during the Crusades, in the name of Christianity, during the 12th and 13th centuries. (Islam is roughly the same age as Christianity was during the Crusades.) Yet the vast majority of Muslims are equally horrified. By 2028 Islam will be the largest religion in the world, with an estimated 2.8 billion followers. I want to understand this large chunk of humanity. The village I live in in Kenya is largely Muslim. They are lovely people on the whole. There are clearly inequalities and restrictions on freedom for women, which seems wrong from a Western perspective. But in our village there is a swimming pool where the girls can learn to swim, a girls' football team and a high level of education, with more girls than boys going on to higher education and getting important jobs. Two of my neighbours are gay. We are making progress.

Today the country with the most English-speaking people is China. Its 1.4 billion population represents 20 per cent of the world's population. I want to understand this culture. I want to know how to say 'How are you?' (*Nee how ma – ni hao ma*) and 'thank you' (*shé shé – xie xie*). On the one hand the Chinese culture has the worst record for human rights violations and on the other its social policies have lifted 600 million people out of poverty, which is arguably the single biggest contribution to human rights over the last three decades.

My work takes me to South Africa. I love the city of Cape Town, surrounded by Table Mountain, with amazing restaurants and houses nestled in small communities around bays. Yet as you fly into Cape Town you see a vast ghetto of corrugated iron huts across the Cape Flats. The Cape Flats contain a vast number of ever-growing communities where the majority of coloured and African people live in varying degrees of poverty as people move from rural areas to the city. Diabetes has become the number one killer, more so than AIDS. More often than not, I'm staying in a gated community with high walls and barbed wire keeping out robbers. It makes me feel uncomfortable. On one of my visits, the mayor of Cape Town, Patricia de Lille, came to one of my workshops and we agreed I'd give a free talk to the Cape Flats communities. I felt both excited and frightened at the prospect. As a middle-class Englishman, how could I say anything useful? But fear, a monk once told me, is just suppressed excitement. Anyway, I did the talk. The mayor bussed in hundreds of people with diabetes and an interest in preventing it, and we are now working together to create an army of community champions who can educate local people in following a low glycemic load (GL) diet using foods that they can afford.

If places like these are an area of your prejudice or discomfort, watch *Tsotsi*, the film I mentioned earlier. It tells the story of a group of South African youths who rob a house and steal a baby. A relationship develops between the main character, an orphan of AIDS brought up in the ghetto with no family, and the baby. It explains a lot. When I'm in South Africa, if I can, I like to give a lecture for NOAH, a charity that is Nurturing Orphans of AIDS for Humanity. They do great work.

What are your prejudices? How can you face them and feel the fear but do it anyway? What actions, however small, can you take in your community to engender more connection?

Morphic Fields and Telepathic Connections

We are actually far more connected than we think. One hypothesis that implies we are much more connected in social groups than conventional science would have us believe is Rupert Sheldrake's morphic resonance, which we explored in Chapter 6 in the context of the mind–body connection.

According to this model, there are morphic fields for social groups, such as packs of dogs or flocks of starlings, which can explain how animals can work in packs across vast distances and how flocks of birds can fly in synchronized formations. There is also a morphic field for our family and friends. Once bonded, members can move apart but still be linked to the social group. The morphic field continues to connect them. The same phenomenon has been found in atomic and subatomic particles. When atoms have been part of the same molecule, or subatomic particles part of the same atom, they have what physicists call 'entanglement': when there is a change in one, there is spontaneously a change in the other.

For social groups to form there needs to be a shared past or memory encoded in a pattern of activity that works across a morphic field. This 'morphic resonance' provides a connection across space. Sheldrake refers to it as our 'seventh sense' (the sixth sense being reserved for our electromagnetic sensitivity).

An example is the heart rate variability of pets tending to synchronize with that of their owners. This effect could be explained by a shared electromagnetic field, which we know extends several metres from the heart, although it might just be a consequence of a connection across a morphic field rather than the means of the connection.

However, neither electromagnetic sensitivity nor any of the other senses explains phenomena such as telepathy occurring over long distances, especially between people who are emotionally connected. Mothers often describe telepathy with their babies and children, and many people have reported having a premonition about the death of someone they are close to, at a distance too far to be explained by conventional senses or an electromagnetic field.

The most common example of this sense is telephone telepathy, when someone comes to mind and the phone rings and it is that person. The Nolan Sisters put this to the test on Channel 5 TV in an experiment set up by Rupert Sheldrake and available for all to see.[7] One sister, Coleen, was in a hotel room a considerable distance from the other sisters, who, at the throw of a die, would select who would call her. As the phone rang, before picking it up, she had to guess who was calling. With four sisters, her chances of getting it right each time were one in four, or 25 per cent. However, she guessed right 50 per cent of the time. You can try this out for yourself at www.sheldrake. org/participate/telephone-telepathy-test. You'll need two phones, three people and 15 minutes.

The idea is that if someone within your morphic field thinks of you, or reaches out to you with their intention, you are more likely to pick up on it. Similarly, if there is a big disruption in the morphic resonance of a group, such as a disaster, others pick up on it.

Another example explained by this model is the sense of being stared at, a subject that Sheldrake has extensively researched in his book *The Sense of Being Stared At*.

While the morphic resonance hypothesis is not yet conclusively proven, it certainly provides a much more logical basis for explaining all sorts of phenomena, including how our intention and state of mind have such a profound effect on healing ourselves and others and shaping our world and society. It also puts us much more into the world, as opposed to the dehumanizing hypothesis that limits our mind to the grey matter of our brain and separates us from each other.

Sheldrake summarizes our interconnection in this way:

> *Through vision the external world is brought into the mind through the eyes, and the subjective world of experience is projected outward into the external world through fields of perception and intention. Our intentions stretch out into the world around us and also extend into the future. We are linked to our environment and to each other. Likewise, our minds pervade our bodies, and our body images are where we experience them, in our bodies, not just in our heads. We are not imprisoned within the narrow compass of our skulls, our minds separated and isolated from each other. We are no longer alienated from our bodies, alienated from our environment, and alienated from other species. We are interconnected.*

Find Your Purpose

When asked how he managed to be so vibrant in his nineties, the philosopher Bertrand Russell replied, 'As you get older you must have a purpose larger than yourself. That's what makes life meaningful.'

So, what is it that gives you a sense of purpose? Of course, that may change at different times in your life. For example, taking care of your family may give you your feeling of purpose. But when your children grow up, or leave home, or disappoint you, what then? Similarly, many people gain a sense of purpose through doing work that feels important and meaningful. But often, once they've achieved their goal, they begin to lose their feeling of purpose.

However, there are ways of finding purpose that can carry us through life. For most of us, being of service to others gives us a sense of purpose. This could take many forms. It might be service to our children or grandchildren, or to the community. It could include political action, supporting worthy causes or simply helping people we meet.

Another powerful and ongoing feeling of purpose can come from our connection to nature and doing what we can to nurture the Earth, from gardening to recycling to being involved in environmental issues.

For some, doing everything with love, or with excellence, gives a sense of purpose.

Another purpose can be our own self-development – becoming the best we can be. Sometimes this is originally motivated by our desire to be happy and free of emotional pain, but through the process of our own transformation – however we have achieved it – and learning how to let go of our own limited concepts, negative patterns, selfishness and pettiness, we become more able to be of service to others.

For some, being of service to the greater good is what gives life a sense of purpose. Some people practise this by identifying with a figure who represents what they aspire to be, be it Jesus, the Dalai Lama or whoever. The Dalai Lama once said that every human being had a desire to be happy and to be free of pain, and that his daily practice was to remember that his desire to be happy and free of pain was of no greater or lesser importance than for those he interacted with.

If you are unclear about your purpose, in a moment I'll give you a couple of exercises to help you find it.

An Ever-changing Journey

As we get older, we may realize our purpose is not so much our job, but our calling as to what we are here to do – although they can be one and the same. People who struggle with retirement are often struggling with rediscovering their purpose. I once heard a description of increasing maturity as the expansion of your circle of caring from yourself to your family and immediate friends, to the community and then to the world.

Here's a simple exercise that will help you find your purpose. You'll need a pen and some pieces of paper and a place to sit quietly and comfortably.

Exercise: Finding Your Purpose (1)

1. Sit comfortably in a quiet place. Recollect how you felt at the age of 10. What gave you your sense of purpose then?

2. What was your sense of purpose at ages 15, 20, 26 and 35? Write down whatever comes to mind without too much deliberation, making a list of the different purposes you've been aware of at different times in your life.

3. Now ask yourself, 'What gives me a sense of purpose now?' Write down as many of your current purposes as you can.

4. Now become still, perhaps by doing the Diakath Breathing exercise (*on page 110*), or another meditative practice, and ask your innate wisdom, your higher intelligence, 'What is my true purpose?' Offer this question without 'thinking' the answer and write down, without censorship, whatever comes to your mind, starting with the words 'My purpose in life is…'

Exercise: Finding Your Purpose (2)

Another way to become clear about your purpose is to answer these questions:

1. What do you love to do or enjoy doing?

2. What makes you feel good? What gives you a sense of satisfaction and fulfilment?

3. What are you good at? We all have certain gifts or talents. For some, it's the ability to listen; for others, it's having a clear mind. What are some of your gifts?

4. What is needed now in the world, in your community or your family?

5. How can you use your gifts to help or to serve?

When you contemplate these questions and put the answers together, you'll find some powerful insights into your own purpose and ways of connecting with community spirit.

SUMMARY

In summary, to help generate community spirit and social connections:

- Don't get too involved in the virtual world of social media – meet people face to face instead.

- Have the courage to be vulnerable and share how you really feel.

- Be aware of your prejudices and identify the underlying fears and limited beliefs.

- Take a risk and say hi to strangers, especially people you have a natural prejudice about.

- Find your purpose and be true to it.

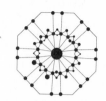

Chapter 13
Men and Women – *Vive la Différence*

There is a natural attraction between the male and female principle and (for most) between men and women, and an eternal 'rub' concerning the differences. Some men are more feminine than others, some women more masculine. Even in homosexual relationships there is usually a more 'male' and 'female' partner. The male and female energy still plays out.

In the Indian tradition, Shiva, the god of consciousness or pure awareness, is male, and Shakti, the goddess of the manifest world, namely energy in its various forms, is female. In many spiritual traditions it is the female principle, the Mother, Shakti, who has the power, even if, in reality, women are subjugated. The material world, and of course the babies, come from the mother. The male principle is the container, the awareness. Men without women are impotent. Women without men can be chaotic and unpredictable. The driven masculine energy is attracted to the free-flowing energy of the feminine. How these two come together and how we work with them is an important part of connection.

Throughout this chapter I am generalizing, which is dangerous in this territory, and, rather than just referring to 'men' and 'women' as if there were such a homogenous thing, I am referring to the masculine and feminine energy that exist in all of us, even though one or other of these forces will be more dominant in any given individual.

The feminine can be considered more an embodiment of an 'attractive' principle and the masculine more an embodiment of an 'active' principle in the game of life. The masculine is more analytical, the feminine more analogical or relational.

It is usually these opposites that attract. Men with more feminine energy will seek women with more masculine energy. More masculine men will be drawn to more feminine women. It is this attraction of the poles, the opposites, that drives passion. Attempts to make your man or woman think, decide or act in the way that you do is a passion killer.

For a man to suppress his natural masculine energy, which includes making his mark on the world, being true to his mission to provide and compete and expressing his natural attraction to the feminine, is disempowering. Often the career or mission comes first, followed closely by sport. The masculine has a killer instinct, which is reflected in business, sport and adventure – conquering mountains, beating the opponent, killing the deal. A young man needs to break away from the mother and set out on his own hero's journey.

For a woman to suppress her natural feminine energy, which is to love, to heal, to nurture, to teach, to create, to trust, to support the family and make a home, is also disempowering. The feminine has more emphasis on relationships, and often the family, the couple and the home come first. Women are much more likely to work in education, medicine and the healing professions.[1] In the UK, 82 per cent of therapists, 67 per cent of PR people, 57 per cent of marketeers and 56 per cent of journalists and editors are women.[2] Women also make up 45 per cent of GPs. Having good social and relational skills are important in all these jobs.

This doesn't mean that women can't be good in business or politics, or that men can't be good teachers or take care of the home and the children. We all have both masculine and feminine aspects in our make-up.

However, it is important to respect that the power base in business, education, government and medicine is still very much male-dominated. It is hard to know how much of this is due to the 'natural' inclination of the masculine and feminine principles and how much reflects the continued subjugation of women. Women are still paid 22 per cent less than men in the USA, 20 per cent less in the UK and 16 per cent less in the EU.[3]

What about connection between these two principles? The masculine finds his deepest love through the feminine. The feminine needs to feel supported, loved, heard and appreciated to give love, to nurture and to heal, as, of course, do we all. It is sometimes said that a man has sex to feel love and a woman needs to feel loved to have sex.

To get a sense of the different qualities of the masculine and feminine energies, try this simple visualization.

Male/Female Visualization

While sitting in a comfortable upright position or, if you prefer, lying flat on the floor, imagine your body is divided in half longways.

Your left half is masculine and your right half is feminine. The left half has the skin, the muscles, the hair and the sex organs of a man.

Imagine how that feels, and how you feel as a man, and how you think.

Your right half has the skin, the form and the sex organs of a woman.

Imagine how that feels, and how you feel as a woman, and how you think. How is this energy different from that of your 'male' half?

Why Men Don't Listen and Women Can't Read Maps

There are some important evolutionary and biological differences between the sexes, apart from the obvious, which help to explain some of these differences. For starters, the corpus callosum, the band of fibres between the two hemispheres of the brain, tends to be thicker in women than men, so women have a more 'connected' brain. This may explain their superior social skills. They are also more in touch with their emotions and how they feel at any given moment.

While there are obviously exceptions, and remember that I am generalizing in this entire chapter, women pick up more social clues than men and are more adept at having more than one conversation rolling. They are more attuned to the subtle undercurrents of interactions, more in the flow of the social landscape and more responsive from the heart. Many studies have reported that men have more advanced visual/spatial skills while women have more advanced language and social skills. Allan and Barbara Pease's book *Why Men Don't Listen and Women Can't Read Maps* explores these differences in an amusing and constructive way. It is well worth a read.

These differences would make sense from an evolutionary perspective if men were the main hunters and women the main gatherers, so we may assume this was the case. As well as gathering herbs, seeds, fruit and vegetables, women would gather information better than men. Socially, they would hold the community together. Hence, today, if you want to know which actor is in which film and who is sleeping with whom, ask a woman. If you want directions, ask a man. Of course some of these traits are culturally programmed, but I suspect more is 'hard-wired' in our design than we would like to admit. Most women prefer rom-coms and most men prefer action movies.

As hunters, the language needed is action speak. 'Lion. To the left. Stop.' Men tend to talk less than women and struggle to follow more than one thread of a conversation. Given too many things to think about simultaneously, they will switch off, hence their frequently perceived inability to listen.

In the past, hunters would hunt game with spears and other weapons. Now men are programmed to hunt for money rather than buffaloes. The fastest car and latest smartphone are today's prizes. Still the hunter must provide. And there is a natural competition between men, hence their love of competitive sports. These kinds of sport are a metaphor for battling against death. Men need to live on their edge and make their own decisions to feel truly alive. They learn through challenges. These are hunter skills.

Gathering, on the other hand, has parallels with shopping. And all gatherers, since the first records, have had bags. To this day most women find it almost impossible to leave home without a bag. I have tested this on numerous occasions in my seminars with hundreds of women. About two in 100 come to a lecture without a bag. And the 'best' bag is highly sought after. How on Earth can one justify £2,000 for a bag – considerably more than the price of the contents? Top gatherer status?

Hunters, on the other hand, need to have their hands free. They'll clip things on their belt, put them in jacket pockets, wear backpacks and sling bags over their shoulders, but will they carry man bags? Despite all the attempts by the fashionistas, these just don't catch on. But when it comes to the fastest, flashiest car, it's another story.

The Feminization of Nature

On a chemical level, testosterone may have quite a lot to do with this. In the world of rats, one in nine female rats are more butch. In normal circumstances, they don't do so well in the pecking order: it is the more 'female' rats who hang out with the king rat. However, when times are hard, the butch rats do better.

Researchers wanted to find out what made these rats more masculine and the answer was that they were sandwiched between two males in the womb and therefore exposed to more testosterone than the other female rats.

The same phenomenon may appear to exist with male and female twins, who are twice as likely to have same-sex attraction.[4] An example of this is Montgomery Clift and his twin sister, Roberta. He had softer feminine features, while she looked masculinized. He was gay, while she was not. However, whether sexual orientation is primarily driven by hormonal, genetic or environmental factors is a subject of much heated debate. Opposite-sex twin girls are not more likely to be gay and opposite-sex twin boys are not more likely to be gay if they have an older brother, suggesting that the family environment is more important than hormonal preconditioning in the womb.

Feminization through hormone exposure has, however, been happening in the animal world as a consequence of exposure to xenoestrogens – environmentally polluting chemicals that latch onto oestrogen receptors and mess up hormonal signalling. This may be a factor in the increase in infertility, as cogently argued in Deborah Cadbury's book *The Feminisation of Nature*.

One in six couples are now having problems conceiving. Sperm counts have almost halved in the last 60 years. In some countries, even sex drive is on the decline. In Japan, for example, almost half of the adult population is not having sex and has little interest in it. A survey in 2013 by the Japan Family Planning Association (JFPA) found that 45 per cent of women aged 16 to 24 'were not interested in or despised sexual contact'.[5] More than a quarter of men felt the same way. The population, which has been shrinking for the past decade, is projected to plunge by a further third by 2060.[6] Why is this? Most blame psychological and social factors resulting in stressed-out men and uninterested women.[7] Whether or not there are environmental or dietary changes at play as well is largely unknown.

Adrenalin Dominance

What is known is that women don't tend to handle chronic stress as well as men. Stress produces lower serotonin levels and depression, and three times as many women are diagnosed with depression as men. Around one in eight women in both the UK and USA have been prescribed antidepressants. Psychologists often say that when stressed, women blame themselves, take their feelings inside and become depressed, and men blame the world, express their anxieties externally and get angry.

Depression is often anger without enthusiasm. Also, in most cultures, expressing anger as a woman is less 'acceptable'. But a simple explanation of the differences in stress response and depression rates may be that men are more adrenalin dominant. Adrenalin is the hunter hormone.

My mentor Dr Abram Hoffer discovered that adrenalin could be turned into adrenochrome in the absence of enough B vitamins, vitamin C and zinc, inducing hallucinations in schizophrenics. Also, too much adrenalin is linked to ADHD symptoms and an inability to sit still and concentrate. Both of these conditions are more prevalent in males.

Adrenalin also makes you stupid. When the brain's energy is continually focused on the amygdala, the 'stress' centre, there's less available for the neo-cortex, the centre for higher thought. That's why smart people do stupid things when stressed.

Adrenalin shuts down digestion too. One in six people suffers from irritable bowel syndrome (IBS) which is more prevalent in women, whose adrenal systems are less programmed to cope with non-stop stress. Stomach acid levels decrease, so much so that the average 50+ year-old suffers from indigestion because they aren't completely digesting proteins. The net result is that bacteria do instead, producing gas and therefore belching, and up comes some of the stomach's acid, producing heartburn.

Ironically, the medical profession's solution is to sell you antacid 'protein pump inhibitor' (PPI) drugs that kill stomach acid. Then you really can't digest your food, or absorb B12, so your brain and bones start shrinking. It's a classic example of disconnected thinking and a lack of understanding of how the body really works. Still, it's a great money-spinner.

Many older people's indigestion and heartburn are resolved by *supplementing* stomach acid (betaine hydrochloride). Then the gas and the belching and the indigestion go away. (You have to be careful with this approach, though, because it'll make you worse if you've got an undiagnosed ulcer.)

Post-menopausal women often end up more adrenalin dominant because progesterone, levels of which plummet when ovulation ceases, switches off adrenal response. Many menopausal symptoms fit in with this theory – anxiety, angry outbursts, insomnia, restless legs, tight muscles, frequent urination, hot flushes. Sometimes it's hard to be a woman.

But men don't come off lightly. The male menopause, the andropause, is far more common than realized as a cause of anger, depression, loss of libido and drive. Dr Malcolm Carruthers, a world expert on testosterone and author of *The Testosterone Revolution*, also reports other 'feminizing' symptoms such as the development of breast tissue, gynaecomastia, in older men. He found this was most common in farmers, especially chicken farmers. Male chickens are castrated, or caponized, which helps them get fatter and tastier with less testosterone and more oestrogens. Perhaps, Carruthers wondered, the farmers had become somewhat caponized themselves. A strange kind of poetic justice.

Reclaiming Feminine Power

In many spiritual traditions the female principle has the power, yet most of the world's current religions are patriarchal. Misinterpretation of religious texts has given authority to a lesser status for women. In most societies, at a base level men exert their authority through financial and physical dominance, including threats and violence, while women manipulate their men through sexual and emotional teasing and withholding. Reclaiming feminine power will bring about a better balance and a deeper connection that will benefit both masculine and feminine energies.

There is a long way to go. We forget how hard women had to fight for the right to vote in the last century, a right still denied in Saudi Arabia. Most major world religions still discriminate against women, for example by not allowing them to be priests. However, much worse than this is the continued sexual abuse and slavery of women for prostitution. Globally, there are over 20 million women in sexual slavery – more than the total number of slaves in the 18th and 19th centuries – with more than half a million trafficked across borders every year. An estimated 140 million girls and women have had genital mutilation.[8] Former US president Jimmy Carter considers abuse and subjugation of women the number one human rights violation in the world. His TED talk[9] and book *A Call to Action: Women, Religion, Violence, and Power* make this point very clear.

One way forward has come from Sweden, which has given sex workers rights but made sex trafficking and purchasing sex illegal. This has been effective in driving down prostitution. However, so much still needs to change. How did we even get to this point?

One possible historical contributor to the story that supports male superiority could be the rather late discovery, in the 19th century, that women made eggs (ova) which were just as important as the male sperm for conception. Before then the general conception, excuse the pun, was that men made the babies and women just carried them to term. This remarkable fact was pointed out to me by Sir Charles Jessel, who says:

We have mostly assumed that this belief was due to the male's superior physical strength and his ability to defend his partner and family in times of danger and to provide them with essential food as a hunter-gatherer while she minded the home. But I have realized that it required something quite different to keep this belief going until quite recent times… It is a matter not of strength or any similar attribute, it is a matter of physiology and the ignorance of the true details of human reproduction and birth.

He goes on to explain that in the 16th century the Swiss-German revolutionary-minded physician Paracelsus (whose full name was Philippus Aureolus Theophrastus Bombastus von Hohenheim) said:

Woman, being nearer to Nature, furnishes the soil in which the seed of man finds the condition required for its development. She nourishes, develops and matures the seed without furnishing any seed herself. Man, although born of woman, is never derived from woman, but always from man.[10]

He was only repeating a belief that had been held at least since the days of Aristotle (384–322BCE), who also favoured the view that the woman merely provided fertile ground for the male seed to grow. It was no doubt also noted that in the Bible God produced Eve by taking a piece of Adam. He did not produce both sexes at the same time.

It was not until the 19th century, according to a review article in the journal *Nature*, that:

Karl Ernst von Baer first confirmed the presence of the mammalian egg under the microscope, and Matthias Jakob Schleiden and Theodor Schwann postulated that egg and sperm are equivalent in that they are both cells. In 1876 Oscar Hertwig made the seminal discovery of fertilization in sea urchins. He observed that the nuclei of sperm and egg fused during fertilization, thereby providing a conceptual base for genetic inheritance and settling the long-standing debate on the role of the egg and sperm in the generation of new life.[11]

While there may have been matriarchal cultures in the past, Sir Charles proposes that it wasn't until the discovery of equal roles for conception were established as scientific fact that the male was deposed from his superior height of importance.

Now, after hundreds of years of male domination both in religion and politics, the pendulum is starting to swing, at least in some countries.

In the traditional Christian story of our times, for example, the Catholic Church has apologized for the depiction of Mary Magdalene as a whore. Was she far more than that – the Shakti, so to speak, to Jesus's Shiva? She is referred to as his favoured disciple, but after his death her role was soon denigrated by the male-dominant power base headed by Peter, who won out over her more egalitarian approach.[12] The Gospel of Mary Magdalene[13] is, however, becoming increasingly recognized as a source of Christian wisdom.

Much, too, has been made of Leonardo da Vinci's painting 'The Last Supper', in which there is clearly a woman, presumably Mary Magdalene, sitting at Jesus's right hand (you can view the painting at tinyurl.com/62obl). Women are even being allowed into the Protestant priesthood, though they are still denied this right in the Catholic Church.

Islam also has a bad rap as far as women are concerned. At its core, however, Islamic philosophy has a deep respect for the female principle and for women, not as equals to men but as complements to them. Not greater or lesser, different. Anyone wanting to delve deeper into this would do well to read the online article *The Male and Female in the Islamic Perspective* by philosopher and Professor of Islamic Studies Seyyed Hossein Nasr.[14]

However, in these days of extremism, Westerners often take offence at the perceived subjugation of women visibly illustrated by the extreme covering up with the veil or *burqa*. This is not actually required in the Koran, which states, for women, cover your chest (24:31) and lengthen your garments (33:59), and for both sexes, the best garment is righteousness and modest conduct (7:26). Some women choose to cover themselves. For those in some Islamic fundamentalist countries, it is, however, obligatory.

Of course, this is the least of the concerns regarding female abuse. Some fundamentalist groups enforce a strict replay of what was happening back in Prophet Mohammed's time, when women couldn't work and had to stay inside.

In the same way that we identify with our own kind as human beings, I believe there is a collective memory and awareness within womanhood of abuse and subjugation, and a history of women who have had to fight, and are fighting, for equality and basic rights, not through war but through protest. Wars are, for the most part, forged by men. In the wake of their destructive power comes the collective grief of millions of mothers who have lost children, sons and husbands. It may be that, ultimately, this is the most constructive force for peace.

Working with the Female Principle

There is a story from the legend of King Arthur that illustrates how to work with the female principle, not only with women in general life, but also with the transforming female power in meditation. It runs as follows:

King Arthur was in a terrible bind. He would lose his kingdom unless he could solve the riddle: What do women want? And he had no idea.

Contemplating this riddle, he was riding through a wood when he came across a hideous old crone.

'I know the answer to your riddle,' she said to him, 'but there is a price to pay – the hand of Prince Gawain in marriage.'

Prince Gawain was Arthur's most favoured and loyal knight and he was hot. All the ladies-in-waiting fancied him. Anyway, King Arthur had to agree.

Then the old hag said, 'Women want their own way.'

The wedding day was set and as Prince Gawain got hitched to the old crone, there were many damsels in distress.

After the ceremonial part, the crone said, 'Now we must consummate the wedding.'

Off they went to the boudoir and did the deed, upon which the crone turned into a beautiful princess.

She said, 'Your loyalty has freed me from a spell I have been under for many years. But I can only be this way for either the day or the night, and for the other I will become the crone once again. So, which do you want? The princess by day or by night?'

Prince Gawain said, 'You choose.'

And with that the spell was broken.

I was first told this story by Sally Kempton, author of *Awakening Shakti: The Transformative Power of the Goddesses of Yoga*, a marvellous book about the Goddess powers as captured in the Indian tradition. Sally is a master of meditation and how to work with the kundalini energy, the energy of creation, the intelligent force that leads us towards fullness and connection – the female power. In the Exercise Appendix she shares one of her most powerful Goddess meditations.

David Deida, author of *The Way of the Superior Man*, says:

The essential masculine ecstasy is in the moment of release from constraint. This could occur when facing death and living through it, succeeding in (and thus being released from) your purpose, and in competition (which is ritual threat of death). The masculine is always seeking release from constraint into freedom. The feminine, on the other hand, is not seeking freedom, but love. A woman's bliss is not emptiness, but in fullness. Her means is not release, but surrender.

We all have aspects of both – the desire for freedom and love, release and surrender. It is the play between these two forces that makes life juicy.

If you are struggling in your relationship and stuck in the polarities, you would do well to read *Sex, Love and the Dangers of Intimacy* by Nick Duffell and Helena Løvendal-Duffell, founders of the Centre for Gender Psychology. They say:

Conflict inevitably arises when partners come together in sexual relationship. It cannot be avoided. It is a chemical process. The joining of male and female energies invokes a deep and universal pattern that has unparalleled power. If we understand how to tap into its creative alchemy, we may flower, otherwise it can destroy us.

Another classic and very helpful book is Harville Hendrix's *Getting the Love You Want*.

It is the interplay and, finally, the marriage of male and female principles, consciousness and the creative force, love and freedom, that is the ultimate alchemy, producing the highest state of connection, emptiness and bliss. We will explore this in more detail in the next chapter.

So, what of the difference between men and women? *Vive la différence!*

PART IV

THE ULTIMATE CONNECTION

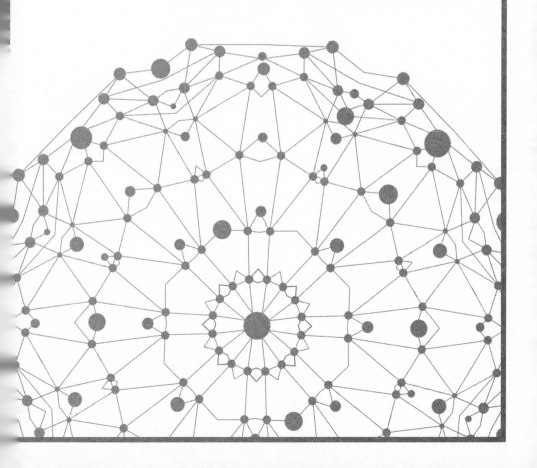

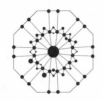

Chapter 14

The Alchemy of Sex and Spirit

A recurring theme in our exploration of connection is the two principles: the material and the spiritual; the relative and the absolute; Earth and Heaven; physicality and transcendence. We experience these two principles every day as subject (I) and object (world).

The merging, the meeting point, the coexistence, the alchemy of these two principles provides the greatest opportunity for a fully connected existence. This is the dance of Shakti and Shiva in the Hindu tradition and the goal of many mystical traditions.

The Essential Trinity

What I find encouraging is that new concepts in science, such as morphic fields and resonance, which require no religious belief, and the revival of Platonic and Neoplatonic philosophy that is influencing a new movement in theology called neo or radical orthodoxy, and Hindusim, the Sufism of Islam and the fundamental tenets of Christianity all share the same 'trinity', which can be expressed as absolute being; the field, or consciousness, which is aware of form and meaning; and energy – the stuff of life, be it external, as in the Universe, or internal, as in thought.

This trinity is expressed in most philosophies of enlightened teachers. Ibn Arabi, the great Sufi philosopher, uses the words *wujud* (being), *wijdan* (consciousness) and *wajd* (bliss) to describe three faces of God as absolute Reality.[1] It is Father, Son and Holy Spirit. Also, God, humanity and the Universe. Also, the Essence (*dhat*) of Allah, the being of God as One in Himself; the Attributes (*sifat*) of Allah, which are the knowable relationships between the Essence and creation; and the Acts of Allah, which are all creatures and all actions of creation.[2]

Similarly, as human beings, we have three aspects: our being or direct experience; our relating (across the morphic fields of humanity, our family and other social groups, and also the relationships we have with our world); and our function or activity. This trinity also exists in our development from our mother, from whom we come into existence, our father, the first person to whom we relate outside the mother–child bond, and our developing sense of self, shaped by siblings or peers, with whom we develop our world views.

When visiting Konya, in central Turkey, on a pilgrimage to Rumi's shrine, I found this symbol above his grave. It is the double 'Hu'. Hu, you will remember, is the ultimate state of union with the divine. We are Hu-Man. Take the HU/U/AU/O, the universal vibration, add in the Rasta and Hebrew name for God, Jah or Jahweh, and you've got Allah Hu Jah – Hallelujah! Three names of God in One! A very multicultural mantra.

Figure 47: Double Hu symbol above Rumi's grave

In Hinduism the trinity is called *Sat-Chit-Ananda*. *Sat* refers to that which sustains the being of all beings. This is God the Father or the absolute truth that is, as the Buddhists call it. The Sufis call this *Al-Haqq*, 'being itself – the source and ground of all things'. In Jewish mysticism it is called 'the root of all roots'. Meister Eckhart called it the 'is-ness'.

Awareness and Energy

That which exists in and is sustained by this pure being has two aspects:

1. There is our awareness of it (as the knower or the subject) – awareness of dimension, structure and order. We can call this the field. For example, light and radiation require an electromagnetic field. Atoms and molecules require the quantum field. We exist across the field of humanity. Ours is a human consciousness. This is the meaning of *Chit*, or the Son, the Word, the Logos. This is Shiva.

2. Then there is energy, the manifestation of the relative, ever-changing world, both inside and outside. This is the object, or the known. This is Shakti. It is the unfolding intention of creation. It is alive. We do not simply register or observe what is happening, we are always organizing it, manipulating our world towards an intention. This is the Holy Spirit, or *Ananda*, which can also mean 'love', 'bliss', 'joy', the expression of the flow of pure energy across the field. What we think of as matter is a vibratory pattern or flow of energy across a morphic field, which makes things change. It's the action. In Buddhist terminology this is the realm of the 'relative' – that which changes.

While for most of us the world is not experienced as blissful – that is, we are trapped in the separateness of 'I' and 'that', or subject and object – the enlightened ones, on the other hand, see no separation. In their view, 'Shakti dances for Shiva's delight'. Everything is just energy, and that recognition is blissful.

Maybe love really does make the world go round.

One Eye Looking Out, One Eye Looking In

Energy itself can be seen as a dual force. The 'Earth' force, or life force, or desire for life, is the fuel of our sex drive. Sex makes life. The 'Heaven' force is the desire and drive for transcendence. They are the same energy, albeit with a different direction. Freedom and love.

Enlightenment in the higher schools of Buddhism and the tantric traditions of India is having a foot in both camps, so to speak. But there is more to it than that.

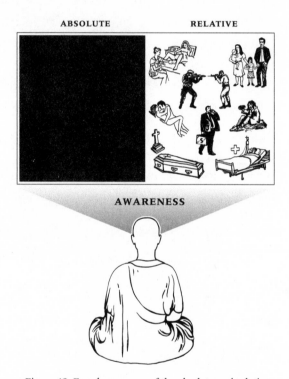

Figure 48: Equal awareness of the absolute and relative

Think of your essential self as a projector – the light of awareness. In one direction, or eye, you are looking out at the world of appearances (and in on the world of thoughts and feelings). This is the mind of concepts. This eye is perceiving the relative world that is always changing through cycles of birth, death and rebirth. Nothing stays the same. This is the *samsara* that the Buddha was referring to when he said, 'All life is suffering.' Due to our attachments, aversions and desires to things being a certain way, we suffer. If you were free from those attachments, you would be watching the film of life with wonder and compassion.

In this analogy, your other eye is aware of that which never changes – the 'empty' screen of pure being or 'is-ness' onto which this film of life is projected. This is absolute, pure awareness. (It is not truly empty, but full of all potentiality. It is no-thing as of yet. It is not, however, nothing.) It exists in all of us as the absolute ground of our being. It has been described as the shadow of the creator, while the manifest world is the creation. It is one eye looking out and one eye looking in.

In Tibetan Dzogchen Buddhism, the *vajra*, or *dorje*, symbolizes this with two eight-petalled lotus flowers emerging from a sphere. One represents the phenomenal world of appearances, called *samsara*, the other pure awareness, or *nirvana*. The sphere in the middle represents the highest enlightenment, as achieved by the Buddha.

Figure 49: The vajra *or* dorje *used in Buddhism*

In the Buddhist teachings these are known as the 'two truths': Everything has an absolute and a relative aspect – the absolute or ultimate is the inherent nature of everything, how things really are; the conventional or relative is how things appear. They are not to be understood as two separate dimensions, rather as two aspects of a single reality.[3] In *The Tibetan Book of Living and Dying* it says:

The posture we take when we meditate signifies that we are linking absolute and relative, sky and ground, heaven and earth, like two wings of a bird, integrating the skylike, deathless nature of mind and the ground of our transient, mortal nature.

<small>SOGYAL RINPOCHE, *THE TIBETAN BOOK OF LIVING AND DYING*</small>

The *vajra* is also called the diamond, as this pure naked awareness cuts through everything but remains unchanged. In rituals the practitioner also has a bell, representing the feminine energy, the world of manifestation, and in this context the *vajra* represents the male energy, awareness. This union of the male and female energy is often depicted as the erotic or sexual union of God/Goddess Shiva/Shakti (*as shown in the figure below*).

Figure 50: A statue of the union of Shiva and Shakti

Carlos Castaneda, whose book *The Teachings of Don Juan* turned a whole lot of people on to mystical ideas in the 1970s, describes this apparent duality as the shaman's folly – the shaman knows that it is all illusory, but acts as if they do not know.

Only the ego is serious.

Of course, the ego, that is consciousness attached, gets caught in our conceptual interpretation of the world and does anything to avoid the 'void' – just being in emptiness. We use all sorts of a-void-dance techniques. That's what *samsara* is – a dance around the void. Yet just being is rather wonderful.

One popular training which takes us towards this stillness is Vipassana meditation from the Buddhist tradition (*see Resources*). Vipassana is, in the words of S.N. Goeka,

> *...observing reality as it is by observing the truth inside – this is knowing oneself directly and experientially. As one practises, one keeps freeing oneself from the misery of mental impurities. From the gross, external, apparent truth, one penetrates to the ultimate truth of mind and matter. Then one transcends that, and experiences a truth which is beyond mind and matter, beyond time and space, beyond the conditioned field of relativity: the truth of total liberation from all defilements, all impurities, all suffering. Whatever name one gives this ultimate truth is irrelevant: it is the final goal of everyone.*

One of my favourite stories is that of Shankara:

> *Shankara, the great Indian master from the eighth century, was taken as a boy to the Maharajah's opulent palace. Looking at the concubines and servants, dancers, peacocks and abundant feast of tasty delights, he said, 'This does not impress me. It is all illusory.'*

> *On his next visit, the Maharajah let out the lions. Shankara narrowly escaped being eaten alive by climbing up a tree.*

> *The lion-tamers caught the lions and the Maharajah walked towards Shankara in the tree and laughingly said, 'Illusory lions, Shankara?'*

> *He replied, 'The illusory lions chased the illusory Shankara up the illusory tree.'*

> *But he had still bothered to climb the tree.*

This is a great example of someone with one eye on the absolute and one on the relative. It is the alchemy of these two that is the greatest connection, when the seer and the seen become one, when nothing exists which is not consciousness.

Alchemical Practices

Alchemy is often taken to refer to the mythical act of converting base metals into gold. But really it is an allegory for the clarification of the human consciousness to the point of enlightenment, the equal awareness of the relative and absolute, and the fullest expression of an individual.

The act of human creation, when the sperm hits the egg, is also alchemy. How exactly does the spark of life produce a new being? It is a mysterious and wonderful thing. But this creative 'Eros' energy is not limited to the act of procreation. It is also the energy of life, the pulse of creation and evolution.

Alchemical practices have existed for thousands of years in mystical traditions going back to the Egyptians and Zoroastrians, the Hindus and Buddhists, the Sufis and the Greeks. Some include acts involving sex, some are internal meditations for transmutation and some have involved sacred elements. All these practices are called *tantra*, which is defined in the dictionary as 'a tradition of beliefs and meditation and ritual practices that seeks to channel the divine energy of the macrocosm or godhead into the human microcosm, in order to attain moksha, liberation'.

Many people mistakenly think that tantra is about sex. While there are tantric practices that do involve sex, even in these the purpose is not to have a wonderful orgasm (not that there is anything wrong with this), but to channel the immense sexual energy, the fire of life, in order to create a spiritual opening and an expansion of consciousness. In some traditions monks would engage in a specific ritual with a young and very sexy consort, fully trained in the art, who would incite the monk to the point of crystallized pre-explosion, but then that energy would be sent up the central energy channel in the body to force an opening in the crown chakra and a spiritual awakening.

The idea that alchemists were turning base metals into gold may have come from a misunderstanding of the original Siddha tantra practitioners in northern India and Tibet, from the third to 11th centuries, who did very interesting things with mercury and sulphur. Mercury was considered to represent Shiva's sperm and sulphur is one of the most abundant elements spewed forth by volcanoes – eruptions from Mother Earth. By combining mercury with sulphur in specific and ritualized ways, it was believed that immortality would be achieved. This is definitely one of those practices that deserves the caution: *Do not try this at home!* Mercury is extremely toxic and can kill you, but first you go mad. Hatters used to polish top hats with mercury and, absorbing the mercury, become 'as mad as a hatter'.

Another alchemical practice from the ancient tantric traditions of India involved the ritual combination and consumption of sperm (aka Shiva) and menstrual blood (aka Shakti). Blood, coloured red, the colour of flaming magma, the blood of the Earth, represented the Mother Earth principle.[4]

This one may not seem that appealing either. But I am only filling you in on a bit of tantric lore and history, not recommending anything as such! At least, not yet.

Figure 51: The ouroboros (© Ashnandoah)

In many traditions, from the Egyptians to the Greeks, the symbol of the ouroboros, the snake eating its own tail, represented the tantric practice of the assimilation of apparent opposites – the desire for life, love and lust and the desire for transcendence, the ultimate freedom – that is, the union of Heaven and Earth.

The snake also frequently appears as the great transforming intelligence in the visions of those undertaking *ayahuasca* ceremonies (*see page 36*). Many people have reported 'alchemical' transformations as a result. One well-written, informative and entertaining book is *Shaman in Stilettos* by Anna Hunt. It describes her transformation from a celebrity journalist into a shaman.

The Mayan culture's Hunab Ku symbol, meaning 'only God' has the hallmarks of two forces uniting. In Taoism the union of these two principles is symbolized in the yin–yang symbol.

Figure 52: Hunab Ku (left) and yin–yang symbol (right) (Thinkstock/ MariaTkach)

The wilder, also known as 'left-handed', path of tantra has pretty much died out now and has been replaced by specific practices involving yogic breathing, hatha yoga positions, yantras, mantras – and initiation from a master or guru. These are the roots of the yoga we know today, which is more often than not seen as a holistic exercise routine than preparation for deep tantric experiences.

The Shree Yantra (*see page 147*) has, however, been widely used in this context. It shows the union of the two energies, represented as upward- and downward-pointing triangles. It also represents the female force of attraction and desire, hallmarks of the goddess Lalita in the Hindu tradition.

Lessons from Lalita

Among the Indian gods and goddesses, Lalita Tripura Sundari, to use her full name, has many empowered feminine qualities, including authority, sensuality and the power to bestow extraordinary inner blissfulness. Shankara describes her like this:

You are consciousness, ether, air, fire, water and earth.
You are the Universe, O Mother.
But in order to perform your play as the Universe,
You take the form of the wife of Shiva
And appear before us as exquisite happiness.

Her appearance is queenly, as befits a goddess who epitomizes world-creating feminine power. In *Awakening Shakti*, Sally Kempton describes her like this:

She sits on a lotus, which emerges out of a bed supported by the reclining form of Sadashiva (her consort). The legs of the bed are four male Gods: Brahma the creator, Vishnu the sustainer, Rudra the destroyer, and Shiva in his form as destroyer and the Lord of Yoga. Her commanding position symbolizes her status as supreme Power, worshipped even by those who govern the cosmos itself.

Figure 53: Lalita
(© Ekabhumi Charles Ellik. Reprinted with permission of Sounds True, Inc.)

*Delicately featured, she has a luminous, rosy body. Her rosy colour
signifies she is flush with both sexual fulfilment and spiritual delight,
and her body is moist with nectar and bliss. She has heavy breasts and a
narrow waist. The crescent moon adorns her forehead, and her smile, it is
said, overwhelms Shiva.*

Sally goes on to say that:

*One key to connecting with Lalita is to recognise her as the electric energy
that pulses through your body which you can draw on for creative action
as well in relationship. To realise the empowered erotic in relationship
demands first that it is realised inwardly as autonomous power of self-
love. Bringing Lalita alive as an inner archetype, through meditation, is
the first step toward incarnating her in your relationship with your own
body and in relationship with another.*

With that in mind, Sally, who is a master of meditation, gives a powerful
meditation on Lalita to embody her alchemical power (*see page 238*).

The most internally dynamic expression of Lalita's power is as
kundalini Shakti, the transforming power that sleeps at the base of the
spine until it is awakened by the force of the Goddess. Sally points out
that natural desire creates life; it is generative:

*When properly understood and channelled, the energy of desire can
also become the fuel for higher consciousness and creativity. For this
reason, the Tantric and Taoist yogic traditions work with technologies for
transmuting sexual energy into spiritual energy.*

Tantric Paths and Practices

Tantra, as we have seen, refers to the transmutation of the basic
energy of desire, or Eros, into spiritual energy for transformation and
upliftment. It is the same energy. The Eros, or sensual energy, is the
quality of allurement and attraction. It is the gravitational pull that

attracts atomic particles and quarks into their relationships, as well as the pull of sex in a relationship that ultimately creates new life. It is the fuel of the love, joy and wonder of life. Tantric practices are, in essence, working with this quality of desire, starting with sexual energy and bringing it up into the heart, the head and the crown as a means of opening up the higher centres to experience the highest bliss – the ultimate connection to the Divine, to Creation.

This transforming power has the nature of bursting forth. *Tantra* derives from the Sanskrit root *tan*, meaning 'to stretch, span or expand', and out of that tension there is a vibration, known as the *Spanda* (the German word *Spannung* means both 'tension, excitement, suspense' and 'voltage'). This was described in the eighth to 10th centuries in Kashmir by Kshemaraja, a disciple of Abhinavagupta, a disciple of Vasugupta, who is thought to have originated the verses, or *karikas*, of Spanda.[5] Here are a couple of my favourite verses, paraphrased:

> *I am happy, I am sad, I am frustrated, etc. These thoughts are like beads on a necklace of I am.*

> *In states of extreme anger, great laughter and delight, in an impasse when you don't know what to do, or when you are running for your life, there is Spanda.*

Spanda is the creative tension that exists as things come into being – as the potential (Shakti) comes into existence or awareness (Shiva). It is, essentially, orgasmic, bursting forth. Unlike the dual, or separate, concept of traditional science – that there is matter and there is awareness of it (for example subject and object) – these deeper non-dual philosophies say that nothing exists without awareness, that there is a flow of potential into awareness and that potential is always latent in awareness. Everything is connected.

Former rabbi, philosopher and scholar of Judaism Dr Marc Gafni, author of the highly acclaimed book *The Mystery of Love*, describes the journey to wholeness from the teachings of the Kabbalah in the

Jewish mystical tradition. This results in your 'unique self', the highest expression of who you can be, tapping into the erotic energy of life. This is further explained in his book *Your Unique Self*. He gives a simple exercise involving an orange to give you an experience of the erotic nature of life in the mundane (*see page 241*).

Marc explains that there are four basic approaches or attitudes to sexuality, which he calls:

Sex positive – sex is lovely, it's a panacea, a good thing.

Sex negative – it is dangerous, distracting and essentially sinful.

Sex neutral – it is just a human function, observed as the sex researcher Kinsey did.

Sex sacred – which is associated with the fact that sex is the generator of life.

But, as he points out, none of those four exhaust our experience of sexuality – after all, even in 'sacred sex', 99.9 per cent of sexuality is not procreative. I asked him for his take on tantra and how that worked in Jewish mysticism. He explained:

Tantra means to expand the sexual, erotic and explosive nature of life beyond just the sexual domain and into your life. Sex is considered sacred in that it procreates life in a woman's womb, thus sexuality represents the evolutionary impulse, the drive to more emergence, depth and connection. It is the evolutionary drive pulsing inside you. Evolution is happening in you. This is not something generic. It is very personal to you becoming the fullest expression of yourself.

In the Hindu tradition, as we have seen, that evolutionary force is called *ananda*, meaning 'bliss'. This is the public face of Eros, the erotic energy. Eros also has the associated meanings of 'holy', 'death' and 'being on the inside' and is associated with the Goddess. In the Jewish tradition, Kabbalah also means 'to receive'. It too is associated with the Goddess. In the Roman tradition the Goddess is Venus.

Marc explains how this is ritualized in orthodox Judaism:

In the tefillin ritual the practitioner ties a black cube to their arm [as we saw on page 145], *and another to the top of their head, first putting their arm through a loop made of the black leather strap – an act of penetration of a line into a circle – then binds their arm with seven turns of the strap. It is certainly an erotic act. It's bondage with black leather, after all.*

In this ritual:

…you are making an oath to fulfil your birthright to incarnate your fullness, your truest expression of your unique self. In this sense it is not dissimilar to the Bodhisattva vow in Buddhism.

Bodhi is the highest state, the fullest potential as a human being. The Bodhisattva vow is to attain complete enlightenment for the benefit of all sentient beings. It is consistent with Sheldrake's morphic resonance theory, in which the collective memory and evolutionary intention of humanity are evolving. By being the fullness of who you can be, which is unique and personal to you, you are actually shaping humanity's future, bringing the energy of Eros into life.

In Sufism, Hu is the name of God. It is also the first breath, the first word or sound in Egyptian mythology. It is interesting that we are named a 'hu-man-being' – a man being God, or God being man or God-Man, being or becoming our fullest expression.

This tantric approach is quite different from the nihilistic philosophies of early Hinduism and Buddhism, where the goal was the total annihilation of 'ego' or 'personality' to be in the absolute reality, the emptiness or void. While the practitioner, for example of Zen, may actually have an awakening into bliss out of achieving this 'empty' state, the danger, I suggest, is that this denies the natural, full expression, beyond ego, of ourselves. We are all different, yet enthused by the same divine pulsing energy that is life itself, constantly evolving. This state of being, at its highest, is described by the great Shaivite guru Abhinavagupta as:

> *It is Shiva himself, of unimpeded Will and pellucid consciousness, who is ever sparkling in my heart. It is his highest Shakti herself that is ever playing at the edge of my senses. The entire world gleams as the wondrous delight of pure I-consciousness.*[6]

For him, subject and object ceased to be separate.

In truth, this total connection is neither easy to explain in words, nor can I truly do it justice, due both to my own limited understanding and experience and by virtue of attempting to simplify deep truths that can only be experienced. This is the territory and the goal of the non-dual mystical traditions such as Dzogchen Buddhism, Kashmir Shaivism, mystical Judaism, the Neoplatonic schools and the Sufism of Islam as proposed by Ibn Arabi and Rumi among others. They are really accessed through the teachings of masters who embody the state that comes from this higher level of consciousness. Another is the approach of Oscar Ichazo and his Arica School trainings. There are, I am sure, other paths to the same understanding, including the Toltec and Quechuan traditions in South America. I can, at least, point to their existence for those who wish to explore more on their journey towards connection.

I realize this territory is not for everyone and everything happens in its own time. Once layers of the onion start to unravel, we may find ourselves naturally drawn to people, disciplines and paths that can help us reach the highest level of connection.

In much the same way that I have discovered the highest level of health occurs when all 'systems' are working, I believe that the highest expression of who we are, and our greatest ability to live in the world and make a difference to it, occurs when we are truly connected on all levels, as the next and final chapter shows.

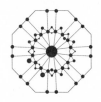

Chapter 15

Five Keys to Connection

The purpose of this book has been to explore different facets of connection and to open up possibilities for evolving into a more connected experience of life. The ultimate goal of our evolution as human beings is to be fully connected.

There are five keys to do this:

1. *Sexual, sensual and erotic connection* – expressing yourself as a sexual and sensual being, in touch with your own enthusiasm for life, true to your longings and desires, enjoying the pleasures of the senses and orienting your life to that which has the most juice for you. This relates to the element fire and the *muladhara* chakra at the base of the spine and perineum. (In the Indian system the *Svadhisthana* chakra in the pelvic area is the centre of sexuality.)

2. *Body and Earth connection* – being in touch with, respecting and nurturing your body with good nutrition and energy-generating exercise, and respecting and protecting the Earth through conscious living. This relates to the element earth and the *hara*, the energy centre below the navel.

3. *Social and self connection* – being in touch with your heart, your love and deepest feelings and reaching out to your social group,

society and humanity as a whole, and also to the realm of animals, to share and make this world a better place. This relates to the element air, which we all breathe, and the *anahata* heart centre.

4. *Intellectual connection* – having clear thoughts, beyond fears, limiting beliefs and limitations, openly enquiring and questioning and learning and tapping into the wisdom of the intellect, the source of insights and the illumination beyond the thinking mind. This relates to the *ajna* chakra, the 'third eye' centre and the element water, as thoughts ripple through the mind.

5. *Spiritual connection* – being in touch with the field of being, the consciousness in which everything is happening, your pure awareness, the all-pervasive benevolent intelligence that is your essential nature. This relates to the crown centre, the *sahasrara*, and the element ether, representing the space in which everything happens.

These keys also relate to the five main anatomical cavities of the body, the five elements, the five Platonic solids, the five energy centres and their corresponding mantras and colours, and the five aspects of our existence.

ASPECT/ KEY	ENERGY	CAVITY	CHAKRA	COLOUR	SOUND	SHAPE
Spiritual	Unity	Dorsal	Sahasrara	Violet	Ah or Aum	Dodecahedron
Intellectual	Clarity	Cranial	Ajna	Blue	Om	Icosahedron
Emotional	Love	Thoracic	Anahata	Green	Yam	Octahedron
Physical	Vitality	Abdominal	Hara	Yellow/ orange	Ram	Cube
Sexual/ sensational	Eros	Pelvic	Muladhara	Red	Lam	Tetrahedron

Figure 54: The five keys and how they relate to the various aspects of our existence

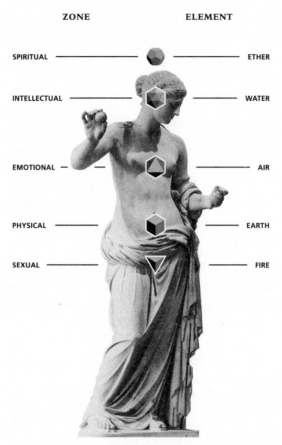

Figure 55: The five zones of connection and their associated elements.
(Reproduced with the kind permission of Malcolm Stewart
from Symbols of Eternity.*) See colour section.*

You may recognize those aspects that you are least in touch with and those that are your strengths. Remember that the Connection Quiz at www.patrickholford.com/connectionquiz gives you an assessment of where you are now, showing your strengths and weaknesses. Some people are full of heart but quite ungrounded. Others are intellectually sharp but out of touch with their deepest feelings. Some are focused on transcendence and out of touch with their body and/or sexuality. We all have our strengths and weaknesses – the weaknesses being our greatest potential areas for evolution.

Some of the ideas expressed in this book are on the edge of our understanding and often challenge the status quo. They are unlikely to be the whole truth and no doubt will also evolve in time. We have explored them in the spirit of enquiry.

One fundamental idea is that we, as humanity, are connected and that our learnings, and sufferings, are shared. Judging by the state of the world, the awful conflicts and wars, the unsustainable consumption of resources, the lack of respect for the Earth and its animals, insects and trees, the denial of the sacred and mysterious, the vast disparity of wealth and the epidemics of man-made diseases, it is clear that we need a way forward that is not based on separation and greed but on mutual respect and an understanding of our connectedness and interdependence.

As well as taking what you can from this book for your own benefit and evolution, my hope is that it will inspire you to take some action that will make a difference, however small, for the benefit of all. So we can work together, each of us in our unique way, to make this world a better paradise.

To that I dedicate this book. Thank you for being part of it. I hope you have enjoyed reading it as much as I have writing it.

The perfect prayer

Om
Purnamadah Purnamidam
Purnat Purnamudachyate
Purnasya Purnamadaya
Purnameva Vashishyate
Om shanti, shanti, shanti

This (the absolute) is perfect.
That (the relative universe) is perfect.
If you take the perfect from the perfect,
only the perfect remains.

Peace, peace, peace.

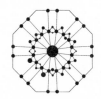

Exercise Appendix

Exercise 1: Clearing Emotional Charge

This exercise is a simple and effective way to clear emotional charge with a friend or partner.

There are three parts to the exercise:

- The first establishes the shared basis of love with your friend or partner, which is important for creating a space for listening with an open heart or mind.

- The second, from this position of love, allows each person to express their emotional charge.

- The third allows for any agreements or intentions to be set.

- It is important that you end the exercise by re-establishing the love that underlies your relationship.

It is helpful, but not essential, to first do HeartMath's Quick Coherence® Technique (*on page 168*).

So, here is how it goes:

1. Sit facing each other. Make a connection with your partner, recognizing your shared love. For example, look them in the eye, either hold hands or say 'I love you', or make a gesture establishing your connection.

2. One partner is active and speaks while the other listens totally, without comment. If you are the listener, check that your intention is to take responsibility for your part in the situation, not to defend yourself. Do your best to maintain eye contact and also a heart connection throughout. Then, for the identical amount of time, you switch roles. You may wish to set a limit of 10 minutes each. The time limit encourages getting to the bottom of emotionally charged incidents.

3. When it is your turn to speak, bring to mind a charged incident. It helps to be very specific. 'When you raised your voice at me yesterday, I felt angry...' or 'When you answered the phone in the middle of me sharing something important with you, I felt abandoned.' Describe whatever you have charge with, basically whatever makes you feel separate from the other person.

4. If you are the listener, your job is simply to empathize with the validity of the other person's point of view, even if you don't agree with it. This is not how most people listen most of the time – we often listen for how we can defeat the other person's argument. The purpose at this point is simply to understand that how the situation occurs for the other person is valid. Even if you think, *How could you possibly think or feel that?*, it is important to respect that if another person says that's how it is for them, that is valid. Agreeing with it or not at this stage is not particularly relevant, nor

is debate. The job of the listener is simply to get the story from the other person's point of view. Do not interrupt. Show that you are actively listening by maintaining eye contact and keeping your body language open.

Sometimes it is helpful, especially if a person is feeling unheard or misunderstood, to repeat back to them what they have said without adding or taking anything away, attempting to capture the content and the feeling exactly. The person sharing the emotionally charged incident then responds to either say yes, they feel understood, or to give helpful feedback for the listener to retune their replication of their experience.

5. If necessary, you can keep going back and forth (always taking equal time) until there are no more incidents of emotional charge coming to mind. If someone does interrupt, just give them a gentle reminder of the agreement so that they go back to listening.

6. At the end, each person may share, if they wish, any agreements or intentions regarding their own actions they wish to make. Avoid getting into heated discussions or forcing agreements on each other.

    Come to a point where you re-establish the love and connection you share. Acknowledge this in some way and close the exercise.

If you don't have an emotional charge with a particular person, or the opportunity to clear it face to face, but have a charge from a particular event, you can adapt this exercise by having a listening friend who will not interject but truly hear you.

Exercise 2: Negative Transference Exercise

This exercise from the Hoffman Process (*see page 161*), used with permission, explores what is called *transference*. This is reacting to others the way we learned to react to our parents.

We are often unaware when we are in transference with someone and tend to make assumptions about them – their thoughts, feelings and behaviour. When we're in transference with someone we're in an altered state – we're unconsciously reacting to that person as though they are a parent and we are once again a child.

In this state we see in others what we are unwilling or unable to see in ourselves. The patterns we see in the other person are our own patterns, 'You spot it, you got it.' We feel certain we know what's going on in the other person – what they are thinking and/or feeling. We hear, see, and perceive things that are not always there – and don't hear the things that are being said. We're no longer in relationship with the other person. We end up going into a vicious cycle – one pattern triggers another pattern and another pattern and so on.

Being free of transference doesn't mean we are going to like everyone and everything. Bad things will still happen. However, we can sort out what our transference is in these situations. For example, someone may push in front of us in line or make a rude remark – nobody likes that. But when we have had a parent who pushed us around all the time, got in our space, embarrassed us or was humiliating, we have historical wounds around this behaviour that make the present-day bump feel like a huge shove, and we have a very big reaction. When we can divest the present interaction of our history, our wounds, we can get a better sense of what we actually need to say, what belongs to the relationship, what's present and what is past and historical and is our own to hold responsibly.

This exercise is a wonderful tool when we find ourselves being triggered by another person. Often just recognizing and/or writing out our transference can end it.

There is a saying in the Hoffman Process: 'Never waste a good trigger.' These triggers can lead us onto a personal path of discovery. Given that our life is our responsibility, it is worth taking the time to see what triggers us, identify the patterns and do our patterns work. This is not a communication tool. This is a tool of self-reflection.

This exercise will provide you with an invaluable structure for resolving negative emotional reactions with others by understanding where your patterns of negative reactions come from and taking that responsibility.

Preparation

On page 233 you will see a worksheet for writing down an incident that evoked a negative reaction. Copy this page, and write down a few incidents that are still bothering you. This is for your own use only, as this exercise is copyrighted to Hoffman International and cannot be used without their written permission. Here are some notes to help you get the most from this exercise.

- *'I had a negative reaction to you'* – write down the person's name.

- *'in'* – only write down the time and place the reaction happened. This is factual information. For example: 'Saturday morning in bed.'

- *'I experienced you as'* – this is where you write everything else; your experience and perceptions:
  - ~ judgements you made about the person
  - ~ what you thought they were thinking, feeling, doing
  - ~ what you experienced them saying

Name-calling is not useful – bitch, asshole. Don't do that. Instead, name the perceived qualities: cold, unfeeling, writing me off, etc.

- *'Like my'* – now read what you've written and trace each pattern back to a parent or surrogate parental figure. Then write that parent, or any combination of parents, in the space.

- *'The patterns I went into were'* – is the section for you to name all the patterns you went into in that moment.

- Now list the patterns you went into and trace each pattern back to a parent.

- Then write that parent, or any combination of parents, in the space that reads, 'Which I learned from my…'

Taking Responsibility

Now look at what you wrote and choose one. Could be:

- your strongest/biggest reaction
- one that is familiar to you – this one happens in your life regularly
- one where you still feel a charge
- one where you feel you have a lot to learn

If you want to take this a step further in clearing the air in a relationship, arrange a dedicated time with the person involved where you can be with them, uninterrupted.

Say that you'd like to share an experience of a reaction that you had and ask them to listen as much as possible with understanding and without judgement.

Take a deep breath and make eye contact. Be fully with them and share with them some of your inner experience as long as both of you feel safe. We suggest that you keep this light, but at the same time honest. People have very different thresholds of what they can listen to and receive without feeling criticized. Be clear that your intention is to let go of the past.

When you have said what you need to say, look at the person again, check in with your feelings, and acknowledge for yourself whether you are free of transference or still in transference. Meaning right then, in that moment, are you free from or still in the old reaction?

NEGATIVE TRANSFERENCE

I had a negative reaction to you_____
name

in_____
where and when only

I experienced you as_____

_____
my perceptions, judgements and questions

_____

_____

_____

_____

like my_____
mother/father/surrogate

The patterns I went into were _____

_____

_____

_____

_____

_____

Which I learned from my _____
mother/father/surrogate

Figure 56 © Hoffman International 2015. Used with permission. This exercise is the copyright of Hoffman International and cannot be used or reproduced without their expressed permission.

Exercise 3: Healing the Body Visualization

This is a simple exercise to bring your awareness to any part of your body that needs healing.

1.   The first step is to go into a deep state of relaxation.

     Lie down on your back on the floor, making yourself comfortable with cushions or mats if need be, with your hands slightly away from your body, and your legs uncrossed and slightly apart. Close your eyes. Focus on your breathing and allow your breaths to deepen slightly.

     Take a moment to scan through your body and relax it in the following way, starting with your feet:

     Relax the muscles in your feet. Feel your feet growing heavy and sinking towards the floor.

     Move your focus to your calves. Again, sense their weight. Consciously relax them and feel them sinking into the floor.

     Now focus on your knees. Sense their weight and let them sink into the floor.

     Repeat this for each part of your body as you move up towards your head.

     Upper legs and thighs, then buttocks and pelvis.

     Abdomen (above your pelvis but below your chest).

     Chest.

     Hands, lower arms, then upper arms.

     Shoulders, then neck.

Face, eyes, cheeks, mouth and jaw. Pay particular attention to your jaw muscles and unclench them if they are tense.

Consciously relax them and feel your head growing heavy and sinking towards the floor.

Become aware of the space between your body and the floor. Where your body touches the floor. Focus on this space that is not your body and not the floor.

2. Now visualize that your body is made out of billions of tiny cells and each cell is made of energy in the form of light. All your cells are working tirelessly to keep your healthy.

3. Become aware of your heart space at the centre of your chest. As you inhale, imagine that you an inhaling pure white light into the heart space. As you exhale, imagine that light is spreading throughout your body, filling your cells with light.

4. Scan your body and if there is an area that feels blocked, or needs healing, focus on the light accumulating in your heart as you inhale and moving into that area of your body as you exhale.

5. Imagine that the surrounding cells also share their light with this area. Allow the cells in your entire body to fill with light.

6. To end this exercise, bring your awareness back to the room, the sounds around you, the sensation of your body against the floor. Open your eyes and in your own time sit up.

Do this exercise whenever you feel the need to help heal your body.

Exercise 4: Diakath Breathing™

This breathing exercise (reproduced with the kind permission of Oscar Ichazo) connects the Kath Point™, the body's centre of equilibrium, with the diaphragm muscle, so that deep breathing becomes natural and effortless. You can practise this exercise at any time, while sitting, standing or lying down, and for as long as you like. You can also practise it unobtrusively during moments of stress. It is an excellent natural relaxant and energy-booster, helping you to feel more connected and in tune.

The diaphragm is a dome-shaped muscle attached to the bottom of the ribcage. The Kath Point is located three finger-widths below the belly and 2.5cm (1 inch) in. If you place your index finger just below your navel, your ring finger will be at the level of the Kath point. When you put your awareness in this point, it becomes easy to be aware of your entire body.

Ideally, find somewhere quiet first thing in the morning. When breathing, inhale and exhale through your nose. As you inhale, you will expand your lower belly from the Kath Point and your diaphragm muscle. This allows the lungs to fill with air from the bottom to the top. As you exhale, the belly and the diaphragm muscle relax, allowing the lungs to empty from top to bottom.

1. Sit comfortably, in a quiet place with your spine straight.

2. As you inhale and exhale slowly through your nose, focus your attention on your Kath point.

3. Let your belly expand from your Kath point as you inhale slowly, deeply and effortlessly. Feel your diaphragm being pulled towards the Kath as your lungs fill with air from the

bottom to the top. On the exhale, relax both your belly and your diaphragm, emptying your lungs from top to bottom.

4. Repeat at your own pace.

Every morning, sit down in a quiet place before breakfast and practise Diakath Breathing for a few minutes. Whenever you are stressed throughout the day, check your breathing. Practise Diakath Breathing for nine breaths. This is great to do before an important meeting or when something has upset you and you need to calm yourself.

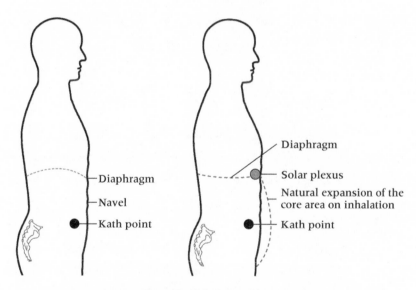

Figure 57: Diakath Breathing
(© 1972, 2016 by Oscar Ichazo. Used with permission. All rights reserved. The Diakath Breathing illustration is a copyright of Oscar Ichazo. Diakath, Diakath Breathing, Kath, and Kath Point are trademarks of Oscar Ichazo.)

Exercise 5: Lalita Meditation

Find a comfortable posture in a quiet place to contemplate the goddess Lalita.

Figure 58: Lalita (© Ekabhumi Charles Ellik. Reprinted with permission of Sounds True, Inc.)

As always with the goddesses, begin by invoking her unique presence.

Imagine her form: slender, delicate, with large breasts. Her skin is luminous and rosy. She wears a red-silk sari without a blouse. Her eyes are large, round, fringed by long lashes. She's smiling. She wears a necklace set with rubies, pearls and diamonds as well as a golden crown on her long, waving hair. She sits in the air in front of you, and you feel her power infusing your body.

As you draw her Shakti in with your breath, you draw into yourself the power of radiance, fascination, and wisdom. You feel the rosy light of Tripura Sundari flowing into your entire sacral region. As it does, she clears all forms of sexual wounding and the traumas that freeze your sexuality or create different forms of sexual addiction, that create shame, fear or avoidance.

As you exhale, the energy of Tripura Sundari flows as empowered sexual energy from your sacrum up the centre of your body, filling you with rose-coloured light.

Inhaling, you breathe in the Shakti of Tripura Sundari through your heart. Her rosy light fills your heart, dispelling the wounds of being misunderstood, washing away your timidity and fear of standing in your own [feminine] heart. As Tripura Sundari's energy expands, you feel compassion and love flowing through your heart. With the exhalation, you recognize that everything within the field of your experience is connected. As your heart expands, the sense of 'we' expands. In whatever way possible, and to whatever degree that you can, you let go of the skin boundaries and feel yourself expanding out to encompass the world around you.

Now you inhale the light flowing from the goddess's third eye into your third eye, drawing in her power of discernment, of discrimination. As her radiance spreads through your brain, you realize that your body is made of her light and that everything you can see or know is irradiated with her light.

Now you draw the image of the goddess into your own body. Feel yourself filled with her radiant erotic energy, dancing through you in every atom and molecule of your body. Feel yourself suffused with divine pride, as she empowers you with her dignity and joy. Feel your innate freedom as her freedom dances through you, loosening every block and area of tightness that constricts the energy in your body. Feel yourself filled with her joy and with her tears as you recognize that her radiant body connects you to everybody in the world.

Used with permission of Sally Kempton, from Awakening Shakti: The Transformative Power of the Goddesses of Yoga. *Visit www.sallykempton.com for more meditations and details on her books and workshops. Visit www.soundstrue.com and search for 'Sally Kempton's* Awakening Shakti' *for a four-CD audio download. The Lalita meditation introduction and the meditation is on the fourth CD (0402 and 0403 on the audio).*

Exercise 6: Erotic Orange Exercise

This simple exercise helps you to connect with the erotic nature of simple acts in life. You need to obtain a fresh orange, tangerine or satsuma.

1. Hold the orange. Feel the shape of it, feel its texture. Delight in its shape and colour.

2. Smell its fragrance.

3. Now start to peel it, to undress it, very slowly. Become aware of the delicate white underside of its skin. Feel its softness.

4. When you have completely disrobed the orange, again feel its roundness. Be aware of its contours and segments and smell, its fragrance and latent juiciness.

5. Split the sections. Feel the delicacy of the inner skin separating.

6. Before you place it in your mouth, be aware that this orange will become you, energizing you, healing you with its nutrients, supporting your life. Offer your gratitude.

7. Now take a section and simply place it in your mouth. Be aware of its texture.

8. As your bite into the segment, feel the sweet juices and the fibres in your mouth. Taste the nectarean sweetness.

9. Continue in this way until you feel completely satisfied.

A nice variation is to do this with a partner, each with their own orange, and then, instead of feeding yourself, feed your partner.

This simple exercise may remind you to be more present and to offer gratitude when you prepare and eat a meal. However, the same sensory delight exists in many mundane daily acts.

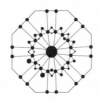

References

Preface

1. M.E. Register *et al.*, 'Development and psychometric testing of the register – connectedness scale for older adults', *Research in Nursing & Health* (2011); 34(1), 60–72

2. M.E. Register and J. Herman, 'A middle-range theory for generative quality of life for the elderly', *Advances in Nursing Science* (2006); 29(4): 340–50; www.ncbi.nlm.nih.gov/pubmed/17135802

Introduction: From Disconnection to Connection

1. www.telegraph.co.uk/women/sex/1-in-10-of-us-check-our-smartphones-during-sex---seriously/

2. Timothy D. Wilson, *et al.*, 'Just think: The challenges of the disengaged mind', *Science* (2014); Jul 4; 345(6,192): 75–7; www.ncbi.nlm.nih.gov/pmc/articles/PMC4330241/

3. www.theguardian.com/science/2016/mar/01/british-win-neuroscience-prize-grete-lundbeck-tim-bliss-graham-collingridge-richard-morris

4. *See* pps.sagepub.com/content/7/6/528.

Chapter 2: Love is the Proof that Consciousness is Shared

1. T. Shomrat and M. Levin, 'An automated training paradigm reveals long-term memory in planarians and its persistence through head regeneration', *J. Exp. Biol.* (2013), 15 Oct; 216(Pt 20): 3,799–810. *See also* now.tufts.edu/articles/total-recall.

2. *See* www.bbc.co.uk/news/science-environment-13452711.

3. *See* this film at www.djsadhu.com/the-helical-model-vortex-solar-system-animation/.

4. For the latter, *see* classics.mit.edu/Plotinus/enneads.html.

5. Oscar Ichazo, *The Human Process for Enlightenment and Freedom*, Arica Institute, 1972, p.74

Chapter 3: The Chemistry of Culture and Consciousness

1. *See* scienceblogs.com/gregladen/2012/12/02/how-many-people-were-killed-as-witches-in-europe-from-1200-to-the-present/.

2. R.L. Carhart-Harris, 'Neural correlates of the LSD experience revealed by multimodal neuroimaging', *Proc. Natl. Acad. Sci. USA* (2016) Apr 26; 113(17): 4,853–8; *also* L. Roseman *et al.*, 'The effects of psilocybin and MDMA on between-network resting state functional connectivity in healthy volunteers', *Front. Hum. Neurosci.* (2014) May 27; 8: 204

3. *See* www.newbirthcompany.com/wp-content/uploads/2013/10/Undisturbed-Birth.pdf.

4. P. Oehen *et al.*, 'A randomized, controlled pilot study of MDMA-assisted psychotherapy for treatment of resistant, chronic Post-Traumatic Stress Disorder (PTSD)', *J. Psychopharmacol.* (2013), Jan; 27(1): 40–52; www.ncbi.nlm.nih.gov/pubmed/23118021

5. M.B. Young *et al.*, '3,4-Methylenedioxymethamphetamine facilitates fear extinction learning', *Transl. Psychiatry* (2015), 15 Sep; 5: e634; www.ncbi.nlm.nih.gov/pubmed/26371762

6. K.A. MacLean *et al.*, 'Mystical experiences occasioned by the hallucinogen psilocybin lead to increases in the personality domain of openness', *J. Psychopharmacol.* (2011), Nov; 25(11): 1,453–61; www.ncbi.nlm.nih.gov/pmc/articles/PMC3537171/

7. P. Gasser *et al.*, 'LSD-assisted psychotherapy for anxiety associated with a life-threatening disease: a qualitative study of acute and sustained subjective effects', *J. Psychopharmacol.* (2015), Jan; 29(1): 57–68; jop.sagepub.com/content/29/1/57

8. Young, op. cit.

Chapter 4: Say No to Drugs

1. Council for Evidence-based Psychiatry (CEP), 2013 data; cepuk.org/2015/04/10/latest-prescription-data-shows-consumption-psychiatric-drugs-continues-soar/

2. C. Coupland *et al.*, 'Antidepressant use and risk of adverse outcomes in older people: population-based cohort study', *British Medical Journal* (2011), 2 Aug; 343: d4,551; www.ncbi.nlm.nih.gov/pubmed/21810886

3. *See* www.telegraph.co.uk/news/health/news/12126146/Antidepressants-can-raise-the-risk-of-suicide-biggest-ever-review-finds.html; *also* T. Sharma *et al.*, 'Suicidality and aggression during antidepressant treatment: systematic review and meta-analyses based on clinical study reports', *British Medical Journal* (2016), 27 Jan; 352: i65; www.ncbi.nlm.nih.gov/pubmed/26819231

4. M. Pirmohamed *et al.*, 'Adverse drug reactions as cause of admission to hospital: prospective analysis of 18,820 patients', *British Medical Journal* (2004), 3 Jul; 329(7,456): 15–19; www.ncbi.nlm.nih.gov/pubmed/15231615

5. 'Medical error is the fifth-leading cause of death in the US', *Medical News Today*, Jun. 2007; www.medicalnewstoday.com/releases/75042.php

6. M.A. Makary and M. Daniel, 'Medical error: the third leading cause of death in the US', *BMJ* (2016); May 3; 353: i2,139

7. J. Le Noury *et al.*, 'Restoring Study 329: efficacy and harms of paroxetine and imipramine in treatment of major depression in adolescence', *British Medical Journal* (2015); 351: h4,320; study329.org/wp-content/uploads/2015/09/Study-329-Final.pdf

8. *See* cepuk.org/.

9. *See* secure.avaaz.org/en/petition/Stop_Drug_Companies_Killing_for_Profits/%5D.

10. *See* www.dailymail.co.uk/health/article-3234334/Prescription-pills-Britain-s-biggest-killer-effects-drugs-taken-insomnia-anxiety-kill-thousands-doctors-hand-like-Smarties.html#ixzz3mAz6KDRz.

11. *See* www.youtube.com/watch?v=_9cfjKOmPF8.

12. A.D. Smith and K. Yaffe, 'Dementia can be prevented: statement supported by international experts', *Journal of Alzheimer's Disease* 38 (2014); 699–703; file:///Users/admin/Downloads/igedpreventionstatementg8_2014__2_.pdf

13. M. Beydoun *et al.*, 'Epidemiologic studies of modifiable factors associated with cognition and dementia: systematic review and meta-analysis', *BMC Public Health* (2014), 14: 643; bmcpublichealth.biomedcentral.com/articles/10.1186/1471-2458-14-643

14. The research councils spent £156,000. For Food for the Brain's campaign, *see* www.foodforthebrain.org/alzheimers-prevention.aspx.

15. M.A. Arroll *et al.*, 'Nutritional interventions for the adjunctive treatment of schizophrenia: a brief review', *Nutr. J.* (2014), 16 Sep; www.ncbi.nlm.nih.gov/pubmed/25228271

16. J. Sarris *et al.*, 'Nutritional medicine as mainstream in psychiatry', *The Lancet* (2015); 23), 271–4; dx.doi.org/10.1016/S2215-036614)00051-0

Chapter 6: The Mind–Body Connection

1. E. Langer, *Mindfulness*, Addison Wesley, 1989

2. *See* en.wikipedia.org/wiki/Creative_visualization.

3. D. Radin *et al.*, 'Distant healing intention therapies: an overview of the scientific evidence', *Global Advances in Health Medicine* (2015), 4 Nov; (Suppl): 67–71. *See also* D. Radin *et al.*, 'Distant healing intention: definitions and evolving guidelines for laboratory studies', *Altern. Ther. Health Med.* (2003), May–Jun; 93 (Suppl): A31–43; www.ncbi.nlm.nih.gov/pubmed/?term=distance+healing+efficacy+Schlitz.

4. S. Feldman, 'Phantom limbs', *American Journal of Physiology* (1940), 53: 590–92

5. *See* www.sheldrake.org/research/morphic-resonance/introduction.

6. E.J. Giltay *et al.*, 'Dispositional optimism and all-cause and cardiovascular mortality in a prospective cohort of elderly Dutch men and women', *Archives of General Psychiatry* (2004); 61: 1,126–35

7. G.V. Ostir *et al.*, 'Emotional well-being predicts subsequent functional independence and survival', *Journal of American Geriatric Society* (2000); 48(5): 473–8

8. D. Danner *et al.*, 'Positive emotions in early life and longevity: findings from the nun study', *J. Pers. Soc. Psychol.* (2001), May; 805: 804–13. *See also* psychcentral.com/blog/archives/2010/10/27/proof-positive-can-heaven-help-us-the-nun-study-afterlife/.

9. N. Ranjit *et al.*, 'Psychosocial factors and inflammation in the multi-ethnic study of atherosclerosis', *Archives of Internal Medicine* (2007); 167: 174–81

10. L. Brydon *et al.*, 'Hostility and cellular aging in men from the Whitehall II cohort', *Biol. Psychiatry* (2012), 1 May; (719): 767–73; www.ncbi.nlm.nih.gov/pubmed/21974787

11. *See* M.J. Glade and K Smith, 'Role of omega-3 fatty acids in the treatment of depressive disorders: a comprehensive meta-analysis of randomized clinical trials', *PLoS ONE* (2014), 7 May; (95):e96905; www.ncbi.nlm.nih.gov/pubmed/24805797; *also* S. Garcia-Calzon *et al.*, 'Dietary inflammatory index and telomere length in subjects with a high cardiovascular disease risk from the PREDIMED-NAVARRA study: cross-sectional and longitudinal analyses over 5 y1', *Am. J. Clin. Nutr.* (2015) 9 Sep; doi: 10.3945/ajcn.115.116863; ajcn.nutrition.org/content/early/2015/09/09/ajcn.115.116863; *and* J. Zhang *et al.*, 'Ageing and the telomere connection: an intimate relationship with inflammation', *Ageing Res. Rev.* (2016), Jan; 25: 55–69; www.ncbi.nlm.nih.gov/pubmed/26616852

12. T.L. Jacobs *et al.*, 'Intensive meditation training, immune cell telomerase activity, and psychological mediators', *Psychoneuroendocrinology* (2011), Jun; 365: 664–81; www.ncbi.nlm.nih.gov/pubmed/ 21035949

Chapter 7: Methyl Magic and the Brain-Makers

1. F. Jerneren et al, Americasn Journal of Clinical Nutrition, 2015. Used with permission. See www.foodforthebrain.org/hcyevidence

2. K. Yurko-Mauro *et al.*, 'Docosahexaenoic acid and adult memory: a systematic review and meta-analysis', *PLoS ONE* (2015); 10(3): e0120391; www.ncbi.nlm.nih.gov/pmc/articles/PMC4364972/

3. W. Stonehouse, 'Does consumption of LC omega-3 PUFA enhance cognitive performance in healthy school-aged children and throughout adulthood? Evidence from clinical trials', *Nutrients* (2014), 22 Jul; 6(7): 2,730–58; www.ncbi.nlm.nih.gov/pubmed/25054550

4. M.J. Glade and K. Smith, 'Role of omega-3 fatty acids in the treatment of depressive disorders: a comprehensive meta-analysis of randomized clinical

trials', *PLoS ONE* (2014), 7 May; 9(5): e96905; www.ncbi.nlm.nih.gov/pubmed/24805797

5. Ibid.

6. V. Knott *et al.*, 'Neurocognitive effects of acute choline supplementation in low, medium and high-performer healthy volunteers', *Pharmacol. Biochem. Behav.* (2015), Apr; 131: 119–29; www.ncbi.nlm.nih.gov/pubmed/25681529

7. S.L. Ladd *et al.*, 'Effect of phosphatidylcholine on explicit memory', *Clin. Neuropharmacol.* (1993), Dec; 16(6): 540–49; www.ncbi.nlm.nih.gov/pubmed/9377589

Chapter 8: Generating Vital Energy

1. S. Cook *et al.*, 'High heart rate: a cardiovascular risk factor?', *Eur. Heart J.* (2006); 27(20): 2,387–93, doi: 10.1093/eurheartj/ehl259

2. Loyola University Health System, 'Boost your immune system, shake off stress by walking in the woods', *Science Daily*, 2013

3. R. Jahnke, F. Lin *et al.*, 'A comprehensive review of health benefits of *qigong* and *tai chi*', *American Journal of Health Promotion* (2010), 24(6), e1–25

4. D. Cohen *et al.*, 'Lifestyle Modification in Blood Pressure Study II (LIMBS): study protocol of a randomized controlled trial assessing the efficacy of a 24-week structured yoga program versus lifestyle modification on blood pressure reduction', *Contemp. Clin. Trials* (2013), Sep; 36(1): 32–40

5. N. Gothe *et al.*, 'The acute effects of yoga on executive function', *Journal of Physical Activity & Health* (2013)

6. P. Jin, 'Efficacy of *tai chi*, brisk walking, meditation, and reading in reducing mental and emotional stress', *Journal of Psychosomatic Research* (1992); 36: 361–70. *See also* M. Lee *et al.*, '*Qigong* reduced blood pressure and catecholamine levels of patients with essential hypertension', *International Journal of Neuroscience* (2003); 113: 1,691

7. C.C. Streeter *et al.*, 'Effects of yoga on the autonomic nervous system, gamma-aminobutyric-acid, and allostasis in epilepsy, depression, and post-traumatic stress disorder', *Medical Hypotheses* (2012)

Chapter 9

1. *See* www.i-sis.org.uk/SS-glyphosate.php.

2. R. McCraty, *Science of the Heart: Exploring the Role of the Heart in Human Performance, Volume 2*, HeartMath Institute

3. K. Sokal and P. Sokal, 'Earthing the human body influences physiologic processes', *Journal of Alternative and Complementary Medicine* (2011); 174: 1–8; www.ncbi.nlm.nih.gov/pmc/articles/PMC3154031/

4. G. Chevalier *et al.*, 'Earthing (grounding) the human body reduces blood viscosity—a major factor in cardiovascular disease', *Journal of Alternative and Complementary Medicine* (2013), Feb; 192: 102–10

5. C. Ober, 'Grounding the human body to neutralize bio-electrical stress from static electricity and EMFs', *The ESD and Electrostatics Magazine*; www.bioenergyproducts.co.uk/wp-content/uploads/Sleep_1.pdf

6. M. Ghaly and D. Teplitz, 'The biologic effects of grounding the human body during sleep as measured by cortisol levels and subjective reporting of sleep, pain and stress', *Journal of Alternative and Complementary Medicine* (2004), 105: 767–76; www.Earthinginstitute.net/wp-content/uploads/2013/06/Ghaly__Teplitz_cortisol_study_2004.pdf

7. *See* www.patrickholford.com/advice/are-you-being-electrified.

8. *See* www.patrickholford.com/advice/cut-carbon-for-health-and-happiness.

Chapter 10: The Shape and Sound of Connection

1. *See* www.newscientist.com/article/mg21528795-500-dna-could-have-existed-long-before-life-itself/.

2. *See* info.visiblebody.com/bid/321039/Anatomy-and-Physiology-Anatomical-Planes-and-Cavities.

3. *See* www.youtube.com/watch?v=3yE4d7O17wE *and also* www.youtube.com/watch?v=qB8m85p7GsU.

4. www.youtube.com/watch?v=0jGaio87u3A

5. There are many possible explanations for seven circumambulations. In the Islamic religion the number of layers of the Earth is seven, the number of skies is seven, the number of levels in heaven and hell are seven, the number of doors to hell is seven (for heaven the number of doors is eight); in verse 12:46 of the Koran, Joseph (Yusef) is asked to interpret the king's dream of seven fat cows being devoured by seven skinny cows and seven fat ears of corn being replaced by seven shrivelled ones. Then there are seven days in our week, seven chakras in our body and seven other planets in our solar system (eight in total).

6. *See* kabbalahstudent.com/mecca-and-kabbalah/.

7. *See* attunedvibrations.com/432hz-healing/.

Chapter 11: Opening the Heart

1. *See* www.newbirthcompany.com/wp-content/uploads/2013/10/Undisturbed-Birth.pdf.

2. R. McCraty *et al.*, 'The Electricity of Touch: Detection and Measurement of Cardiac Energy Exchange Between People' in K.H. Pribram, ed., *Brain and Values: Is a Biological Science of Values Possible?*, Lawrence Erlbaum Associates, Publishers, Mahwah, NJ, 1998, pages 359–79. *See* www.heartmath.org/research/research-library/energetics/electricity-of-touch/.

3. N. Aiba *et al.*, 'Usefulness of pet ownership as a modulator of cardiac autonomic imbalance in patients with diabetes mellitus, hypertension, and/or hyperlipidemia', *Am. J. Cardiol.* (2012), Apr. 15; 1,098: 11,64–70; doi: 10.1016/j.amjcard.2011.11.055. Epub, Jan. 24, 2012; www.ncbi.nlm.nih.gov/pubmed/?term=pets+heart+rate+variability

4. B. Brad, 'Some biological effects of laying on of hands: review of experiments with animals and plants', *J. Am. Soc. Psychical Res.* (1965); 59: 95–171

5. R. Sheldrake, 'The "psychic pet" phenomenon', *Journal of the Society for Psychical Research* (2000); 64: 126–8

6. R. Sheldrake, *Dogs That Know When Their Owners Are Coming Home and Other Unexplained Powers of Animals*, Hutchinson, 1999

7. *See* en.wikipedia.org/wiki/Hexagram#Anahata:_The_Heart_Chakra.

Chapter 12: Community Spirit

1. Juliet B. Schor, 'Can You North Stop Consumption Growth? Escaping the Cycle of Work and Spend' in *The North, the South and the Environment*, V. Bhaskar and A. Glyn (eds), Earthscan, 1995; tinyurl.com/gnbj3rg

2. C.E. Sanders *et al.*, 'The relationship of Internet use to depression and social isolation among adolescents', *Adolescence* (2000) Summer; 35(138): 237–42

3. *See* www.academia.edu/266205/Un-Friend_My_Heart_Facebook_Promiscuity_and_Heartbreak_in_a_Neoliberal_Age.

4. *See* www.ted.com/talks/brene_brown_on_vulnerability?language=en.

5. J. Holt-Lunstad *et al.*, 'Social relationships and mortality risk: a meta-analytic review', *PLoS Medicine* (2010); 77: e1000316

6. J. Holt-Lunstad *et al.*, 'Loneliness and social isolation as risk factors for mortality', *Perspectives on Psychological Science* (2015) March; 10(2): 227–37; pps.sagepub.com/content/10/2/227.abstract

7. *See* www.sheldrake.org/videos/telephone-telepathy-with-the-nolan-sisters.

Chapter 13: Men and Women – Vive la différence

1. *See* www.oecd.org/std/37964549.pdf.

2. *See* www.bbc.co.uk/news/uk-17287275.

3. *See* www.equalpayportal.co.uk/statistics/.

4. *See* www.soc.duke.edu/~jmoody77/205a/ecp/bearman_bruckner_ajs.pdf.

5. *See* www.theguardian.com/world/2013/oct/20/young-people-japan-stopped-having-sex.

6. *See* www.japantimes.co.jp/opinion/2013/04/17/editorials/japans-depopulation-time-bomb/#.Ule5mhY_XzY.

7. *See* ibid., *also* www.theguardian.com/world/2013/oct/20/young-people-japan-stopped-having-sex.

8. *See* womenshealth.gov/publications/our-publications/fact-sheet/female-genital-cutting.html.

9. *See* www.ted.com/talks/jimmy_carter_why_i_believe_the_mistreatment_of_women_is_the_number_one_human_rights_abuse?language=en.

10. Franz Hartman, MD, 'Life of Paracelsus'; *see* www.globalgreyebooks.com/Pages/life-of-paracelsus.html

11. D. Clift and M. Schuh, 'Restarting life: fertilization and the transition from meiosis to mitosis', *Nature Reviews Molecular Cell Biology* (2013); 14(9): 549–62

12. Ann Graham Brock, *The First Apostle: Struggle for Authority*, Harvard Divinity School, 2003

13. Karen L. King, *The Gospel of Mary Magdala*, Polebridge Press, 2003

14. *See* www.studiesincomparativereligion.com/uploads/ArticlePDFs/351.pdf.

Chapter 14: The Alchemy of Sex and Spirit

1. David Bentley Hart, *The Experience of God: Being, Consciousness, Bliss*, Yale University Press, 2013

2. *See* www.lovewisdom.net/philosophical%20topics/Arabi%20-%20man%20 and%20truth.html.

3. *See* www.rigpawiki.org/index.php?title=Absolute

4. David Gordon White, *The Alchemical Body: Siddha Traditions in Medieval India*, University of Chicago Press, 1996

5. *See* www.thenewyoga.org/spanda_karikas_e-book.pdf.

6. This quote comes from the *Mahartthamanjari*, page 25, but Abhinavagupta's teachings, contained in the *Pratybhinjnhrdayam*, are best explained in *The Doctrine of Recognition* by Ksemaraja, translated with a great introduction and notes by Jaideva Singh, State University of New York Press, 1990.

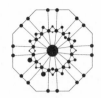

Recommended Reading

Eben Alexander, *Proof of Heaven*, Piatkus, 2012

David Ash, *The New Science of Spirit*, The College of Psychic Studies, 1995

David Bentley Hart, *The Experience of God: Being, Consciousness, Bliss*, Yale, 2013

Brené Brown, *Daring Greatly*, Avery, 2012

David Deida, *The Way of the Superior Man*, Sounds True, 2004

Nick Duffell and Helena Løvendal-Duffell, *Sex, Love and the Dangers of Intimacy*, Lone Arrow Press, 2012

Marc Gafni, *The Mystery of Love*, Atria, 2004

Marc Gafni, *Your Unique Self*, Integral Publishers, 2012

Sue Gerhardt, *Why Love Matters*, Routledge, 2004

Peter Gotzche, *Deadly Psychiatry and Organised Denial*, People's Press, 2015

Stanislav Grof, *Healing Our Deepest Wounds*, Stream of Experience Productions, 2012

Esther Harding, *The Way of All Women*, Rider, 1971

Harville Hendrix, *Getting the Love You Want*, Owl Books, 1988

Hermann Hesse, *The Glass Bead Game*, 1943; English edition Holt, Rinehart & Winston, 1970; Vintage Classics, 2000

Hermann Hesse, *Siddhartha*, 1922; English edition New Directions, 1951; Brownstone Books, 2009

Patrick Holford, *Optimum Nutrition for the Mind*, Piatkus, 2007

Patrick Holford, *10 Secrets of 100% Healthy People*, Piatkus, 2009

Patrick Holford and Dr James Braly, *The Homocysteine Solution*, Piatkus, 2012

Patrick Holford, Dr James Braly and Dr David Miller, *How to Quit without Feeling S**t*, Piatkus, 2008

Patrick Holford and Jerome Burne, *Food is Better Medicine than Drugs*, Piatkus, 2007

Patrick Holford and Dr Hyla Cass, *Natural Highs*, Piatkus, 2011

Anna Hunt, *The Shaman in Stilettos*, Penguin, 2012

Aldous Huxley, *Brave New World*, Chatto & Windus, 1932; Diesterweg Moritz, 2010

Aldous Huxley, *The Doors of Perception*, Harper and Brothers, Publishing, 1954; Frontal Lobe Publishing, 2011

Oscar Ichazo, *P-Cals/Psychocalisthenics®: Exercises to Awaken your Core Fire*, The Oscar Ichazo Foundation, 2011

Jerry Jampolsky, *Love is Letting Go of Fear*, Celestial Arts, 2004

Carl Jung, *Memories, Dreams and Reflections*, 1962; English edition Pantheon Books, 1963; Flamingo, 1995

Sally Kempton, *Meditation for the Love of It*, Sounds True, 2011

Sally Kempton, *Awakening Shakti: The Transformative Power of the Goddesses of Yoga*, Sounds True, 2013

U. G. Krishnamurti, *The Mystique of Enlightenment*, Sentient Publications, 2002

Tim Laurence, *You Can Change Your Life*, Hodder Paperbacks, 2004

Ervin Lazlo, *Science and the Akashic Field: An Integral Theory of Everything*, Inner Traditions, 2007

Patrick McKeown, *The Oxygen Advantage*, William Morrow & Company, 2015

Lynne McTaggart, *The Field*, HarperCollins, 2001

Lynne McTaggart, *The Bond*, Hay House, 2013

Swami Muktananda, *The Play of Consciousness*, Siddha Yoga Publications, 1974; third revised edition, SYDA Foundation, 2000

Clinton Ober, Stephen Sinatra & Martin Zucker, *Earthing*, Basic Health Publications, 2010

Allan and Barbara Pease, *Why Men Don't Listen and Women Can't Read Maps*, Broadway Books, 2001

Proclus, *Elements of Theology*, Oxford University Press, second edition, 1992

Sogyal Rinpoche, *The Tibetan Book of Living and Dying*, HarperCollins, 1992

Sophie Sabbage, *The Cancer Whisperer*, Coronet, 2016

Greg Sams, *The Sun of gOd*, Weiser, 2009

John Sarno, *The Mindbody Prescription*, Little, Brown, 1999

Rupert Sheldrake, *The Sense of Being Stared At*, Park Street Press, 2009

Rupert Sheldrake, *Dogs That Know Their Owners are Coming Home*, Arrow Books, 2011

Rupert Sheldrake, *The Science Delusion*, Coronet, 2013

Rupert Spira, *The Transparency of Things*, Non Duality Press, 2008

Malcolm Stewart, *Patterns of Eternity*, Floris Books, 2009

Malcolm Stewart, *Symbols of Eternity*, Floris Books, 2011

Rick Strassman, *DMT: The Spirit Molecule*, Park Street Press, 2000

David Gordon White, *The Alchemical Body*, The University of Chicago Press, 1998

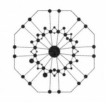

Resources

The 100% Health Programme

Are you 100% healthy? Find out with our FREE online health check and comprehensive 100% Health Programme, giving you a personalized action plan, including diet and supplements. The 100% Health Programme costs £25, but as a reader of this book, at the time of going to press you can save £5 by putting in the following discount code: CONNECT16. Visit www.patrickholford.com.

Arica Institute, Inc.

You may be interested in Arica trainings or the work of Oscar Ichazo. For further information visit www.arica.org, where you can find an Overview, the Arica System, Training Info, the Store, and Articles. Look in the 'Training Info' section for the worldwide schedule of trainings and your nearest training sponsor.

The Brain Bio Centre

This is an outpatient clinic of the charitable Food for the Brain Foundation in Putney, London. It specializes in the nutritional treatment of mental health issues, ranging from depression to schizophrenia, anxiety to ADHD. Support is available for people in the UK and all over the world (via Skype). Visit www.brainbiocentre.com or call +44 (0)20 8332 9600.

Earthing

Earthing is the landmark discovery that disconnection may make us more vulnerable to stress and illness. Contact with the Earth appears to uphold the electrical stability of our bodies and serve as a foundation for vitality and health. In an age of rampant chronic inflammation and disease, 'grounding' ourselves by reconnecting with the Earth beneath our very feet provides a way back to better health. For further information and products visit www.earthinginstitute.net.

The Food for the Brain Foundation

A non-profit educational charity founded by Patrick Holford which aims to promote awareness of the link between learning, behaviour, mental health and nutrition. The website has details on nutritional approaches to anxiety, insomnia and depression, as well as a free Cognitive Function Test that takes 15 minutes to complete. For more information, visit www.foodforthebrain.org.

Marc Gafni

Marc Gafni is a former rabbi, philosopher and scholar of Judaism and author of many books including the highly acclaimed book *The Mystery of Love*, which describes the journey to wholeness from the teachings of the Kabbalah in the Jewish mystical tradition, resulting in your 'unique self', the highest expression of who you can be. This is further explained in his book *Your Unique Self*. For more details, visit www.marcgafni.com.

HeartMath

An organization that focuses on connecting heart and science in ways that empower people to greatly reduce stress, build resilience and unlock their natural intuitive guidance for making better choices. Visit www.heartmath.co.uk or www.heartmath.com for details of events, training, HeartMath coaches and products. If you're looking for research and related information, go to www.heartmath.org.

The Hoffman Process

This is an eight-day intensive residential course in which you are shown how to let go of the past, release pent-up stress, self-limiting behaviours and resentments, and start creating the future you desire. Visit www.hoffmaninstitute.co.uk, address Box 72, Quay House, River Road, Arundel, West Sussex, BN18 9DF UK or call +44 (0)800 068 7114. For details on these and international centres visit www.hoffmaninstitute.com.

Holford Workshops and Retreats

Patrick Holford runs workshops and retreats details on which are given in the events section of www.patrickholford.com. He also runs a retreat centre near Abergavenny in Wales in beautiful, wild and natural surroundings, offering a space for retreats and workshops with the theme of helping people reach their full potential and connecting with nature. He also offers natural holidays and retreats on safari in Kenya. Details on these are also given at www. holfordnaturalholidays.com.

Holotropic Breathwork™

This is a powerful approach to self-exploration and healing that integrates insights from modern consciousness research, anthropology, various depth psychologies, transpersonal psychology, Eastern spiritual practices, and mystical traditions of the world. Visit www.holotropic. com for details. *(See also Transformational Breathwork on page 259.)*

Homocysteine Tests

These are available through YorkTest laboratories. Using a home-test kit, you can take your own pinprick blood sample and return it to the lab for analysis. Visit www.yorktest.com.

Sally Kempton

Sally Kempton is one of today's most authentic spiritual teachers. She teaches devotional contemplative tantra, an approach to practice that creates a fusion of knowing and loving. Known for her ability to transmit inner experience through transformative practices and contemplation, Sally has been practising and teaching for 40 years. To learn more, visit www.sallykempton.com.

Methyl Support Supplements for Homocysteine

A good methyl nutrient complex should contain at least B6, B12 and folic acid in high doses. Some formulas also contain vitamin B2, tri-methyl-glycine (TMG), zinc and N-acetyl-cysteine. Three products that fulfil these criteria are Patrick Holford's Connect, which contains them all (see www.holfordirect.com); Solgar's Gold Specifics Homocysteine Modulators, which contains TMG, vitamin B6, vitamin B12 and folic acid; and Higher Nature's H Factors, which contains B2, B6, B12, folic acid and zinc, plus TMG. See Supplement Suppliers below.

Psychocalisthenics

Psychocalisthenics is an excellent exercise system that takes less than 20 minutes a day, and develops strength, suppleness and stamina, as well as generating vital energy. For further information see www. pcals.com. For training in the UK, visit www.integralview.org and also www.patrickholford.com.

You can also teach yourself from the *Psychocalisthenics* DVD, available from www.pcals.com or www.holfordirect.com. There is also a CD with music and prompts to follow once you have learned the exercises, a book which explains each exercise and a wall chart for quick reference.

© 1972, 2003, 2016 by Oscar Ichazo. Used with permission. All rights reserved. Psychocalisthenics® is a registered trademark of Oscar Ichazo in The United States of America. P-Cals® is a registered trademark of Oscar Ichazo in Canada.

Psychosynthesis

A therapeutic approach that derives from psychoanalysis. It was developed in the early 20th century by Italian psychiatrist Roberto Assagioli, who, unlike Freud, believed in a more inclusive concept of humanity, one that integrated spiritual as well as psychological elements. For information on training or to find a practitioner, visit www.psychosynthesistrust.org.uk or www.psychosynthesis.org. In the USA, visit www.synthesiscenter.org or www.psychosynthesispaloalto. com. For other regions, search on 'psychosynthesis'.

Qigong

The Qigong Institute has a list of teachers around the world ('Teachers and Therapists' link), plus much more information and details of research. Visit www.qigonginstitute.org.

Sophie Sabbage

Sophie Sabbage, the author of *The Cancer Whisperer*, helps others navigate the course of their treatment and recovery by offering online Udemy courses on some parts of the compass (*see page 86*) as well as cancer whispering coaching and workshops on other parts of the Compass such as 'Dancing with Grief'. Information about Sophie Sabbage's talks, courses and coaching can be found at www. sophiesabbage.com/events.

Tai Chi

The Tai Chi Union lists many UK-based instructors on its website at www.taichiunion.com.

Transformational Breathwork

A self-healing technique that helps people to access the full potential of their breathing system for better physical, emotional and mental wellbeing. The connected pattern of conscious breathing is a natural, safe and easy-to-learn technique. As human beings we hold on to tension within our bodies and in doing so create physical, mental and emotional blockages. This technique helps to release the blockages and transform your life and energy. To learn more, visit www.breathtree. co.uk in the UK or www.transformationalbreathwork.com in the USA and internationally. Also see Holotropic Breathwork above.

Vipassana Meditation

A meditative approach for seeing things as they really are and becoming free from suffering. There are three-day and 10-day retreats. For further information about Vipassana meditation, including forthcoming courses in the UK and worldwide, contact www.dipa.dhamma.org and/or www. dhamma.org. In the UK, call +44 (0)1989 730234.

Supplement Suppliers

In the UK

The following companies produce good-quality supplements that are widely available in the UK.

Patrick Holford

Offers a full range of nutritional products for all needs. His daily 'packs' give you everything you need in a daily strip and are good for travelling or when you are away from home. They are available by mail order from www.holfordirect.com and in selected health food stores.

Higher Nature

Available in most independent health-food stores or visit www. highernature.co.uk or call +44 (0)800 458 4747.

Solgar

Available in most independent health-food stores or visit www.solgar-vitamins.co.uk or call +44 (0)1442 890355.

Totally Nourish

An 'e'-health shop that stocks many high-quality health products, including home test kits and supplements. Visit www.totallynourish. com or call +44 (0)800 085 7749 (freephone within the UK).

Viridian

For stockists, visit www.viridian-nutrition.com or call +44 (0)1327 878050.

In Other Regions

Australia

Solgar supplements are available in Australia. Visit www.solgar.com. au or call 1800 029 871 (free call) for your nearest supplier. Another good brand is Blackmores.

Kenya

Patrick Holford supplements are available in all Healthy U stores. Visit www.healthy-U2000.com.

New Zealand

Patrick Holford products (see above) are available in New Zealand through Pacific Health, PO Box 56248, Dominion Road, Auckland 1446. Visit www.pachealth.co.nz or call +64 9815 0707.

Singapore

Patrick Holford and Solgar products are available in Singapore through Essential Living. Visit www.essliv.com or call +65 6276 1380.

South Africa

The original Patrick Holford vitamin and supplement brand from the UK is now available in South Africa through leading health-food stores, Dis-Chem and Clicks retail pharmacies. They are also available online direct from www.holforddirect.co.za or call +11 2654 554 for deliveries by courier direct to your door.

UAE

Patrick Holford supplements (see above) are available in Dubai and the UAE from Organic Foods & Café, PO Box 117629, Dubai, United Arab Emirates; visit www.organicfoodsandcafe.com or call +971 44340577.

USA and Canada

Solgar, Source Naturals, Douglas Laboratories, Natural Factors and Whole Earth & Sea offer a full range of products based on optimal levels consistent with Patrick Holford's principles. These lines are available in health stores and online.

Index

Page references in *italic* indicate Figures.

A

Abhinavagupta 222
achuma (San Pedro) 31, 41–2, 43–4, 49, 107
acupuncture 105
adrenalin xxi, 33, 42, 63, 97, 159, 165
    dominance 196–8
Advaita 11–12, 67
aging xxii
Ahmadiyya Muslim community, Tilford 14
alchemy
    practices 214–16
    of sex and spirit 207–22
    tantric 214–15, 216, 218–22
alcohol xxii, 31, 106, 107
Alexander the (not so) Great 30
Alexander, Eben 17–18, 20
Alexandria, Library of 30
algae xix, 5, *5*, 104
Alzheimer's disease xx, xxiv, 58–60, 82, 100
Amanita muscaria 31
amino acids 38, 39, 61, 92
Amondawa tribe 10–11
amphetamines 107
anahata 172
ananda 209, 220
andropause 198

anger 25, 164, 165, 198, 219
    and depression xx, 197
antacids 197
anti-consumerism 183
anti-psychotics 51, 63
antidepressants 51–3, 56–7, 63, 64, 107, 197
antioxidants 61, 82, 124
Arica School xii, 14, 69, 222, 255
Aristotle 30, 200
Arthur, King 202–3
Ash, David 22
Assagioli, Roberto xi–xii, 75, 259
asthma 109, 118
atheistic culture 24–5
atheistic scientism (AS) xxiv, 8, 18, 21, 24–5, 117
atoms 6–7, *7*, 23
attachment
    dissolving 158
    ego as 'consciousness attached' 157–8, 212
    and karmic reactions 158–9
Aum *see* Om
awakenings
    enlightenment 210–14, 221
    kenshō 69
    peak experiences *see* peak experiences
    spontaneous 76
awareness *see* consciousness/awareness
ayahuasca 31, 35–7, 46–7, 107

B

bacteria 6, 118, 121
barbiturates 107
barefoot walking 123, 126
Beckley Foundation 45
Beecher-Moore, Nan 19
being, absolute 207–9, 211, 222
beliefs
    fundamental 23, 92
    limiting 87, 159
    negative 85, 165, 176
betaine hydrochloride 198
Big Bang 8
birth trauma 159
Blake, William 42, 77
blood pressure 6, 13, 52, 98, 109, 112
blood sugar 82, 97
Bodhi 221
Bodhisattva vow 221
body/Earth connection xv, 117–31, 223, 224
    through chakras see chakras
    cutting carbon 129
    earthing see earthing
    and food 118–22, 128–9 see also food
    generating vital energy xiii, xv, 105–15
    opening up to nature 127–8
    protecting the Earth 128–30
    sexual connection see sexual/sensual/ erotic connection
    synchronizing with the Earth 127
    with walkabout see walkabout/ walking in natural surroundings
    and waste 129–30
body–mind connection see mind–body connection
brain xxii–xxiii, 9–10, 35
    'brain-maker' nutrients 101–4
    brainwaves 127
    connectivity/neural connections 31, 97, 159, 165–7
    corpus callosum 194
    and entheogens 32–40
    essential brain fats 103
    heart and brain connections 165–7
    limbic system 165

neurotransmitters 33, 38, 61, 63, 103, 112
    shrinkage 100, 101, *101*
Brain Bio Centre 60, 255–6
Braly, James 63, 101, 107
breathing techniques 75–6
    Diakath Breathing 110–11, *111*, 122, 236–7, *237*
    energy-generating 106, 108–11
    holotropic 75–6, 153, 257
    transformational breathwork 259–60
British Medical Journal 52–3, 54
Brown, Brené 181–2
Buddha 211
Buffalo 66 (film) 164
Burne, Jerome xxiv
burqas 201

C

Cadbury, Deborah: *The Feminisation of Nature* 196
caffeine xxi, xxii, 106, 107
cancer xx, xxiv, 82
    Sophie Sabbage's experiences and compass 84–8
cannabis 106
Cape Town 184
carbon 3, 5
    cutting 129
    dioxide 129
Carhart-Harris, Robert 45
Carruthers, Malcolm 198
Carter, Jimmy 199
Cass, Hyla 29
Castenada, Carlos 212
Catholic Church 201
CERN, Hadron Collider xxii, 142–3
chakras 172–5, *173*, *174*, 223, *224*
chemical fertilizers 118
chia 104
China 184
CHOSN elements 3, *4*
chromium 82–4
circle piano *151*
circulation *124*, 125
Clarke, Arthur C. 140
Clift, Montgomery 196

Clift, Roberta 196
cocaine 107
cognitive behavioural therapy (CBT) 165
Cohen, Leonard 160
Cohen, Robert 121
coherence 167–8
cola xxi
collective unconscious 11
community spirit 177–90
conception
    gender role equality in 199–200
    problems 196
conductive materials 126
Connect (nutritional herbal formula)
        39–40
connection
    brain connectivity/neural connections
        31, 97, 159, 165–7
    connected fields *see* morphic fields/
        resonance (Sheldrake)
    from disconnection to xix–xxvi
    and happiness xii–xiii
    keys/zones of xiv–xv, 223–6, *224*, *225*
        see also body/Earth connection;
        intellectual connection; sexual/
        sensual/erotic connection;
        social/self connection; spiritual
        connection
    through love *see* love
    mind–body *see* mind–body connection
    through morphic resonance 11, 93–4,
        168, 185–7, 207, 208, 221
    online Connection Check xiv, 225
    through peak experiences *see* peak
        experiences
    Register's scale of xiii
    shape of *see* geometry, the shape of
        connection
    sound of *see* sound of connection
consciousness/awareness
    absolute, pure awareness 211, 212
    attachment of consciousness *see*
        attachment
    consciousness recognizing itself 27
    and culture 29–50
    energy and awareness 209
    enlightened *see* enlightenment

equal inner and outer awareness, of
        absolute and relative 210–14, *210*
    everything as consciousness 12, 15,
        66
    God, the Great Consciousness 43
        see also God; Shiva
    infinite (Turiya) 20
    love as proof of shared consciousness
        9–28
    and mind-altering drugs 29–50
    and near-death experiences 15–18
    peak experiences *see* peak experiences
    play of consciousness 8
    science of consciousness xxiii
    Shiva as representative of 7, 191, 222
    training to raise consciousness 69–70
    trinity of being, energy and
        consciousness 207–9
consumerism 178–9
    anti-consumerism 183
Copiapo, Volcan 72–3, *72*, *73*
corpus callosum 194
cortisol xxi, 109, 124
Council for Evidence-based Psychiatry
        56
creative visualization 91–2
Crick, Francis 134
cubes 143–4
culture
    atheistic 24–5
    and consciousness 29–50
    consumerist 178–9
    cultural revolutions 29–31
    cultures and mind-altering substances
        29–31
    and migration 183
    pop 154
    and science 81–2
cynicism 95–6

D
Dalai Lama xii, 188
Das, Krishna (born Jeffrey Kagel) 148
Dass, Ram (born Richard Alpert) 11
Dawkins, Richard: *The God Delusion* 24
death
    conscious 19

death (*continued*)
  dealing with your own 18–20
  fear of 20
  near-death experiences 15–18
Deida, David 203
dementia xx, xxiv, 58–60, 82, 96, 100
depression xx, 25, 196–7, 198
deprogramming 160
Descartes, René 32, 67
DHA (docosahexaenoic acid) 103, 104, 121
diabetes xx, xxiv, 82, 84, 123, 184
Diakath Breathing 110–11, *111*, 122,
  236–7, *237*
diet 120–22
  and energy 105–6, 107
  for a healthy brain 103–4
  vegan 120–21, 122
  see also fish; meat; protein
digestion 82, *83*
DMAE (phosphatidyl
  dimethylethanolamine) 103
DMT (di-methyl-tryptamine) 32–7, *34*,
  39, *39*
DNA 133, 134–5, 142, 149
dorje/vajra 211, *211*, 212
drugs xxii
  for Alzheimer's 59–60
  antacids 197
  anti-psychotic 51, 63
  antidepressant 51–3, 56–7, 63, 64,
    107, 197
  classification 49–50
  cultures and mind-altering substances
    29–31
  dependence on prescribed drugs 53,
    63–4
  energy-depleting 106–7
  hypnotizing 51–3
  industry, Big Pharma xxiv, 53–5
  and medical error 54
  mind-altering (entheogens) 29–50,
    34, 70–71, 107
  pharmaceuticals to avoid 51–64
  Psychoactive Drugs Bill (2016) 50
  risks with 48–9, 70–71
  and schizophrenia treatment 60–63
  side effects 61

'street' drugs 49
  tranquillizing 51, 62–3, 76, 106
  'war on drugs' 50
drumming 76
Duffell, Nick and Løvendal-Duffel, Helen
  203–4
Dzogchen xxv, 20, 70, 211, 222

E
Earth connection *see* body/Earth
  connection
earthing 122–8, 256
  changing physiological measures of
    health 123–4
  improving sleep 124–5
  methods 126–8
  protecting form electromagnetic fields
    125
  reducing pain 124–5
Ecstasy (drug) *see* MDMA/Ecstasy
ego 157–8, 212
Einstein, Albert xxvi, 10, 21, 24, 76, 82
electromagnetic fields 125, 127, 168,
  185–6
elements (five classical) 19, 43, *141*, 146,
  146, *225*
elements of the periodic table 3, *4*, 126,
  215
Eleusian mysteries 30
Emiliania huxleyi 5, *5*
emotions
  clearing/releasing emotional charge
    or negative emotions 153–4, 158,
    159–65, 227–33
  and connection *see* social/self
    connection
  writing down the emotion exercises
    163–4
  see also anger; fear; love
emWave device 172
energy xi, xx, 3, *224*
  and awareness 209
  and breathing techniques 106,
    108–11
  centres in the body *see* chakras
  and diet 105–6, 107
  and drugs 49

as a dual force for freedom and love
203, 204, 210
in Eastern philosophies 105, 112
energy-depleting drugs 106–7
energy-generating exercise xiii, xv,
107, 112–14, 122
energy-generating plants *see*
entheogens
everything as 15
expending 106–7
feminine *see* female principle; Shakti
generating vital energy xiii, xv,
105–15
masculine *see* male principle; Shiva
nervous xxii
solar 5, 6, 104
in space 6–8
sustainable sources 129
tantric channeling of 214–15, 216,
218–22
for transformation 77
trinity of being, consciousness and
207–9
union of male and female energies
147, 212–22, *212*
in vibration 21–3 *see also* vibrations
wasted 129
enlightenment 210–14, 221
see also awakenings
entheogens 29–50, *34*, 70–71, 107
environmental destruction xix
EPA (eicosapentaenoic acid) 103, 104, 121
Eros/sexual desire xxiv, 196, 218–22
erotic connection *see* sexual/sensual/
erotic connection
exercise, energy-generating xiii, xv, 107,
112–14, 122

F
Facebook 177, 178–81
factory farming 118, 120
fanaticism 27
farming 128
factory 118, 120
fasting 114
fatigue xx, 102, 109
fats 3, 106

omega-3 xx, 59, 60, 61, 103, 104
fear 20, 107, 164, 165
Feilding, Amanda, Countess of Wemyss
and March 45
female genital mutilation 199
female principle 7, 8, 147, 173
difference between masculine and
feminine energies 191–204
feminization of nature 195–6
reclaiming feminine power 198–202
union with male principle 147,
212–22, *212*
working with 202–4
see also Shakti
Fibonacci series 138
fight, flight syndrome xxi
fish 99, 103, 104, 120, 121, 122
see also omega-3 fats
flatworms 10, 93
fly agaric 31
folate 98, 100, 104
folic acid 98, 101, 104, 258
food 105–6, 118–22
diet *see* diet
intolerances 61, 118
production 118–19, 120, 128–9 *see*
also farming
Food for the Brain Foundation xii, 256
Franklin, Rosalind 134
freedom 203, 204, 210, 215, 240
friendship 94
fundamentalists 25

G
Gafni, Marc 219–20, 221, 256
Galileo Galilei 22
gamma amino-butyric acid (GABA) 112
gatherers 195
genes 97
genetically modified (GM) crops 118
geometry, the shape of connection
133–47, *224*
cubes 143–4
hexagons 34, 133
pentagons *see* pentagons
Platonic solids 146, *146*, 224
shape of God 142–5

Gerhardt, Sue: *Why Love Matters* 159
Gershon, Ilana 179–81
GlaxoSmithKline (GSK) 54
glycation 82, *83*
glyphosate (Roundup) 118
gnosticism xxv
God xiii, xxiii, 7, 8, 17–18, 21, 25, 65
  as a father figure 24
  the Great Consciousness 43 *see also*
    Shiva
  as male principle *see* male principle;
    Shiva
  shape of 142–5
  Sun worshipped as 21, 22
  union with Goddess 147, 212–22, *212*
Goddess 7, 35, 43, 203, 212, *212*, 218,
  220–21
  as female principle *see* female
    principle; Shakti
  Lalita 216–18, *217*, 238–40, *238*
  union with God 147, 212–22, *212*
  see also Shakti
Goeka, S. N. 213
golden number, *phi* 137–41, *137*, *138*,
  139
gong healing 153–4
Gotzche, Peter 56
grief 87–8
Grof, Stanislav 43, 45, 48, 62, 75–6, 153,
  159
guanine 133, *134*
Gurumayi 67, 68
gurus 67–70

H
Hadron Collider, CERN xxii, 142–3
Hancock, Graham: *Supernatural* 135
haoma 30
happiness
  and connection xii–xiii
  and longevity 94
harmony 150
Hart, David Bentley 24
Healey, David 56
Healing the Body visualization 234–5
heart
  accessing the heart 169–72

and brain connections 165–7
central place among energy centres
  172–5, *173*, *174*
coherence and heart-centred focus
  167–8
heart rate variability (HRV) 166–7,
  166, 169, 170
listening to the heart 171–2
meditations 169, 170–71
opening the heart 157–76
and pet power 169–70
positivity and the heart state 120
HeartMath Institute 120, 165, 167–8,
  171, 256–7
Hendrix, Harville 160
  Getting the Love You Want 204
herbicides 118
heroin 107
Hesse, Hermann xi
hexagons 34, 133
higher powers/intelligences xiii, xxiii,
  25, 65, 128
  see also God; Goddess
Hindu tradition 74, 76, 105, 153, 207,
  208–9, 220
  Advaita 11–12, 67
  chakras *see* chakras
  Shri Vidya 147
  Vedas 30
Hippocrates 57
Hoffer, Abram 41–2, 43, 45, 61, 62, 197
Hoffman, Albert 42
Hoffman, Bob 162
Hoffman Process 75, 161–2, 257
  Negative Transference Exercise 162,
  230–33
holotropic breathwork 75–6, 153, 257
homocysteine 59, 60, 98, 100, 101–2,
  257, 258
hope 88, 94
hormone exposure 195–6
HRV (heart rate variability) 166–7, *166*,
  169, 170
Hubbard, Ron 160
Hunab Kanu 216, *216*
Hunt, Anna: *Shaman in Stilettos* 216
hunters 194–5

Huxley, Aldous 42, 45
  Brave New World xx
  The Doors of Perception 42
hydration 82, *83*

I
Ibn Arabi 208, 222
ibogaine 31
Ichazo, Oscar xii, 14, 27, 69, 110,
  113–14, 172, 222
Imago method 160
Incas 31
inflammation
  and cynicism 95, 96
  liver 89–90
  reduced by earthing 125, 256
Inner Balance device 166, *166*, 172
Inside Out (film) 164
Institute for Optimum Nutrition xii
insulin 97
intellectual connection xv, 224, *224*
intention 94
  positive 91–2, 94
internet xx, 177, 178–81
ions/ionizers 109
  negative ions 122, 123
irritable bowel syndrome (IBS) 197
Islam 183, 201
  Sufism *see* Sufism
isolation 177–8
  and loneliness 181–2

J
jaguar 30
Jampolsky, Jerry 20
Japan 196
Jessel, Sir Charles 199–200
jet lag 33
Judaism
  Kabbalah 219–21
  mystical 219–21, 222
  orthodox 221
Jung, Carl Gustav xi, 11, 75

K
Ka'aba, Mecca 143–4, *144*, 145
Kabbalah 219–21

Kahunas 76
Kailash, Mount 74
kanna 39–40
karma 158–9
  learning from others' karmic
    experiences 164–5
Kath Point 110–11, *111*, 122, 172,
  236–7, *237*
kava kava 39–40
Kempton, Sally 203, 258
  Awakening Shakti 217–18
  heart meditation 169, 170–71
kenshō 69
Kenya 178, 183–4
Keys, Ansel 183
Koran 201
Krishna Das (born Jeffrey Kagel) 148
Krishnamurti, U. G. 77
Kshemaraja 219
kundalini Shakti 218

L
Lalita (goddess) 216–18, *217*, *238*
  meditation 238–40
Landmark Forum 161
Laurence, Tim 162
lecithin 104
Leonardo da Vinci: *The Last Supper* 201
Levin, Michael 10
life cycles 5–6
light 21
lightning 122
Lille, Patricia de 184
limbic system 165
lipidation 82, *83*
listening 160–61
  to the heart 171–2
loneliness 181–2
Longevity Project 94
love xxv, 105–6, 181–2, 209, *224*
  changing neuronal connections 159
  focusing on an experience of 170–71
  and freedom 203, 204, 210
  and longevity 94
  opening the heart 157–76
  as proof of shared consciousness
    9–28

love (*continued*)
    sexual *see* sex; sexual/sensual/erotic
        connection
LSD 30, 31, 32, 42–3, 44–5, 48, 70–71
Luciana (trauma therapist) 46–7, 70–71

M
'magic' mushrooms 30–31, *34*, 45
magnesium 60
Mahadeva 144
male principle 7, 147
    difference between masculine and
        feminine energies 191–204
    masculine ecstasy 203
    union with female principle 147,
        212–22, *212*
    see also Shiva
Mandelbrot set 140–41, *140, 141*
mantras 20–21, 69, 72–3, 148, 175
    Om *see* Om
marijuana 107
Mary Magdalene 201
Masai 22
masters 67–70
Matrika Shakti 23
Matrix, The 23
Maya 8
Mayans 30, 216
McKeown, Patrick: *The Oxygen Advantage*
    109
McTaggart, Lynne 11
MDMA/Ecstasy 31, 34, 40–41, 45, 48–9
meat 120, 121, 122
Mecca 143–4, *144*, 145
medicine
    drugs *see* drugs
    limitations xxiv
    systems-based 81–4, *83*
    traditional Chinese medicine 105,
        141, 175
Medicines & Healthcare products
    Regulatory Agency (MHRA) 55
meditation 102
    'empty' 67
    and grounding 122
    heart-focused 169, 170–71
    and kenshō 69

Lalita 238–40
    and telomere length 96
    traditional Chinese medicine 141
    Vipassana 67, 213, 260
melatonin 33, *34, 39*, 124, 125
memory xxii–xxiii, 9–10
    as resonances 94
Mendeleev, Dmitri 3
menopause 198
mental illness 48
    Alzheimer's xx, xxiv, 58–60, 82, 100
    schizophrenia 42, 60–63, 76, 100
mercury 215
mescaline 34, *34*, 40, 42
methylation 82, *83*, 97–104
    support supplements 98, 99–100,
        100, 104, 258
Michelfelder, Aaron 109
migration 183
Milarepa 74
Miller, David 63, 107
mind-altering drugs 29–50, *34*
mind–body connection 81–96
    activating our blueprint for health
        92–4
    mind over body 84–92
    psycho-neuro-immunology 91
    systems-based medicine 81–4
mind clearing 87
    releasing emotional charge or
        negative emotions 153–4, 158,
        159–65, 227–33
mindfulness xxi
    Vipassana 67, 213, 260
Mitchell, Mukti 129
mitochondria 5–6
morphic fields/resonance (Sheldrake)
    11, 93–4, 168, 185–7, 207, 208,
    221
morpho-genesis 92
    morphogenetic fields 92–3
mountains 72–4
Muktananda, Swami 8, 67, 68
mushrooms, 'magic' 30–31, *34*, 45
music 76, 148–54
    fifths 152–3
    gong healing 153–4

harmony of spheres 152
notes 151–3, *151*
primal rhythms and 153–4
songs 148–9
Tetraktys 150, *150*, 152, 153
tuning 149–50, *150*, 153
mysteries 66, 67–70

N
N-acetyl cysteine (NAC) 98, 100, 258
Nasr, Seyyed Hossein 201
nature
feminization of 195–6
opening up to 127–8
walking in *see* walkabout/walking in
natural surroundings
near-death experiences 15–18
negativity 75, 95, 107, 162
negative beliefs 85, 165, 176
Negative Transference Exercise 162,
230–33
releasing negative emotions 153–4,
158, 162–4, 230–33
see also cynicism
neo-orthodoxy 207
Neoplatonism xii, xxiv–xxv, 207, 222
nervous energy xxii
nervous system
parasympathetic 112
sympathetic 160
neurotransmitters 33, 38, 61, 63, 103,
112
niacin 60
nicotine xxi, 106, 107
nirvana 211
nitric oxide 6
nitrogen cycle 6
nitrous oxide 6
Nolan Sisters 186
Nutt, David 45

O
obesity xxiv
oceans 5
oestrogens 196, 198
Om 20–21, 175
Om Namah Shivaya 72–3, 148

omega-3 fats xx, 59, 60, 61, 103, 104,
120–21
opiates 107
optimism 94
Orwell, George: *1984* xx, 25
ouroboros 215, *215*
out-of-body experiences xxiii, 13,
14–15, 143
overbreathing 109
oxidation 82, *83*
oxygen xix, 3, 5, 6, 108–9

P
Pachamama (Mother Earth) 8, 173
pain 124–5
Paracelsus 200
parasympathetic nervous system 112
paroxetine 54
Pauling, Linus 21, 134
Paxil (paroxetine) 54
PC (phosphatidyl choline) 103–4
peak experiences 65–77
with gurus/masters 67–70
meaning of 77
with plant medicine 70–71 *see also*
entheogens
spontaneous awakenings 76
touching the transpersonal 75–6
with walkabout 71–4
Pease, Allan and Barbara: *Why Men Don't
Listen and Women Can't Read Maps*
194
pentagons 34, 133, *133*
five elements of the pentagon 141,
141
and the golden number 137, *137*
starcuts 135–7, *135*, *136*
periodic table 3, *4*
pesticides 118
pets, power to access heart space 169–70
peyote 34, 40, 41–2, 49, 107
Pfeiffer, Carl 61
phi, golden number 137–41, *137*, *138*,
139
Phillips, Barry 145
phones xx
phosphatidyl choline (PC) 103–4

phosphatidyl dimethylethanolamine (DMAE) 103
phosphatidyl serine (PS) 103
phospholipids 103–4
pineal gland 32
plant medicine *see* entheogens
Plato 30, 146
Platonic philosophy/Platonists 26, 207
Platonic solids 146, *146*, 224
Plichta, Peter 142
Plotinus: *Enneads* 24
pop culture 154
positivity
    and heart state 120
    and longevity 94
    positive attitude 94
    positive intention 91–2, 94
pranayama 75–6
prejudices 183–5
primal rhythms 153–4
Proclus: *Elements of Theology* 24
progesterone 198
prostitution 199
protein 3, 122, 197
protein pump inhibitors 197
Proust, Marcel xxvi
PS (phosphatidyl serine) 103
psilocybin 31, 45
psychiatric drugs 51–64
psycho-neuro-immunology (PNI) 91
Psychoactive Drugs Bill (2016) 50
Psychocalisthenics 113–14, 258
Psychosynthesis xi–xii, 75, 259
puma 30
purpose 86–7, 187–90
Pythagoras 133, 150

Q
qigong 108, 112, 259
Quechuan peoples/tradition 31, 173, 222
Quick Coherence technique 168, 169

R
rainforests xix
Ram Dass (born Richard Alpert) 11
randomized controlled studies xxiii–xxiv

recapitulation 161
recycling 130
reductionism 82
Register, Elizabeth xiii
religion xxiv
    fundamentalists 25
    see also specific religions
resilience 82, *83*, 94, 118
resonance
    morphic 11, 93–4, 168, 185–7
    Schumann resonances 149
rhythms 153–4
ribonucleic acid (RNA) 134
RNA (ribonucleic acid) 134
rue 30
Rumi 20, 27, 208, 222
Russell, Bertrand 187

S
S-adenosyl-methionine (SAMe) 99
Sabbage, Sophie 84–8, 259
Sams, Greg: *The Sun of gOd* 22
samsara 210–11, 212–13
San Pedro (*achuma*) 31, 41–2, 43–4, 49, 107
Sarno, John: *Mindbody Prescription* 106
Sceletium tortuosum 39–40
schizophrenia 42, 60–63, 76, 100
Schumann resonances 149
selective serotonin re-uptake inhibitors (SSRIs) 52, 53
self-destructiveness xix–xx, 43, 162, 164
self-esteem 91, 94, 182
self connection *see* social/self connection
serotonin 33, *34*, 196
sex xii, xiii, xx, xxi–xxii, xxv
    alchemy of sex and spirit 207–22
    basic approaches to sexuality (Gafni) 220
    biological/evolutionary differences between the sexes 194–5
    compulsive xxi–xxii
    conception *see* conception
    and connection *see* sexual/sensual/ erotic connection
    female principle *see* female principle
    and hormone exposure 195–6

male principle *see* male principle
sexual abuse 199
sexual desire/drive xxiv, 196, 218–22
sexual dysfunction 52
sexual orientation 195–6
sexual slavery 199
trafficking 199
workers 199
sexual/sensual/erotic connection xiv,
223, *224*
alchemy of sex and spirit 207–22
erotic orange exercise 241
tantric 214–15, 216, 218–22
union of God and Goddess, male and
female energies 147, 212–22, *212*
Shaivism xii, xxv, 222
Shakti 7, 8, 147, 191, 201, 207, 209,
239–40
kundalini 218
Matrika 23
union with Shiva 147, 212–22, *212*
shamans 31, 35–7, 43, 46–7, 212, 216
Shankara 213
sharing 160–61
Shaw, George Bernard 50
Sheldrake, Rupert 11, 12, 92–4, 169–70,
185–7, 221
Shipibo Indians 35–7
Shiva 7, 144, 147, 191, 207, 209, 222
union with Shakti 147, 212–22, *212*
Shree Yantra 147, *147*, 216
Shri Vidya 147
Shulgin, Alexander 38–9, *38*, 40–41,
43, 45
Siberian peoples 30–31
Siddha Yoga xii, 67, 148
Sinha, Chris 10–11
sleep 124–5
social/self connection xv, 177–90,
223–4, *224*
and the internet/social media xx,
177, 178–81
and longevity 94
through morphic resonance 11, 93–4,
168, 185–7
and prejudices 183–5
telepathic 186

social media xx, 177, 178–81
Solanezub 59
soma 30, 35
sound of connection 148–54
mantras *see* mantras
music *see* music
Om *see* Om
space, and energy 6–8
Spanda 219
Spira, Rupert 12
spiritual connection xv, 224, *224*
alchemy of sex and spirit 207–22
peak experiences *see* peak experiences
see also awakenings; enlightenment
starcuts 135–7, *135*, *136*
Stewart, Malcolm 11, 13–14, 15, 51–2,
94, 137, 143, 144, 150, 169
Patterns of Eternity 135–6
Symbols of Eternity 141, 142, 146
Stewart, Nora 14, 52
stimulation, constant xxi
Strassman, Rick 32–3, 37
stress 95, 96, 165
addiction xxi–xxii
and energy depletion 115
and exercise 112
women's handling of 196–7
subatomic particles 6–7, *7*, 23
Sufism xii, xxv, 8, 21, 25, 207, 208, 209,
221, 222
zhikr 76
sugars 3, 107
blood sugar 82, 97
sulphur 215
Sun 21–2, 117
solar energy 5, 6, 104
worship 21, 22, 117
sunbathing 6
Sutton, Dudley: 'Forbidden Fruit'
119–20
sympathetic nervous system 160
systems-based medicine 81–4, *83*

T
tai chi 105, 108, 112, 259
tantra 214–15, 216, 218–22
Taoism xxiv, 172, 173, 216

tefillin 144–5, *145*
telepathy 186
telomeres 95–6, *95*
Terman, Lewis 94
testosterone 195, 198
Tetraktys 150, *150*, 152, 153
thermographs *124*, 125
Tibetan Book of Living and Dying
   211–12
time 10–11
tobacco/nicotine xxi, 106, 107
Toltec tradition 161, 222
topsoil 128
traditional Chinese medicine 105, 141,
   175
tranquillizers 51, 62–3, 76, 106
transformational breathwork 259–60
   see also holotropic breathwork
transpersonal experiences 75–6
   see also peak experiences
transpersonal psychology xi, 43, 257
trauma 159
trimethylglycine (TMG) 98, 100, 104,
   258
tryptamines 33, 34, *34*, 38–9, *39*
Tsotsi (film) 164, 184–5
Turiya 20
Turner, J. M. W. 21

U
unconciousness 9
   collective unconscious 9
unity, experiences of 65
urbanization 177–8

V
vajra/dorje 211, *211*, 212
Vedanta xii
Vedas 30
vegan diet 120–21, 122
veils 201
Venus (goddess) 221
Venus (planet) 139, *139*
vibrations 5, 11, 149
   bodily 127
   electromagnetic 127, 149
   energy in vibration 21, 23

sound vibrations *see* sound of
   connection
Vipassana 67, 213, 260
vision 12–15
visualization
   creative 91–2
   Healing the Body 234–5
   male/female 193
vitamin B xii, xx, 59, 60, 101, *101*, 104
   B2 98, 100, 258
   B3 (niacin) 60
   B6 60, 98, 100, 101, 104, 258
   B12 6, 60, 98, 99, 100, 101, 104, 121,
     197, 258
   folic acid 98, 101, 104, 258
   see also methylation
vitamin C 84
vitamin D xx, 104, 120, 121
vulnerability 182, 183

W
walkabout/walking in natural
   surroundings 71–4, 109
   barefoot walking 123, 126
waste 129–30
Watson, James 134
witches 30
Wizard of Oz 165
work to spend cycle 178–9

X
xenoestrogens 196

Y
yage 31
yantras 69, 147, *147*, 216
yin–yang symbol 216, *216*
yoga 105, 108, 112–13, 175
   Siddha xii, 67, 148

Z
Zen 27, 67, 172, 221
zero-point field 11
zhikr 76
zinc 60, 98, 100, 104, 258
Zipruanna 19
Zoroastrianism 30

ABOUT THE AUTHOR

Patrick Holford BSc, DipION, FBANT, NTCRP is a leading spokesman on health and nutrition in the media, specializing in the field of mental health. He is the author of over 30 books, including *The Optimum Nutrition Bible*, *The Low GL-Diet Bible*, *Optimum Nutrition for the Mind* and *The 10 Secrets of 100% Healthy People*, which have been translated into over 30 languages, selling millions of copies worldwide.

Patrick started his academic career in the field of psychology, focusing on intelligence and schizophrenia, and also studied and explored various philosophies and spiritual paths. He was a student of two of the leading pioneers in nutritional medicine and psychiatry, the late Dr Carl Pfeiffer and Dr Abram Hoffer. In 1984 he founded the Institute for Optimum Nutrition (ION), an independent educational charity, with his mentor, twice Nobel Prize winner Dr Linus Pauling, as patron. For the past 30 years, ION has been researching and helping to define what it means to be optimally nourished and is one of the most respected educational establishments for training nutritional therapists. At ION, Patrick was involved in ground-breaking research showing that multivitamins could increase children's IQ scores – the subject of a *Horizon* TV documentary in the 1980s. He was one of the first promoters of the importance of zinc, antioxidants, high-dose vitamin C, essential fats, low-GL diets and homocysteine-lowering B vitamins and their use in mental health and Alzheimer's disease prevention.

Patrick founded the Food for the Brain Foundation and is director of the Brain Bio Centre, the Foundation's treatment centre, which specializes in helping those with mental issues ranging from depression to schizophrenia. He is an honorary fellow of the British Association of Nutritional Therapy, as well as a member of the Nutrition Therapy Council and the Complementary and Natural Healthcare Council. He is also patron of the South African Association of Nutritional Therapy and a qualified HeartMath® practitioner.

Patrick runs workshops and retreats, and has a retreat centre in South Wales available for workshops and retreats to help people reach their full potential.

www.patrickholford.com

NOT GOOD?

AVERAGE?

REASONABLY HEALTHY?

HEALTHY?

Take my FREE health check right now!

I invite you to take my free online Health Check. You'll get instant results and a practical action plan to transform your health.

This detailed, online questionnaire reviews your diet, lifestyle, and any symptoms you may currently have. It should only take a few minutes to complete. Rest assured participation is entirely free and completely confidential.

The Health Check will give you a current health score between 0-100% and then show you which key areas of your health you can focus on to move towards 100% health. I anticipate you'll see and feel a difference within 30 days. Get started at:

www.patrickholford.com

patrick
HOLFORD
100% HEALTH WORKSHOPS

TOTAL HEALTH TRANSFORMATION

Avoid the mid-life health meltdown. Beat the bulge. Give your body a total transformation. Find out how to radically improve your health in this highly informative and motivating workshop. You leave with your own personalised health plan and the tools to be successful.

OPTIMUM EXERCISE IN 15 MINUTES

How do you keep fit, strong, supple and full of energy? The habit of exercise can be hard to keep up, but how much easier would it be if all you needed was 15 minutes every day? This workshop shows you four simple ways to achieve these goals in 15 minutes a day.

OPTIMUM NUTRITION FOR THE MIND

There is no need to have declining energy, memory, motivation and mood. In this one-day workshop you will learn everything Patrick's learnt in 35 years exploring nutrition for mental health.

THE POWER OF CONNECTION

Is life an adventure or an ordeal? Are you having a good time, full of 'joie de vivre' or are you bored or in discomfort of one sort or another, be it emotional or mental anguish, stress or physical pain? Does life make sense or do you have the feeling there's another level of existence but don't know how to get there? Patrick Holford shares deepest wisdoms that help you feel fully alive and awake and connected on all levels, living a purposeful life.

For latest seminars and workshops visit
www.patrickholford.com/events

We hope you enjoyed this Hay House book. If you'd like to receive our online catalog featuring additional information on Hay House books and products, or if you'd like to find out more about the Hay Foundation, please contact:

Hay House, Inc., P.O. Box 5100, Carlsbad, CA 92018-5100
(760) 431-7695 or (800) 654-5126
(760) 431-6948 (fax) or (800) 650-5115 (fax)
www.hayhouse.com® • www.hayfoundation.org

***

Published and distributed in Australia by: Hay House Australia Pty. Ltd.,
18/36 Ralph St., Alexandria NSW 2015
Phone: 612-9669-4299 • *Fax:* 612-9669-4144 • www.hayhouse.com.au

Published and distributed in the United Kingdom by: Hay House UK, Ltd.,
Astley House, 33 Notting Hill Gate, London W11 3JQ
Phone: 44-20-3675-2450 • *Fax:* 44-20-3675-2451 • www.hayhouse.co.uk

Published and distributed in the Republic of South Africa by:
Hay House SA (Pty), Ltd., P.O. Box 990, Witkoppen 2068
info@hayhouse.co.za • www.hayhouse.co.za

Published in India by: Hay House Publishers India,
Muskaan Complex, Plot No. 3, B-2, Vasant Kunj, New Delhi 110 070
Phone: 91-11-4176-1620 • *Fax:* 91-11-4176-1630 • www.hayhouse.co.in

Distributed in Canada by: Raincoast Books,
2440 Viking Way, Richmond, B.C. V6V 1N2
Phone: 1-800-663-5714 • *Fax:* 1-800-565-3770 • www.raincoast.com

***

Take Your Soul on a Vacation

Visit www.HealYourLife.com® to regroup, recharge, and
reconnect with your own magnificence.
Featuring blogs, mind-body-spirit news, and
life-changing wisdom from Louise Hay and friends.

Visit www.HealYourLife.com today!